POST YORK

Story and art by
James Romberger

AN IMPRINT OF
DARK HORSE COMICS

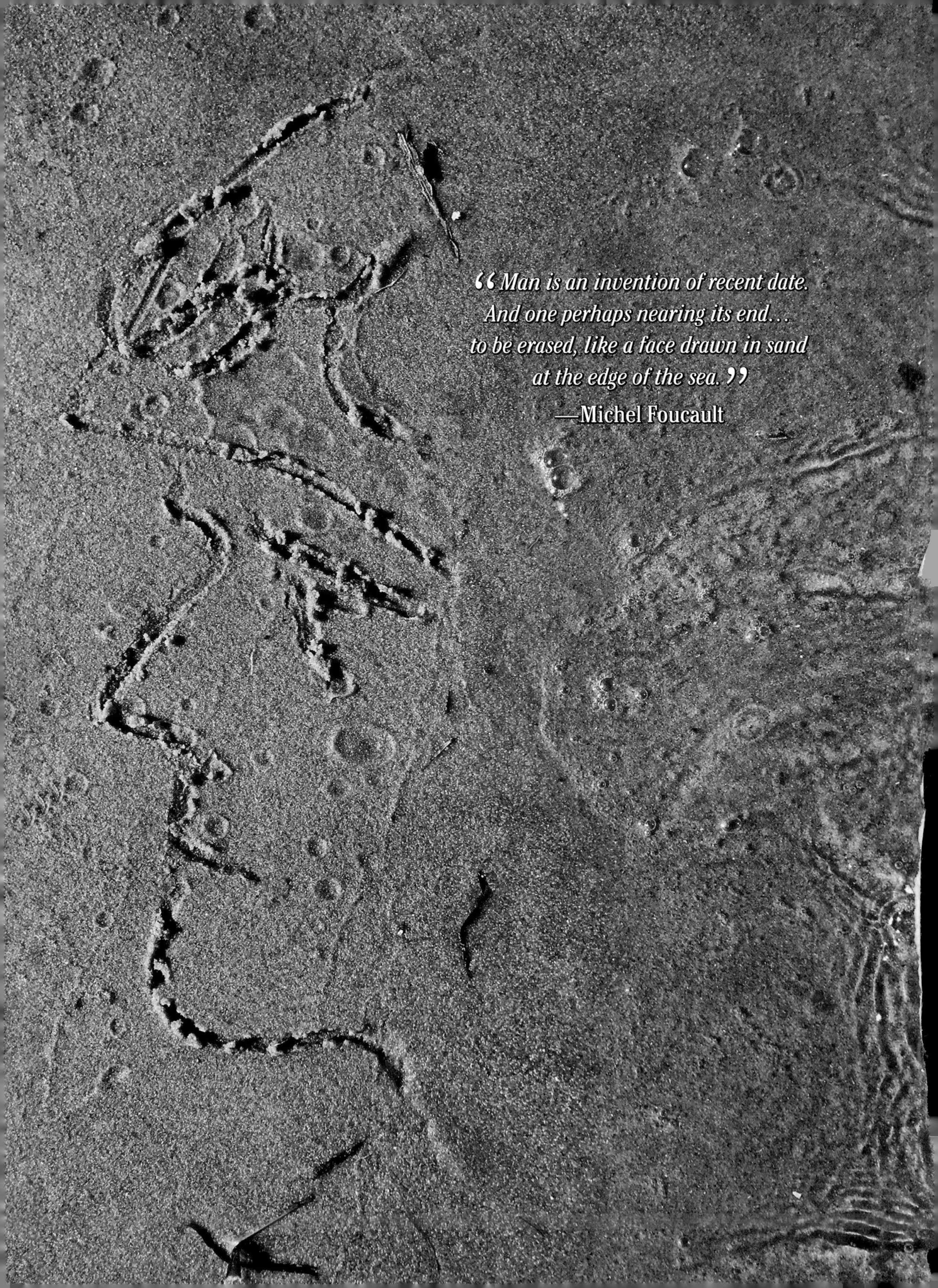

“Man is an invention of recent date.
And one perhaps nearing its end…
to be erased, like a face drawn in sand
at the edge of the sea.”

—Michel Foucault

ZONE A
Residents in Zone A face the highest risk of flooding from a hurricane's storm surge. Zone A includes all low-lying coastal areas and other areas that could experience storm surge from ANY hurricane making landfall close to New York City.

ZONE B
Residents in Zone B may experience storm surge flooding from a MODERATE (Category 2 and higher) hurricane.

ZONE C
Residents in Zone C may experience storm surge flooding from a MAJOR (Category 3 & 4) hurricane making landfall just south of New York City. A major hurricane is unlikely in New York City, but not impossible.

LEGEND
● EVACUATION CENTER
A ZONE
B ZONE
C ZONE

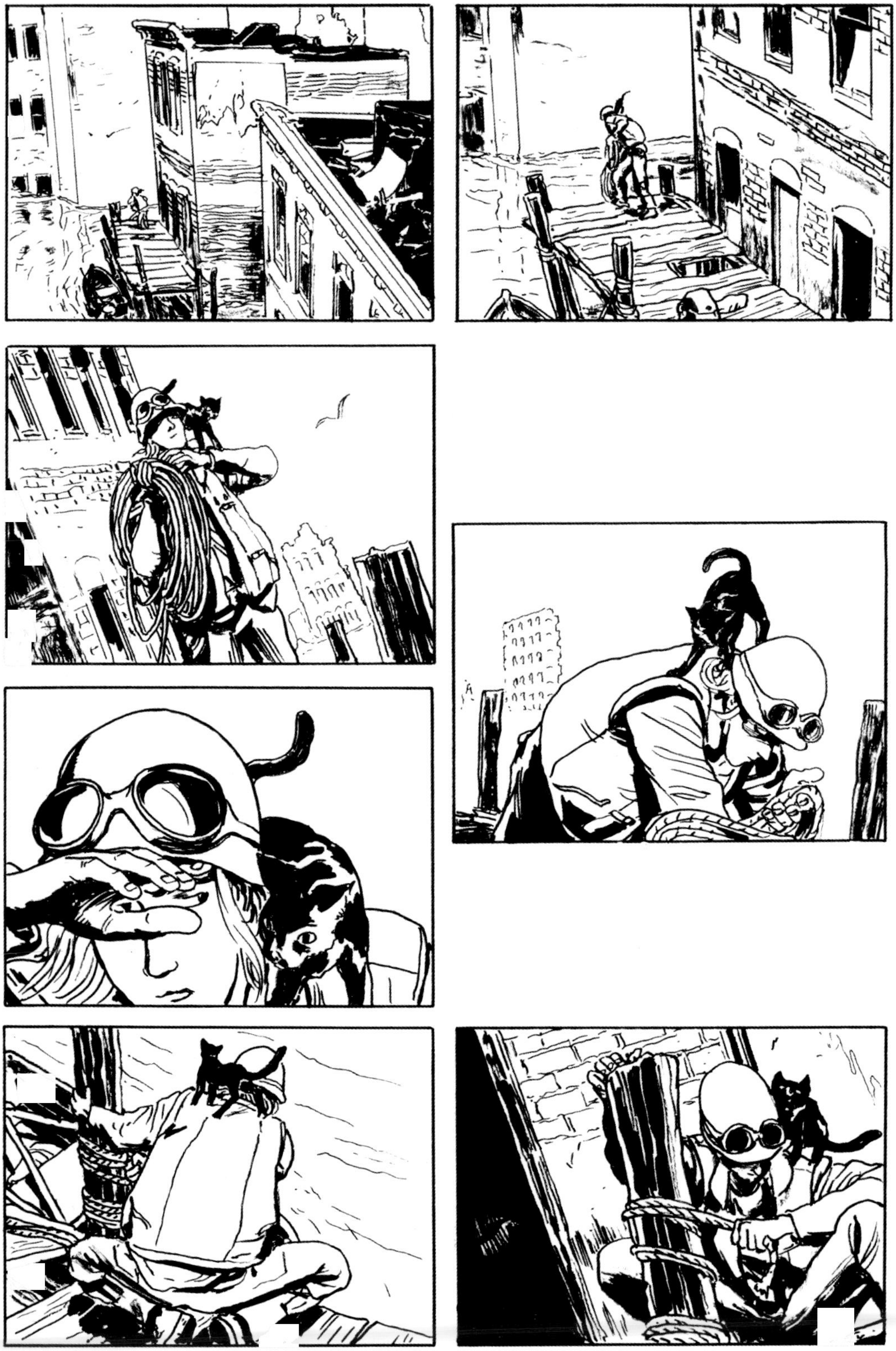

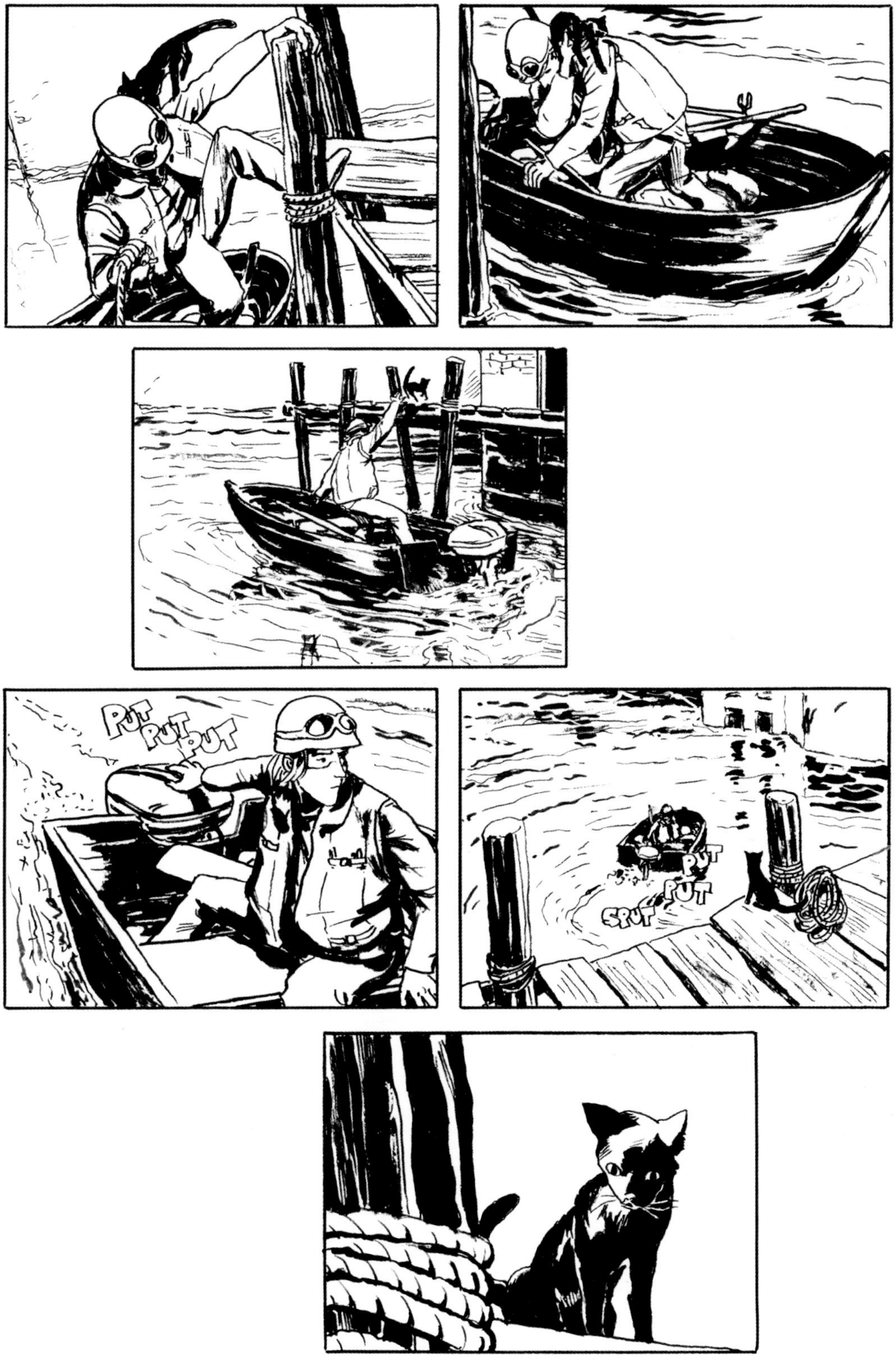
PUT
PUT
PUT
PUT
PUT
SPUT

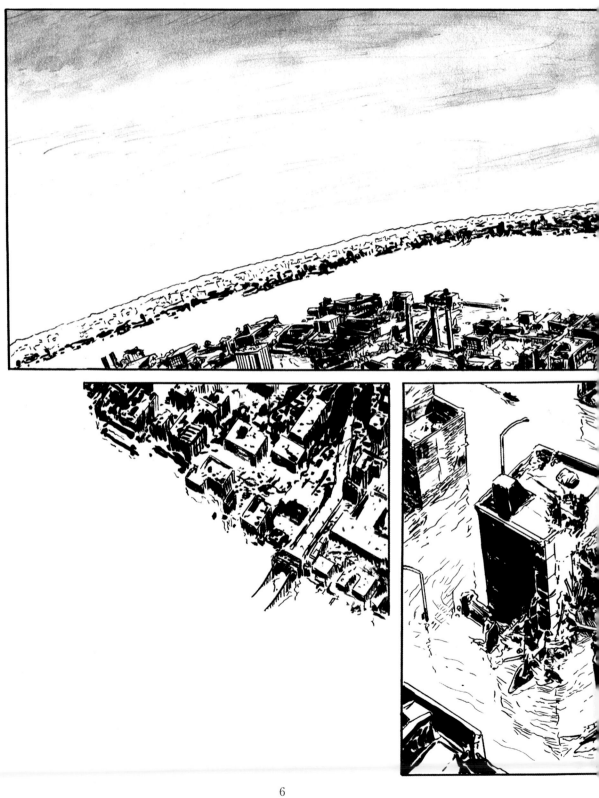

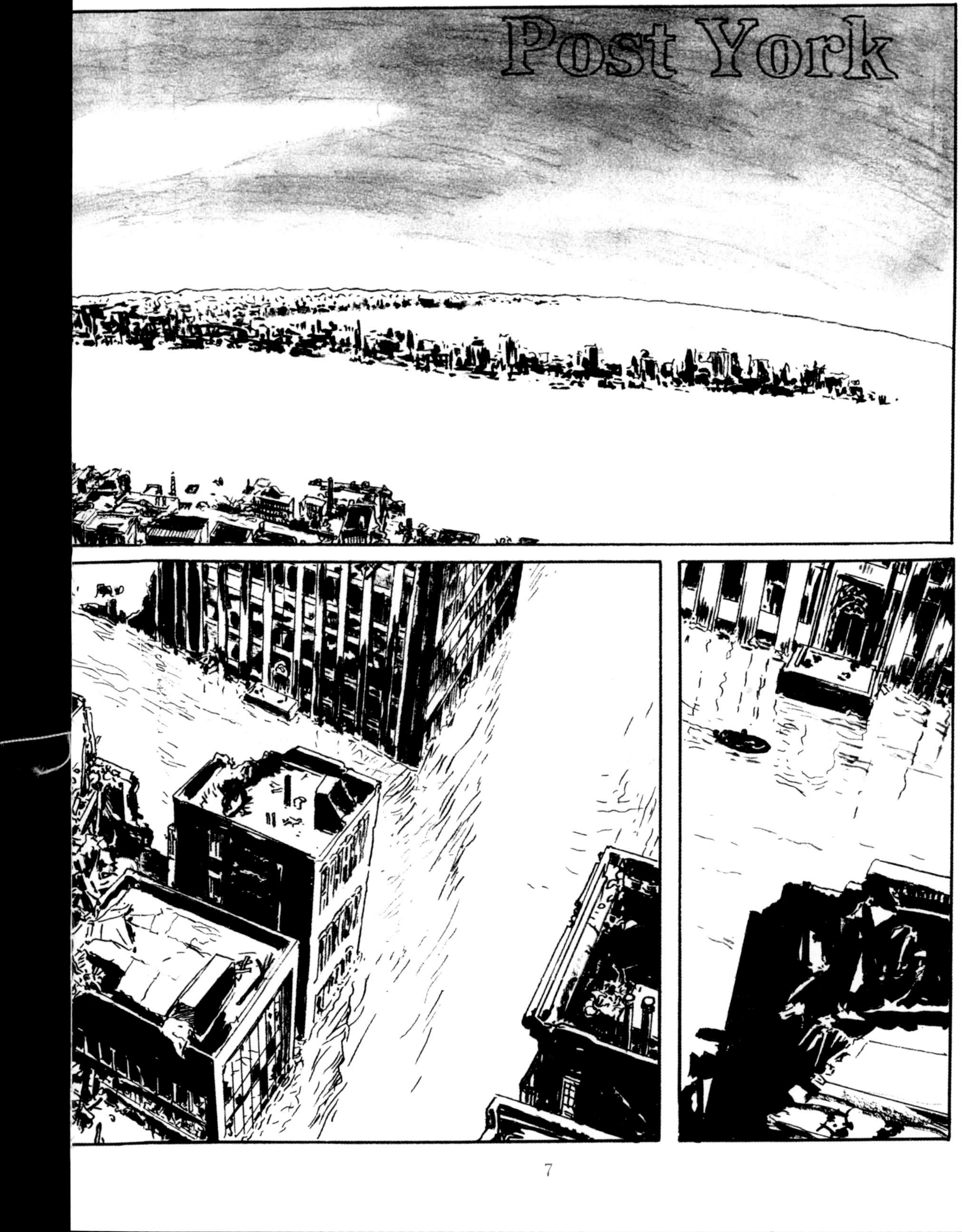
Post York

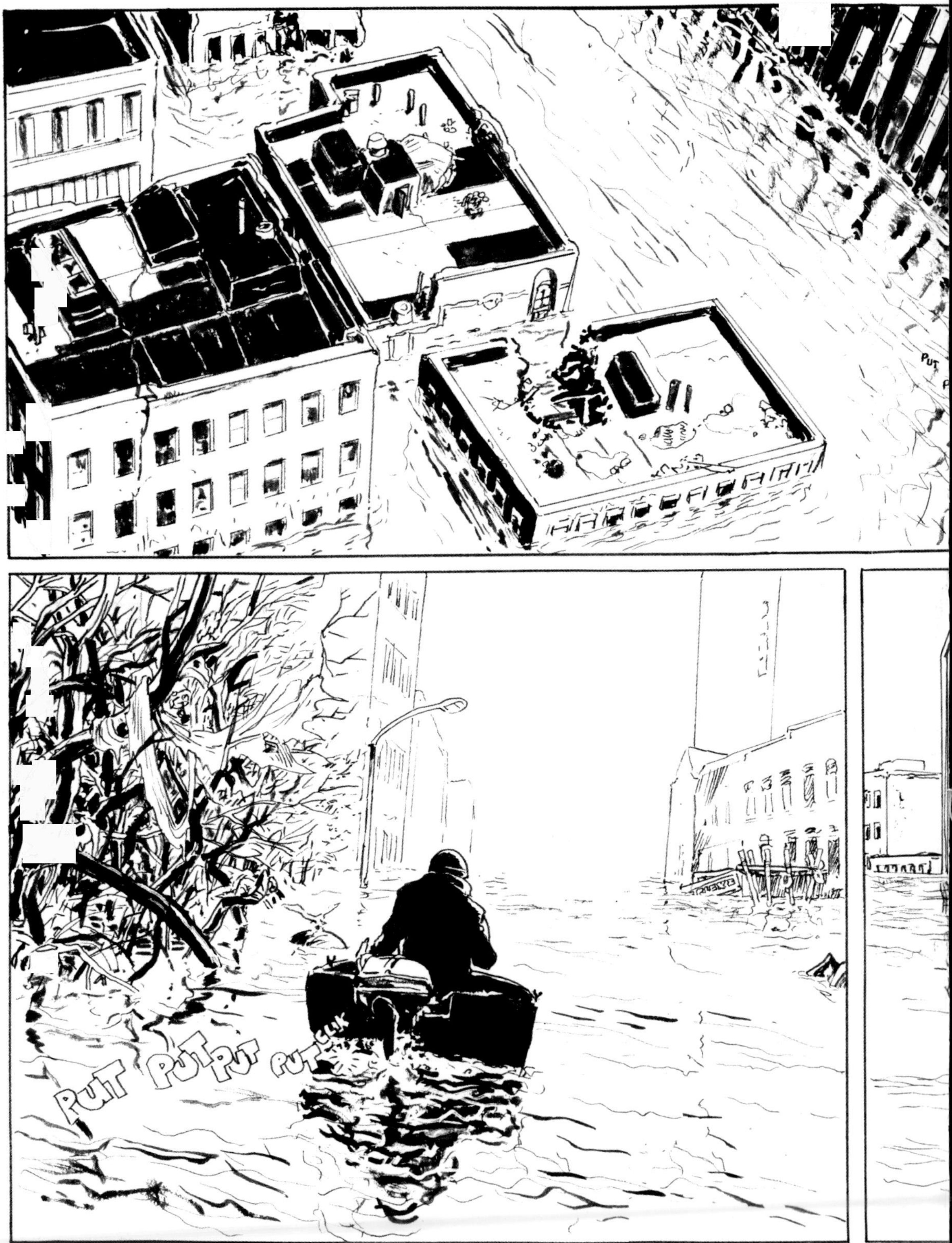
PUT
PUT PUT PUT PUT CLIK

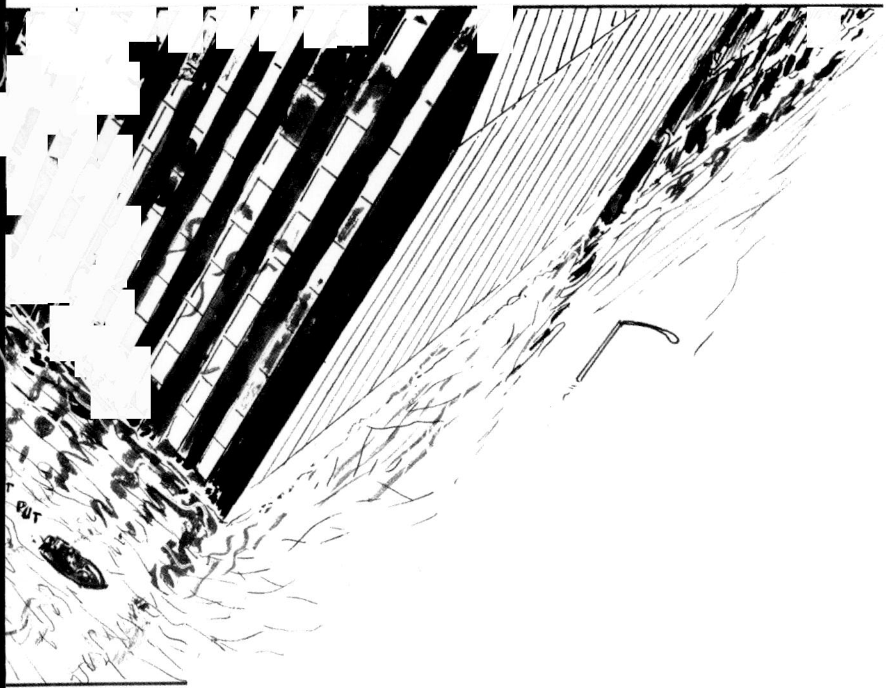

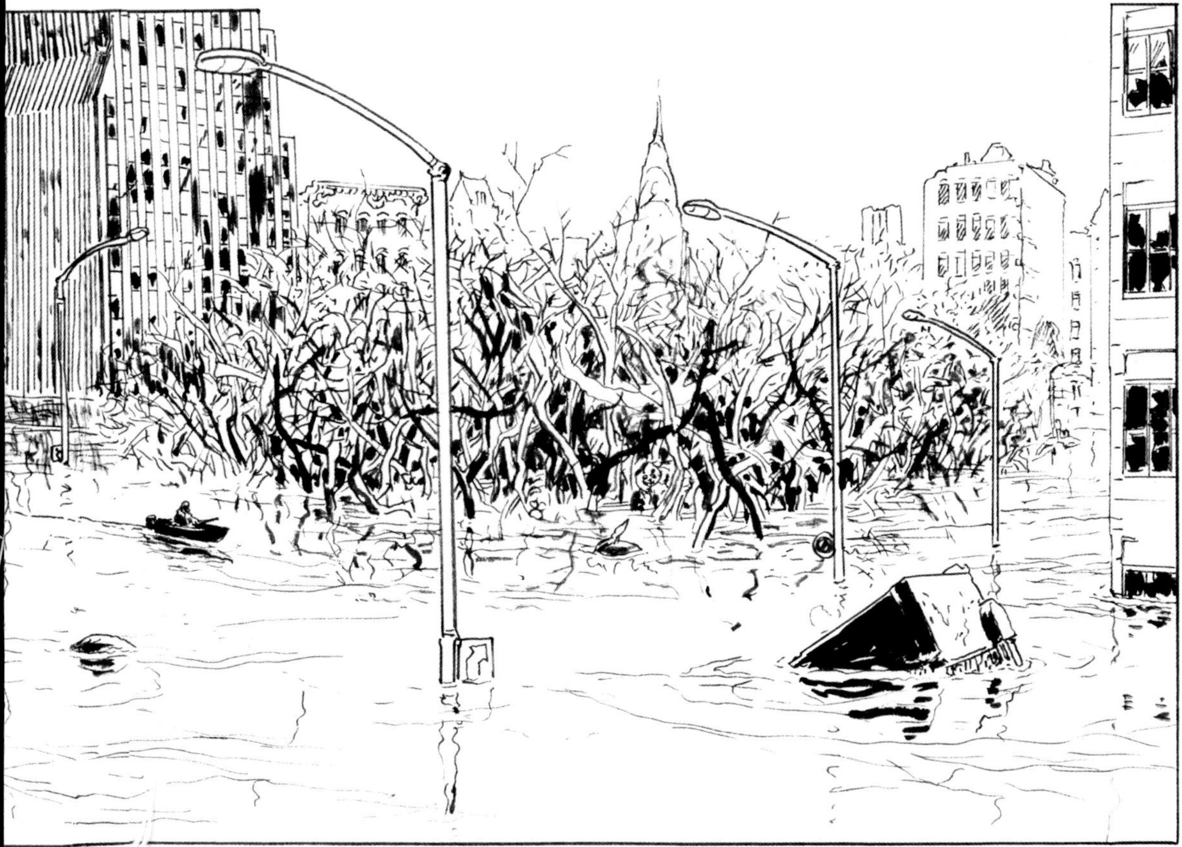

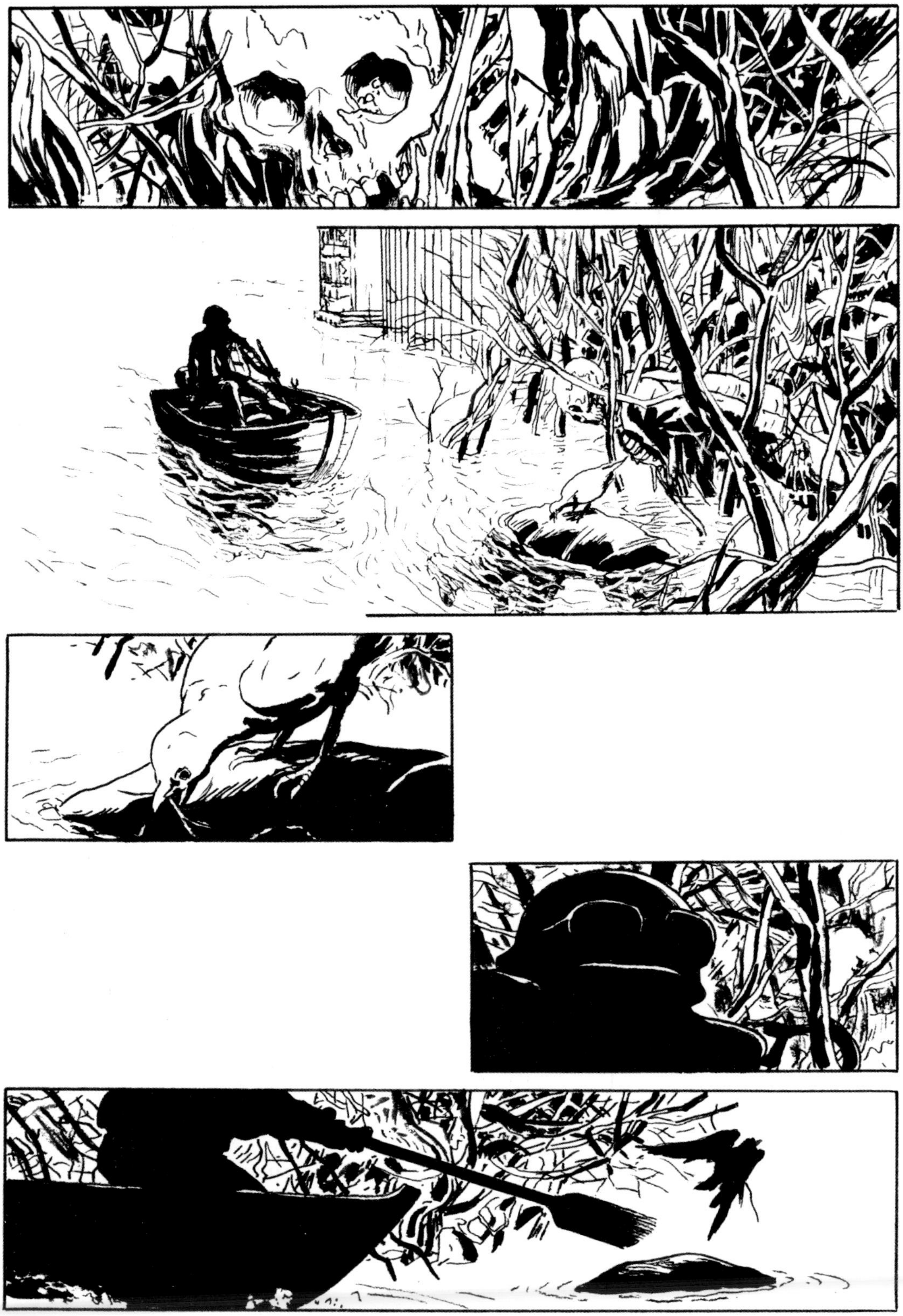

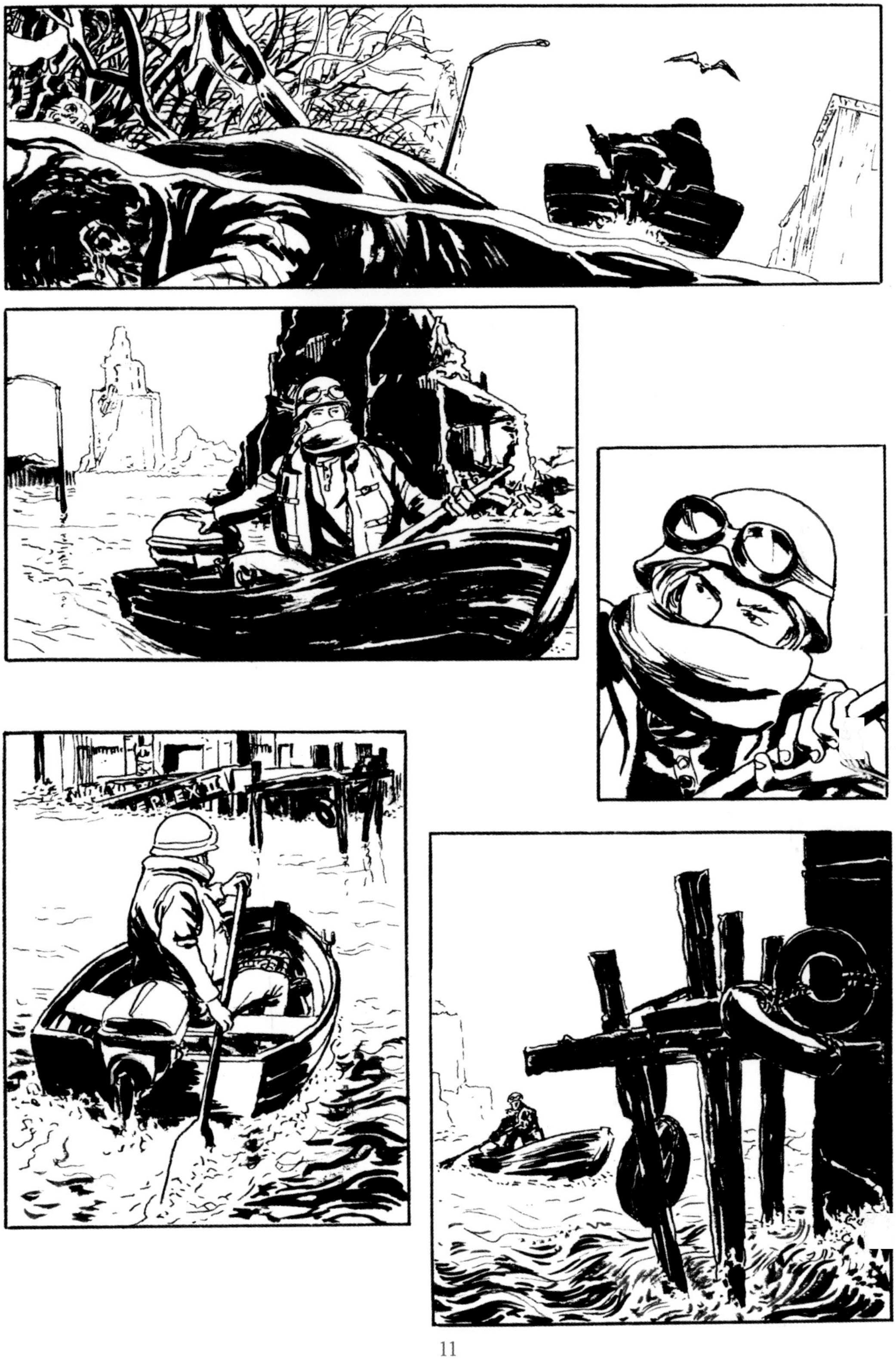
PLEX II

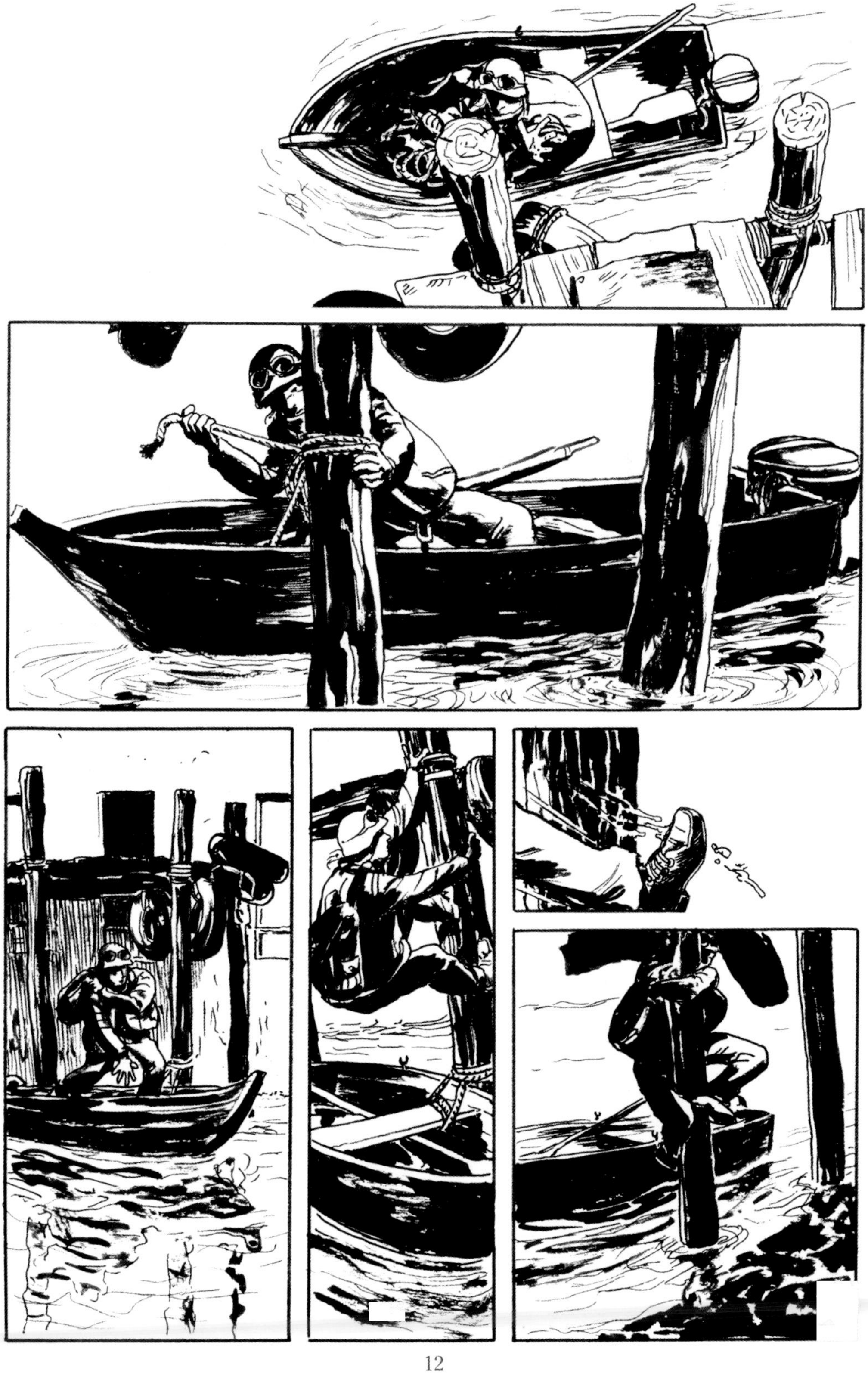

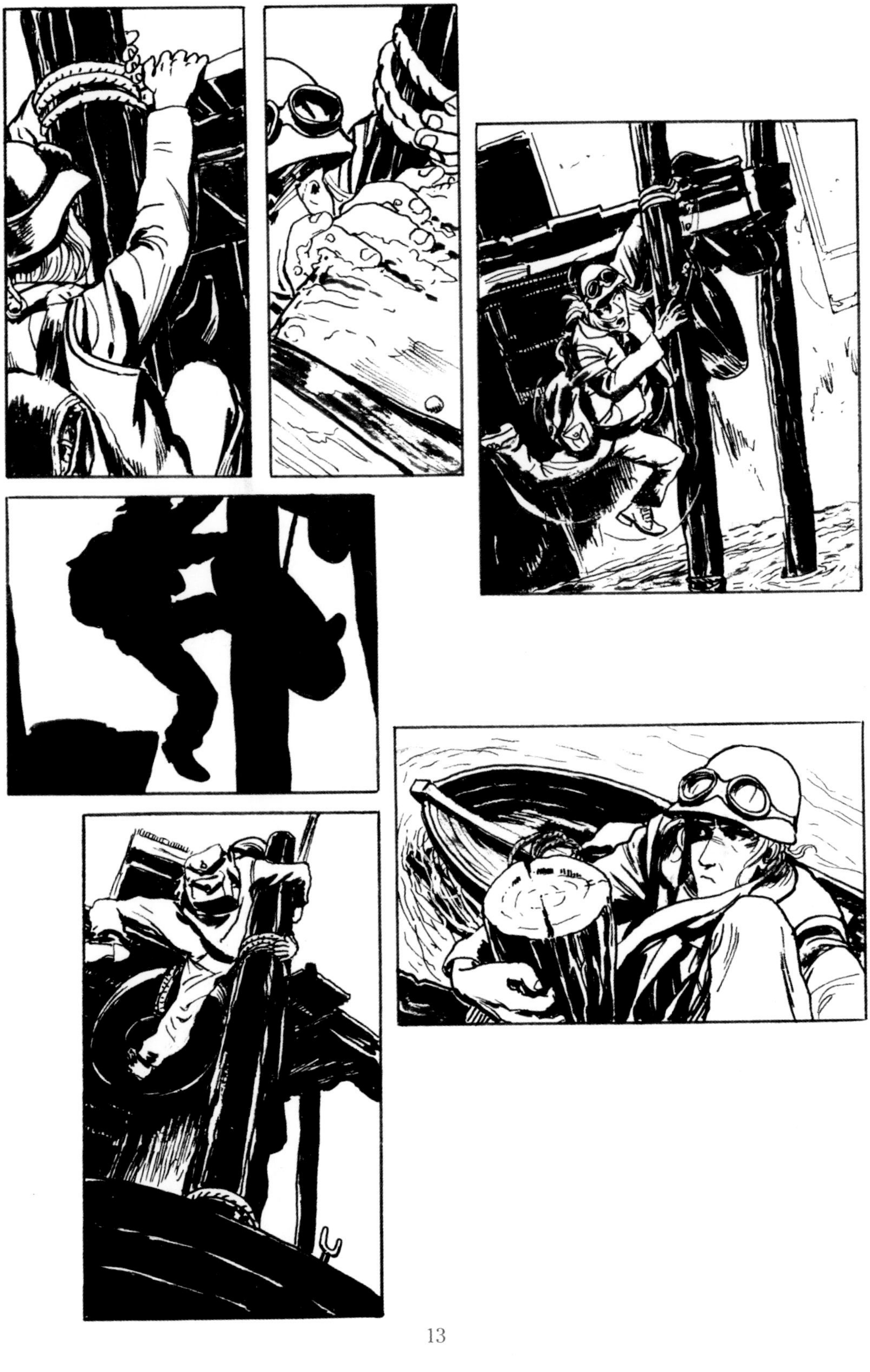

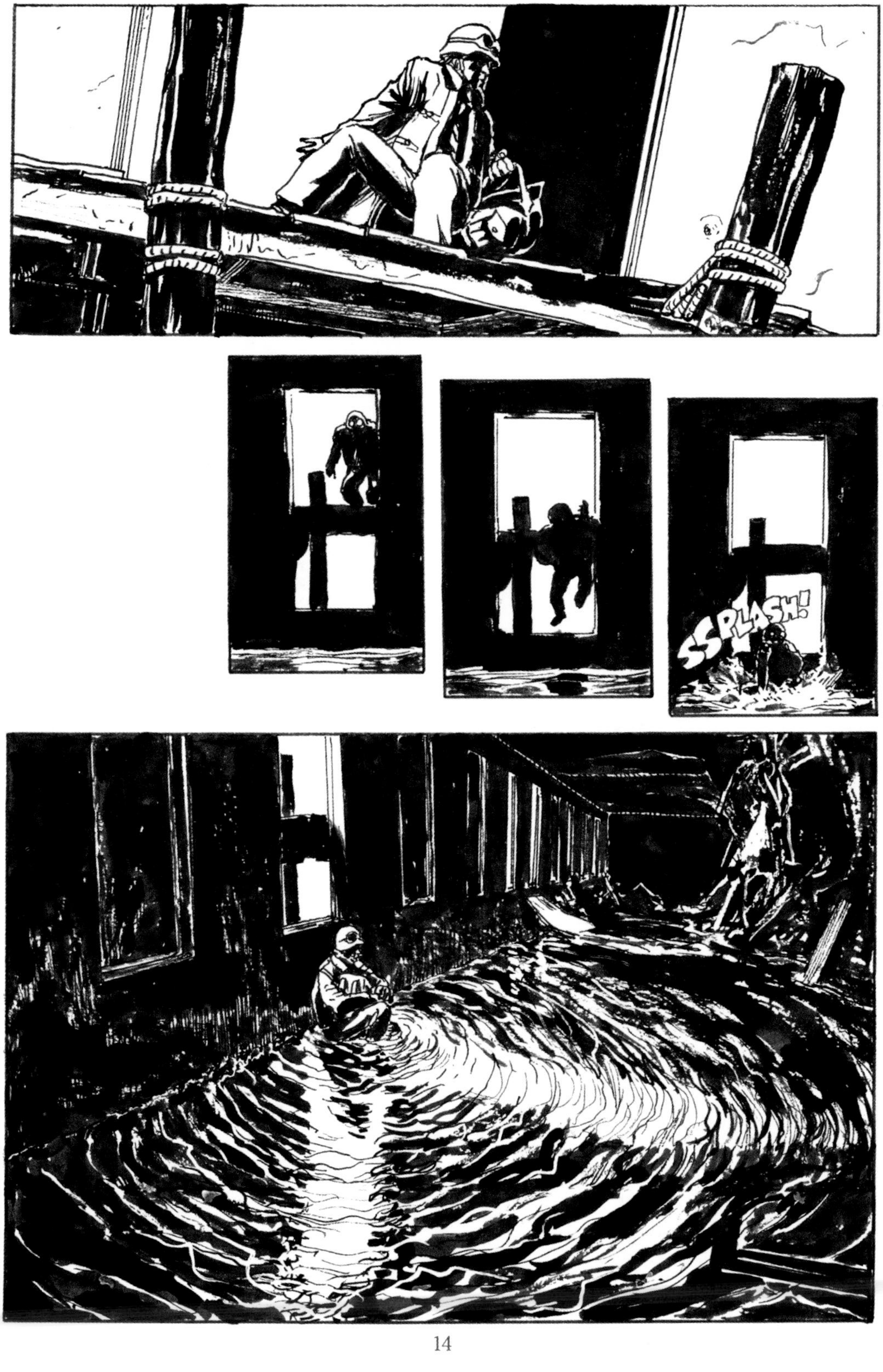
SSPLASH!

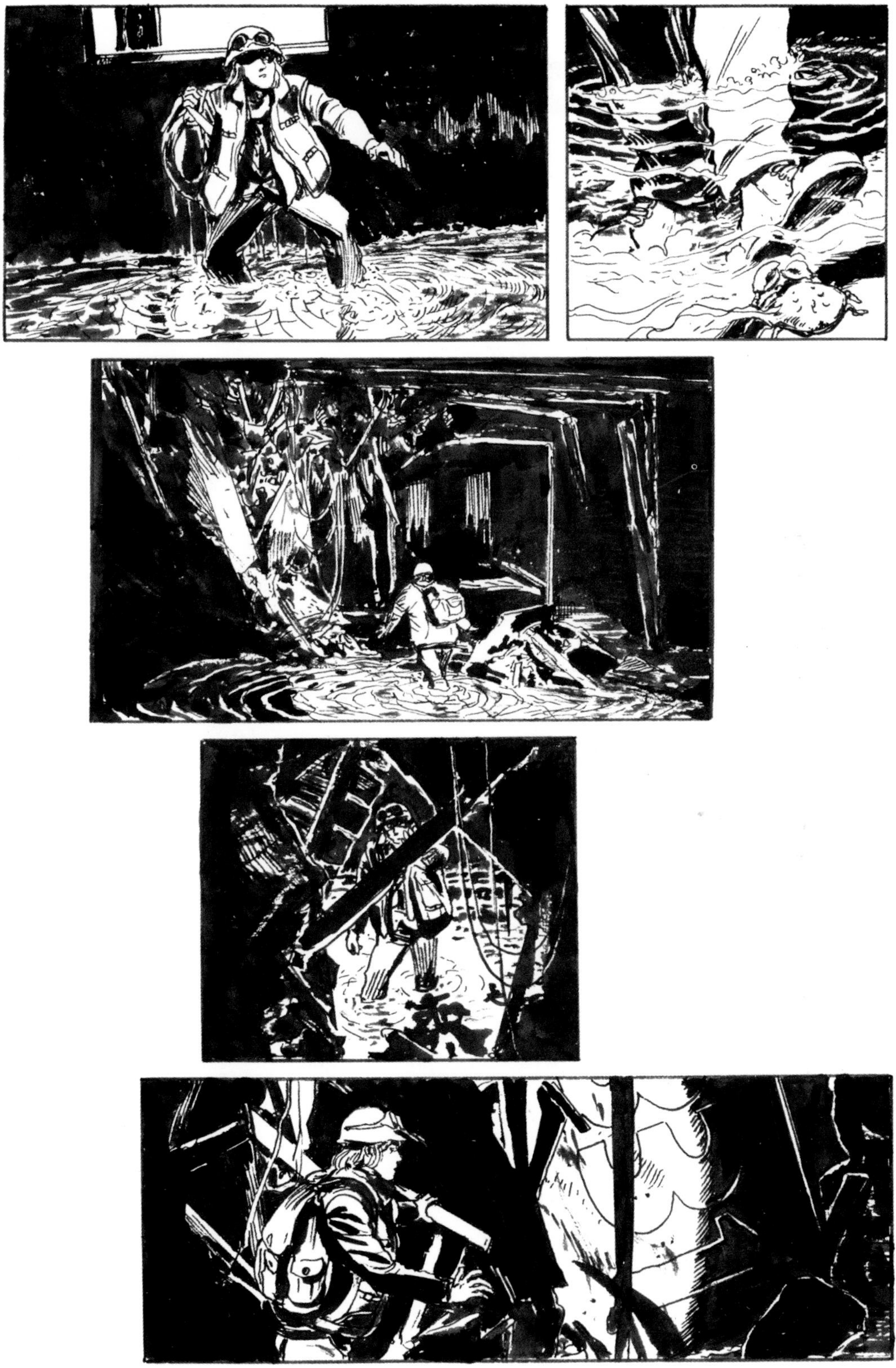

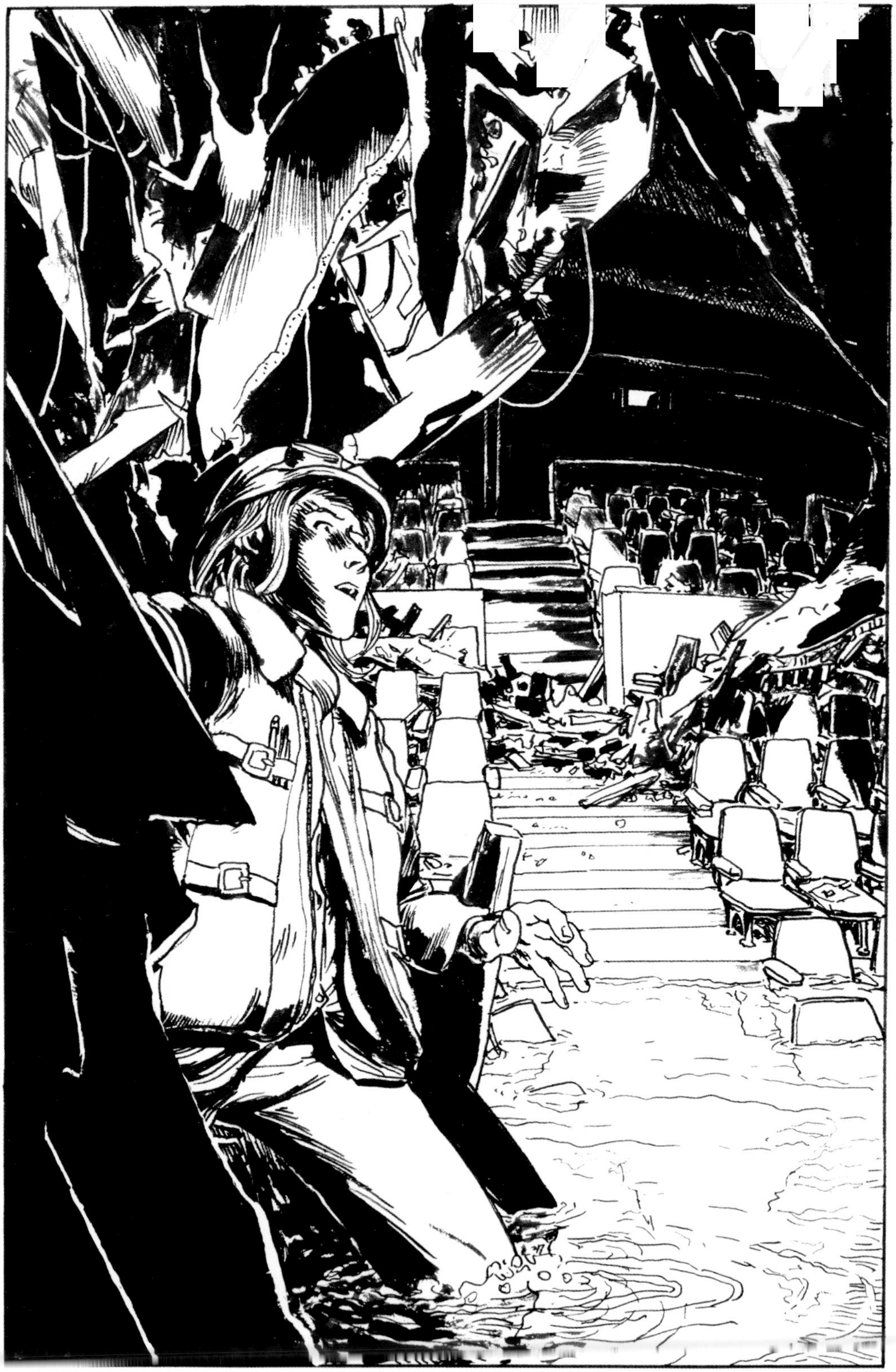

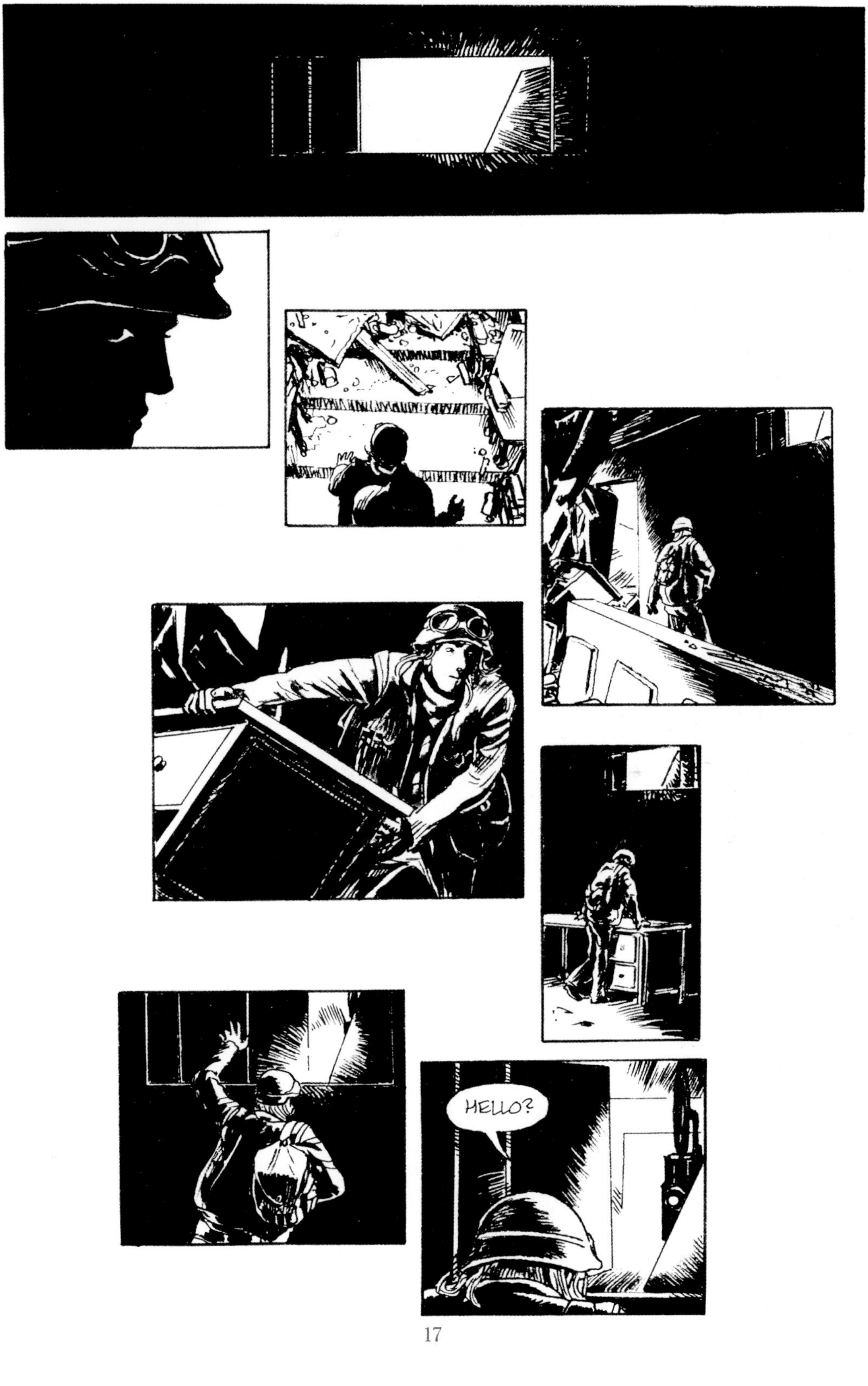
HELLO?

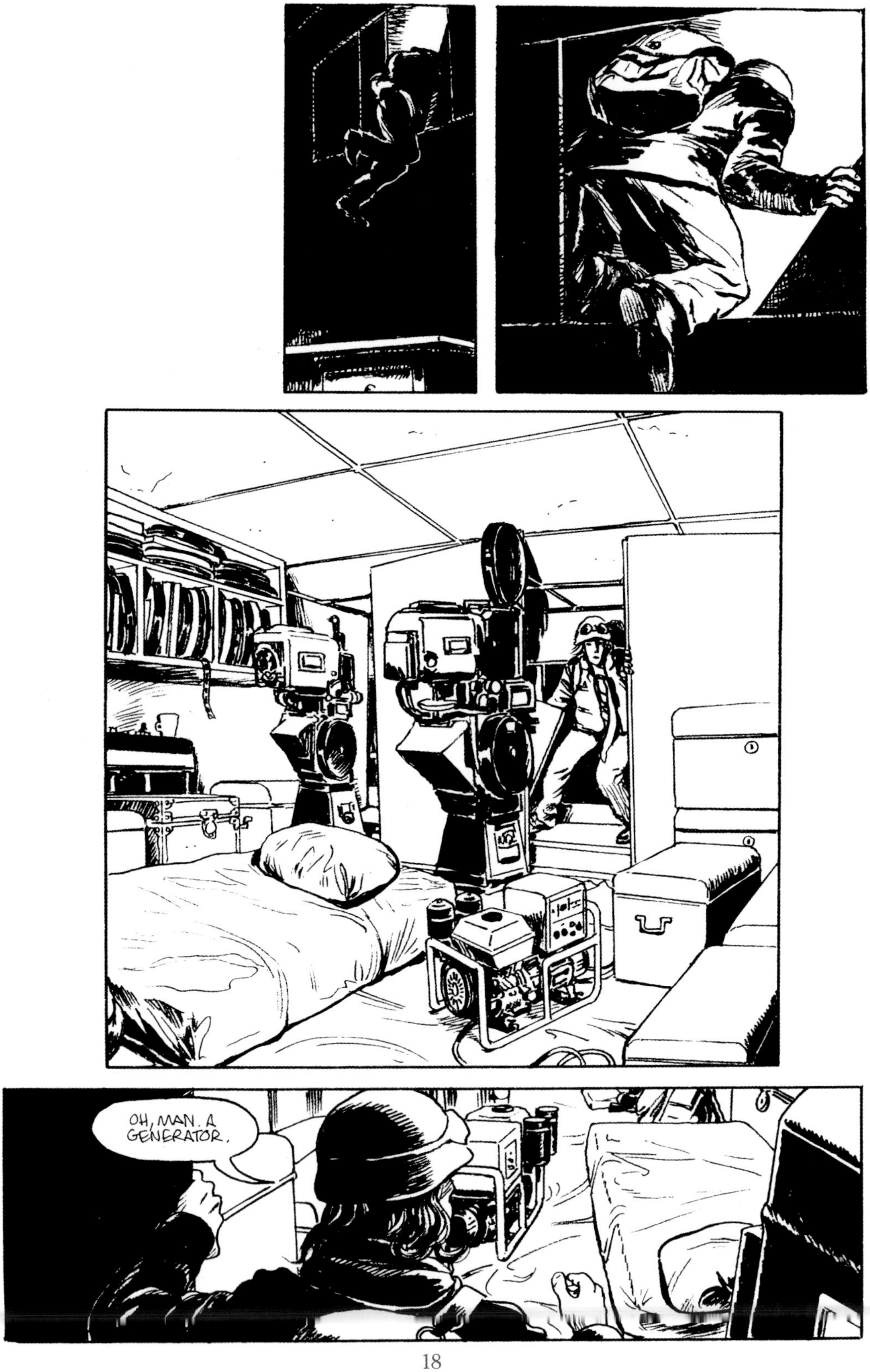
OH, MAN. A GENERATOR.

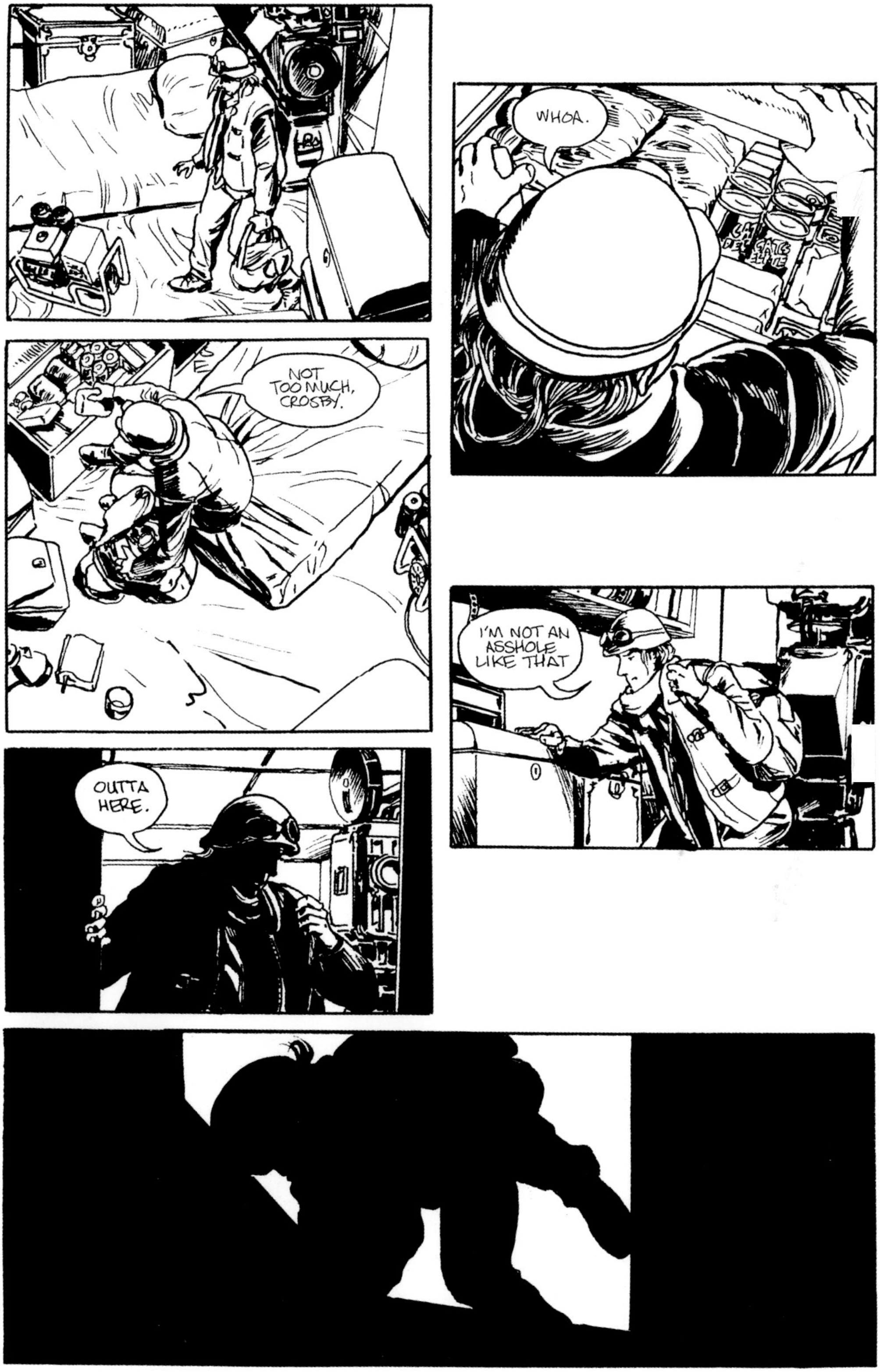
WHOA.
NOT TOO MUCH, CROSBY.
I'M NOT AN ASSHOLE LIKE THAT
OUTTA HERE.

AAAA
OOOF!
WAI---
UUNGH

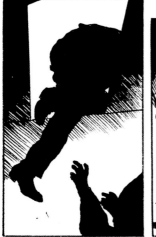

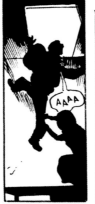

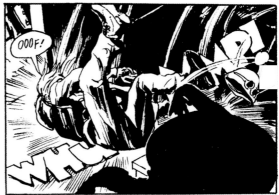

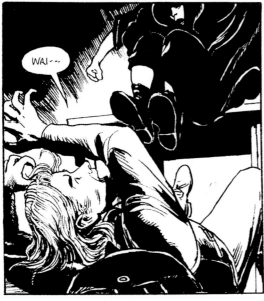

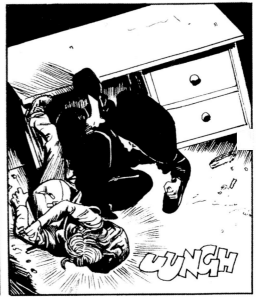

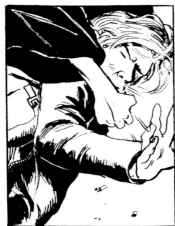

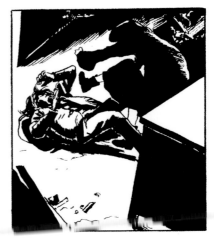

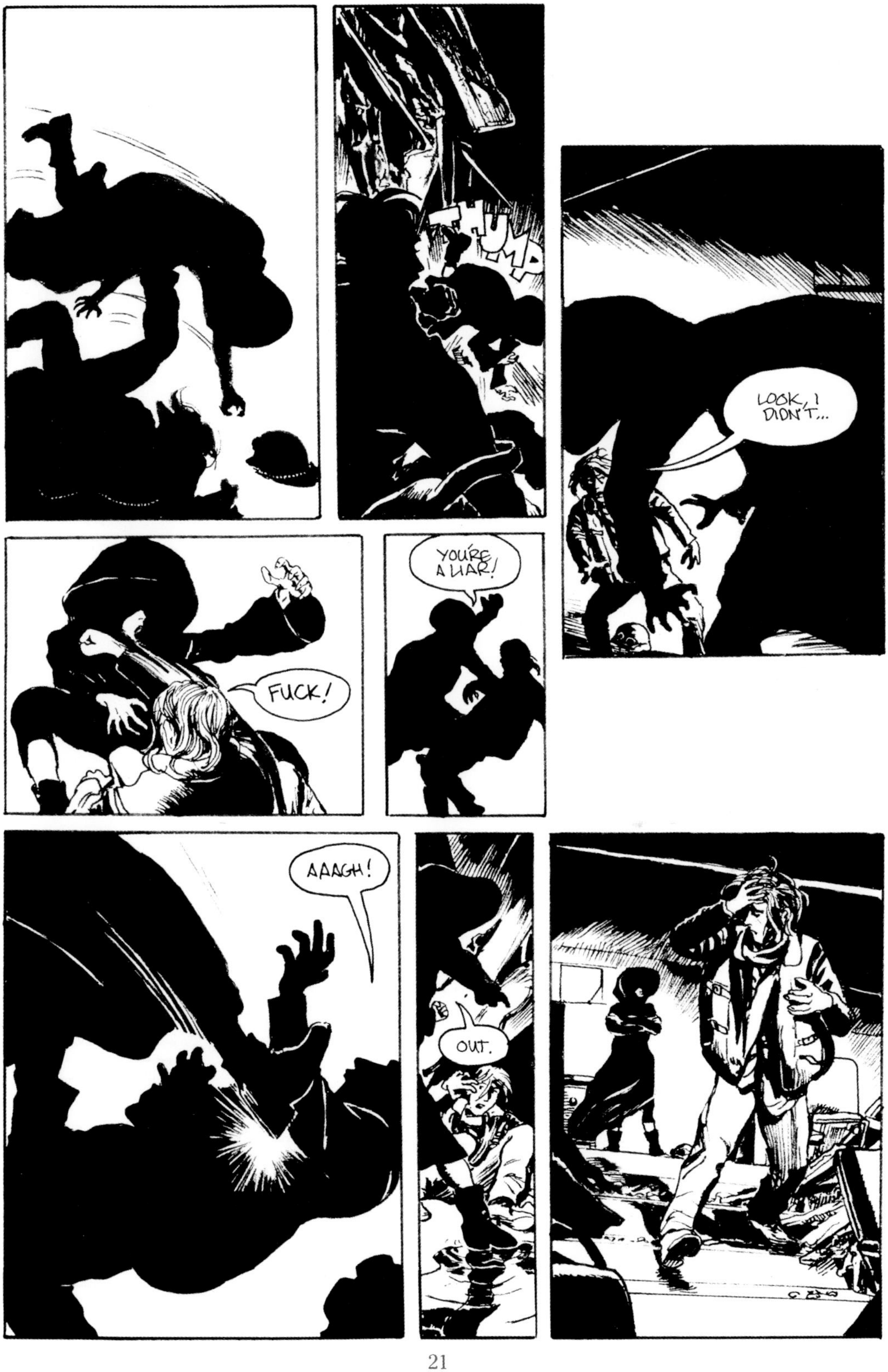
THUMP
LOOK, I DIDN'T...
YOU'RE A LIAR!
FUCK!
AAAGH!
OUT.

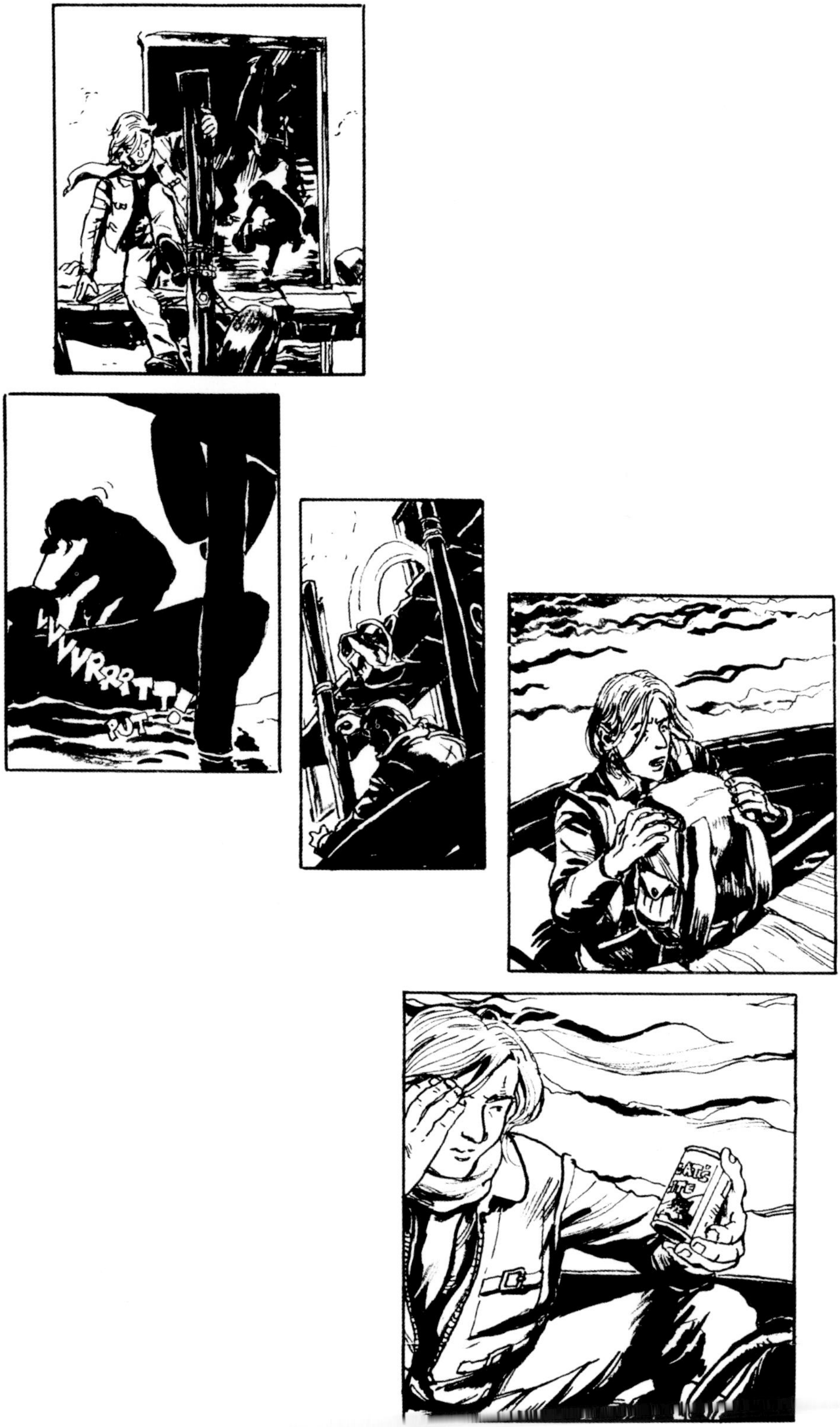
VVVVRRRRTTT!
PUT

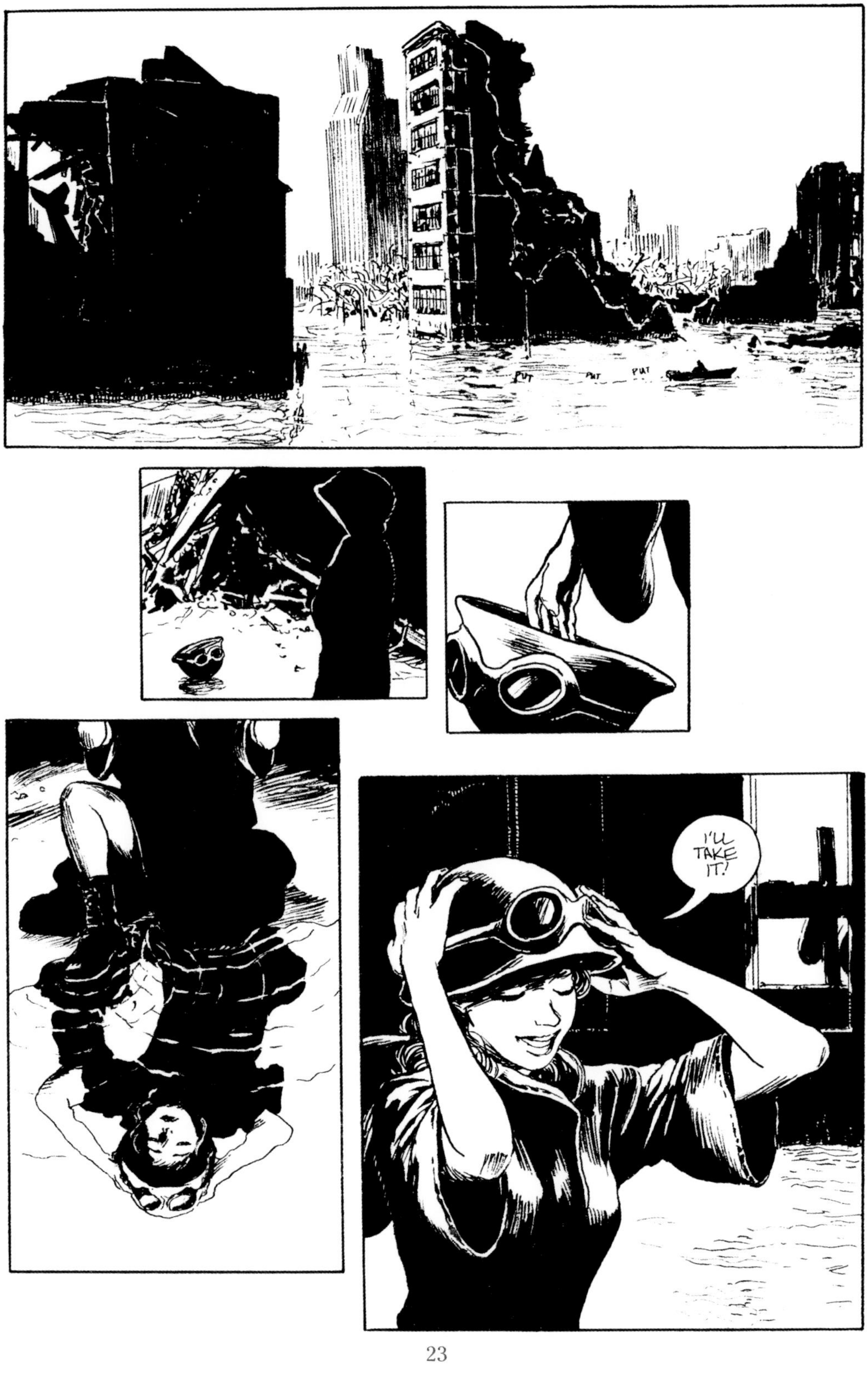
PUT
PUT
PUT
I'LL TAKE IT!

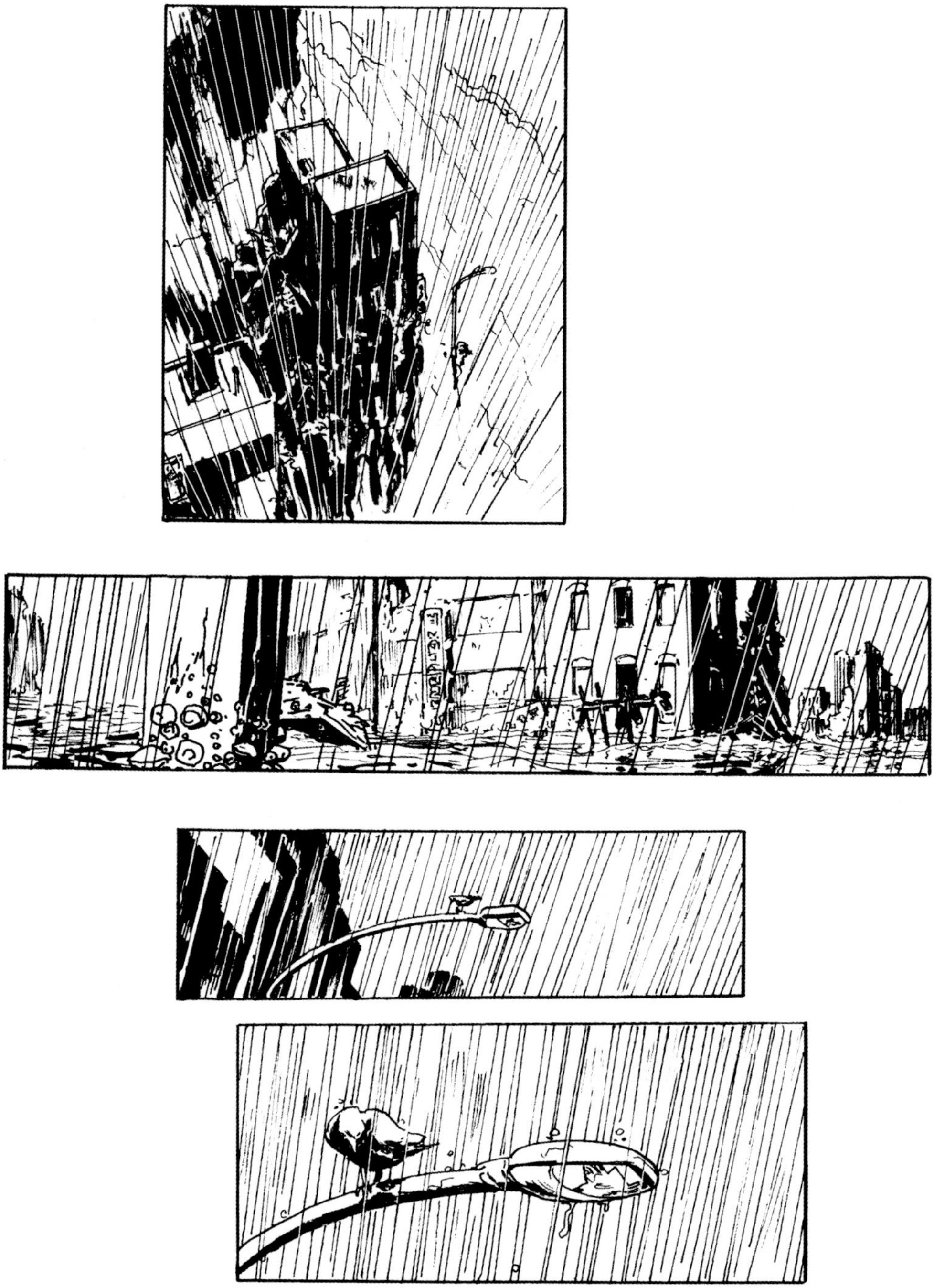

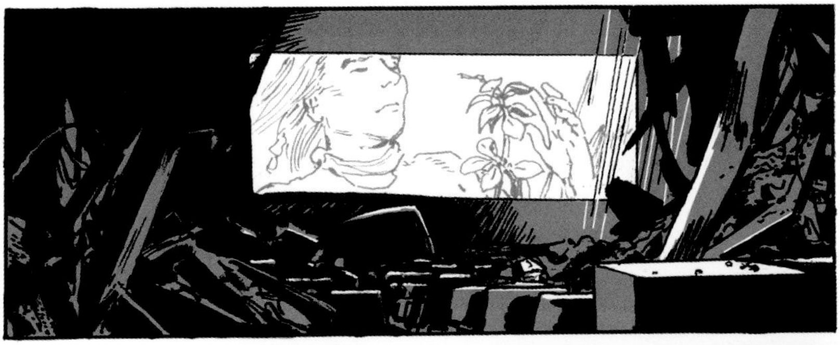

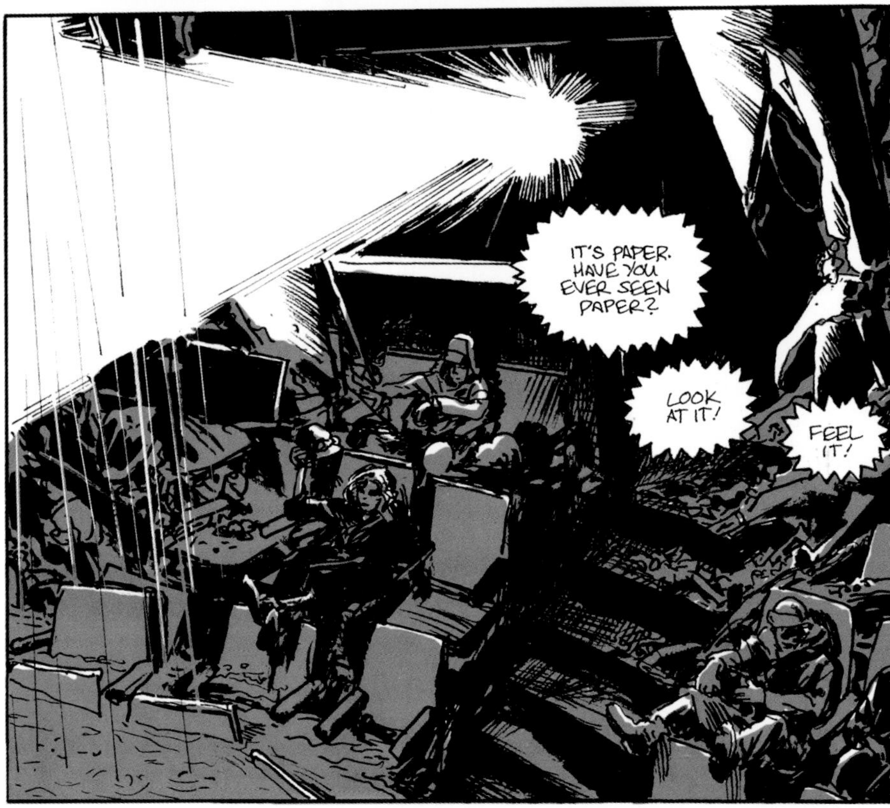
IT'S PAPER. HAVE YOU EVER SEEN PAPER?
LOOK AT IT!
FEEL IT!

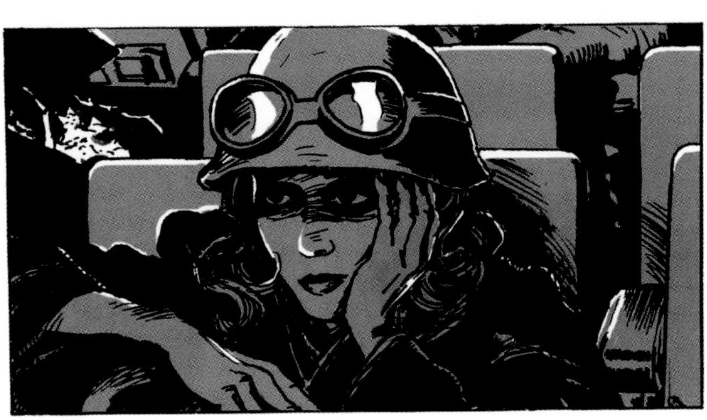

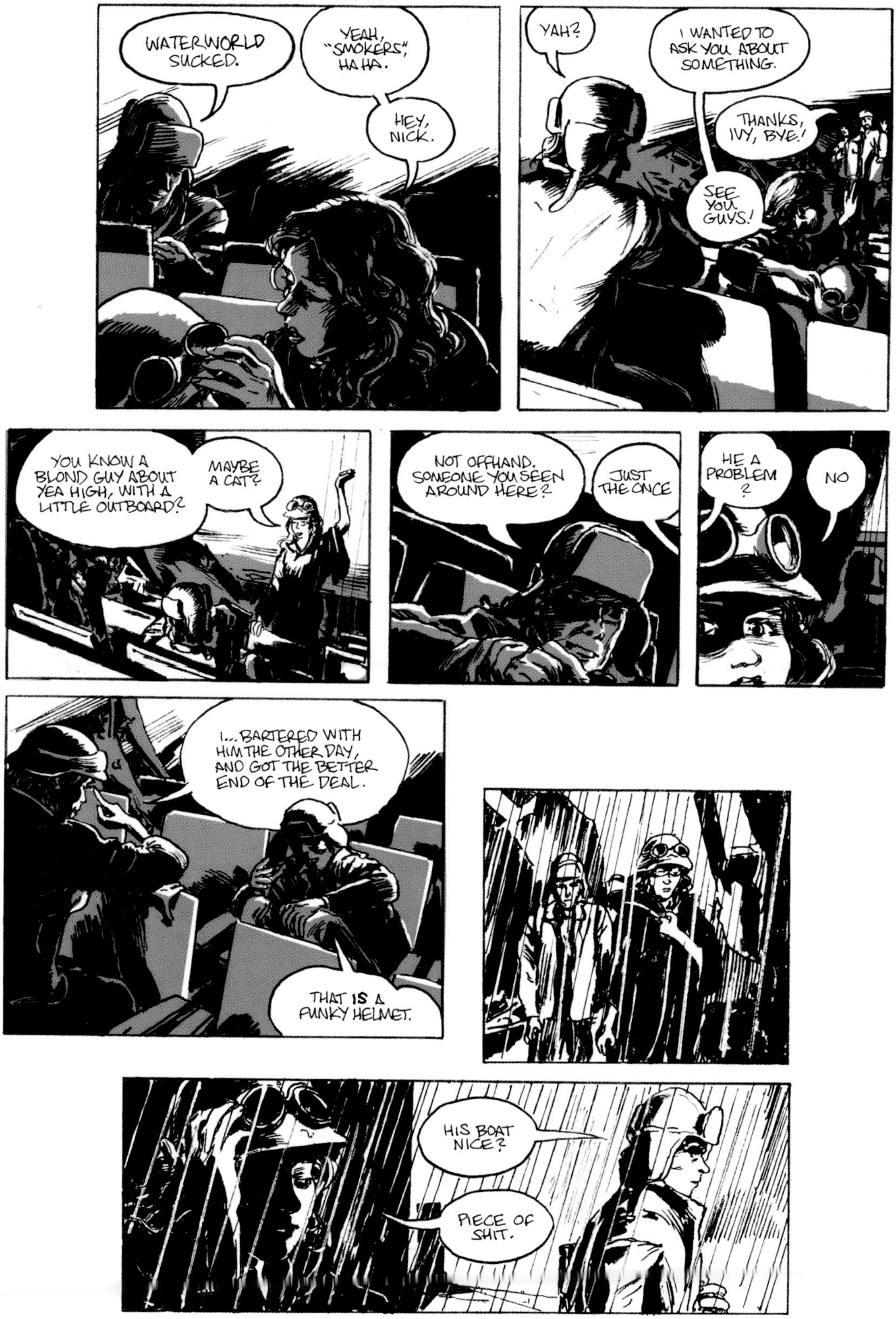
WATERWORLD SUCKED.
YEAH, "SMOKERS", HA HA.
HEY, NICK.
YAH?
I WANTED TO ASK YOU ABOUT SOMETHING.
THANKS, IVY, BYE!
SEE YOU GUYS!
YOU KNOW A BLOND GUY ABOUT YEA HIGH, WITH A LITTLE OUTBOARD?
MAYBE A CAT?
NOT OFFHAND. SOMEONE YOU SEEN AROUND HERE?
JUST THE ONCE
HE A PROBLEM?
NO
I... BARTERED WITH HIM THE OTHER DAY, AND GOT THE BETTER END OF THE DEAL.
THAT IS A FUNKY HELMET.
HIS BOAT NICE?
PIECE OF SHIT.

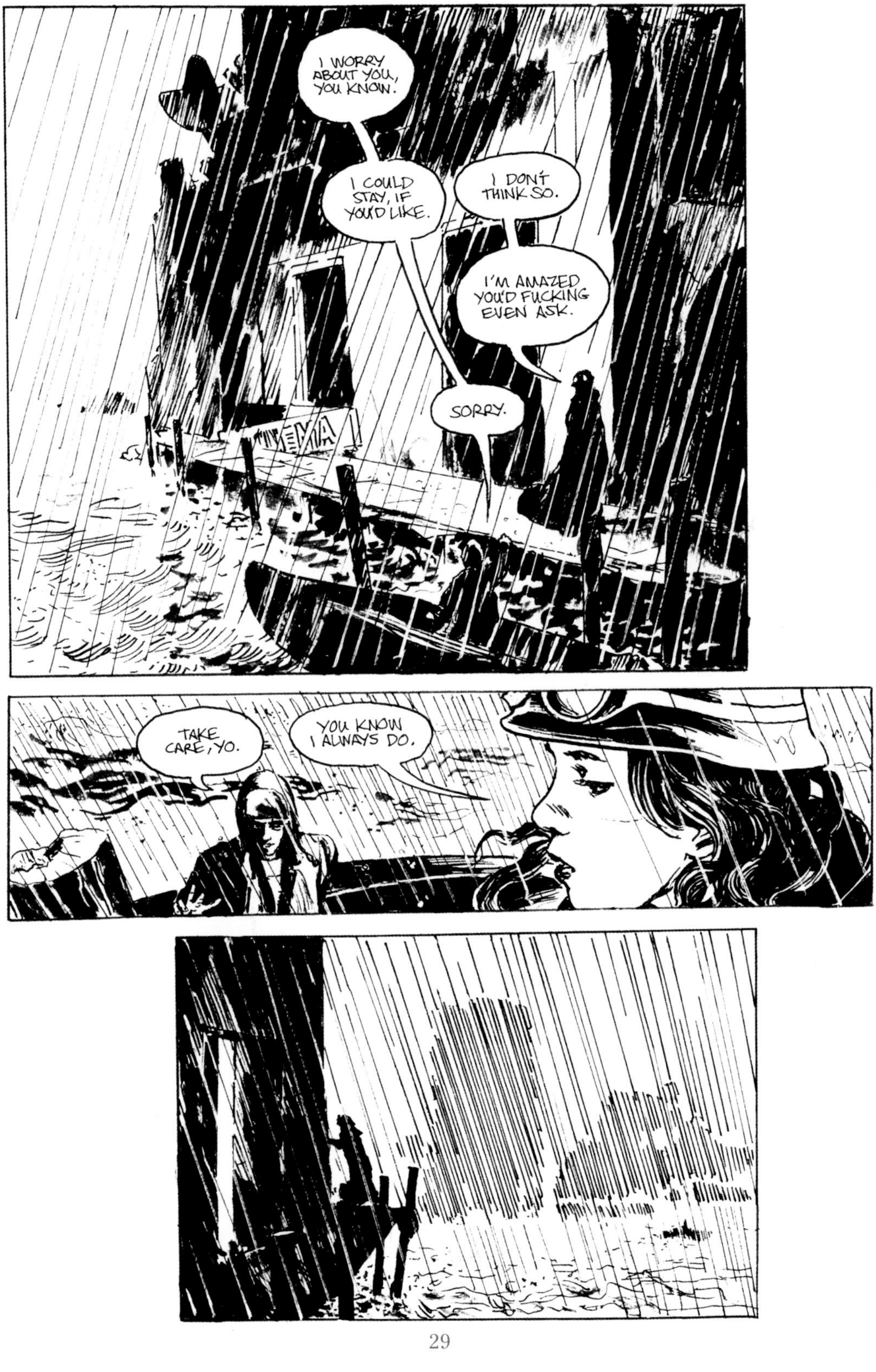
I WORRY ABOUT YOU, YOU KNOW.
I COULD STAY, IF YOU'D LIKE.
I DON'T THINK SO.
I'M AMAZED YOU'D FUCKING EVEN ASK.
SORRY.
TAKE CARE, YO.
YOU KNOW I ALWAYS DO.

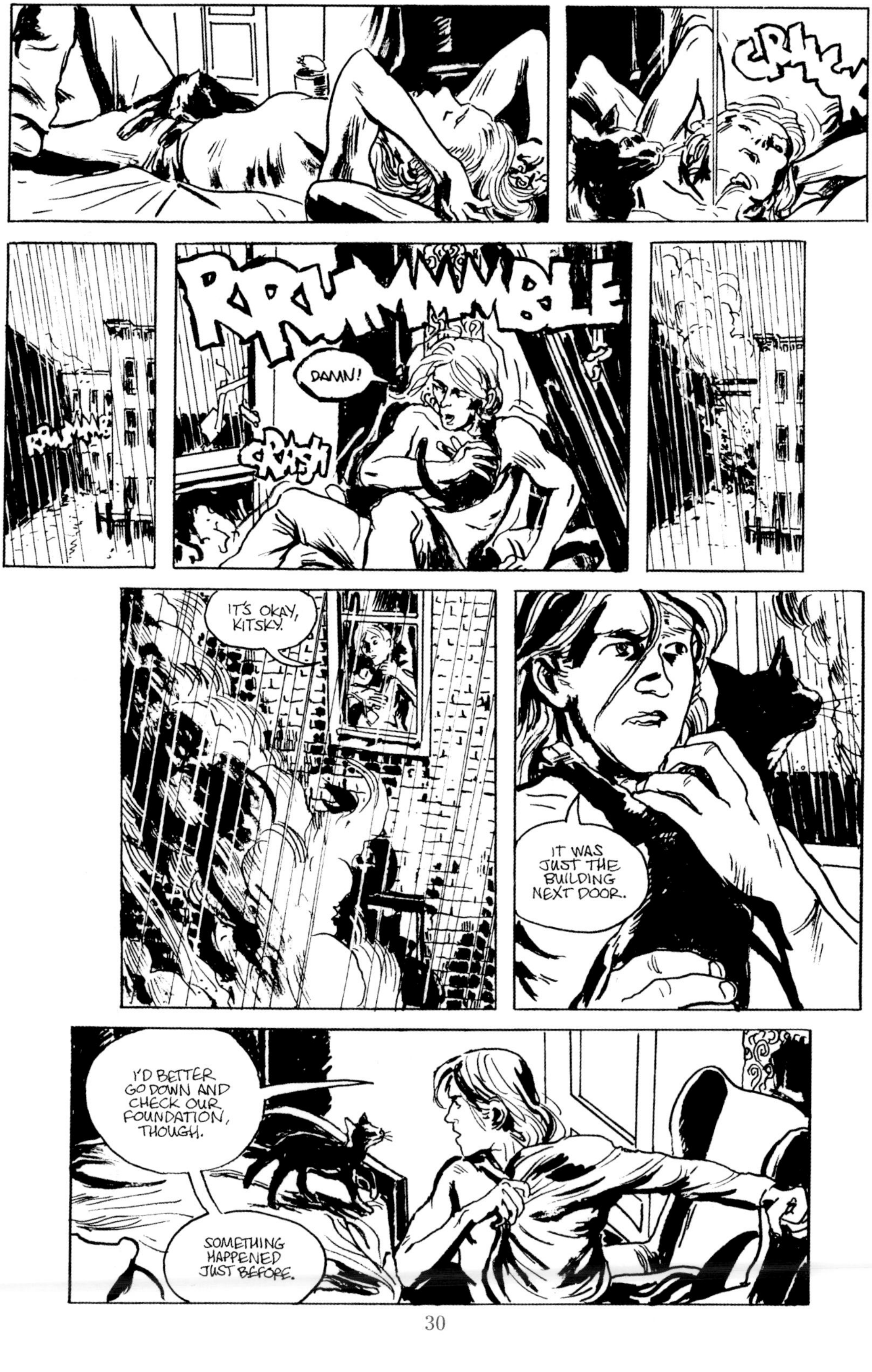
CRACK
RRRUMMMBLE
DAMN!
RRUMMMBLE
CRASH
IT'S OKAY, KITSKY.
IT WAS JUST THE BUILDING NEXT DOOR.
I'D BETTER GO DOWN AND CHECK OUR FOUNDATION, THOUGH.
SOMETHING HAPPENED JUST BEFORE.

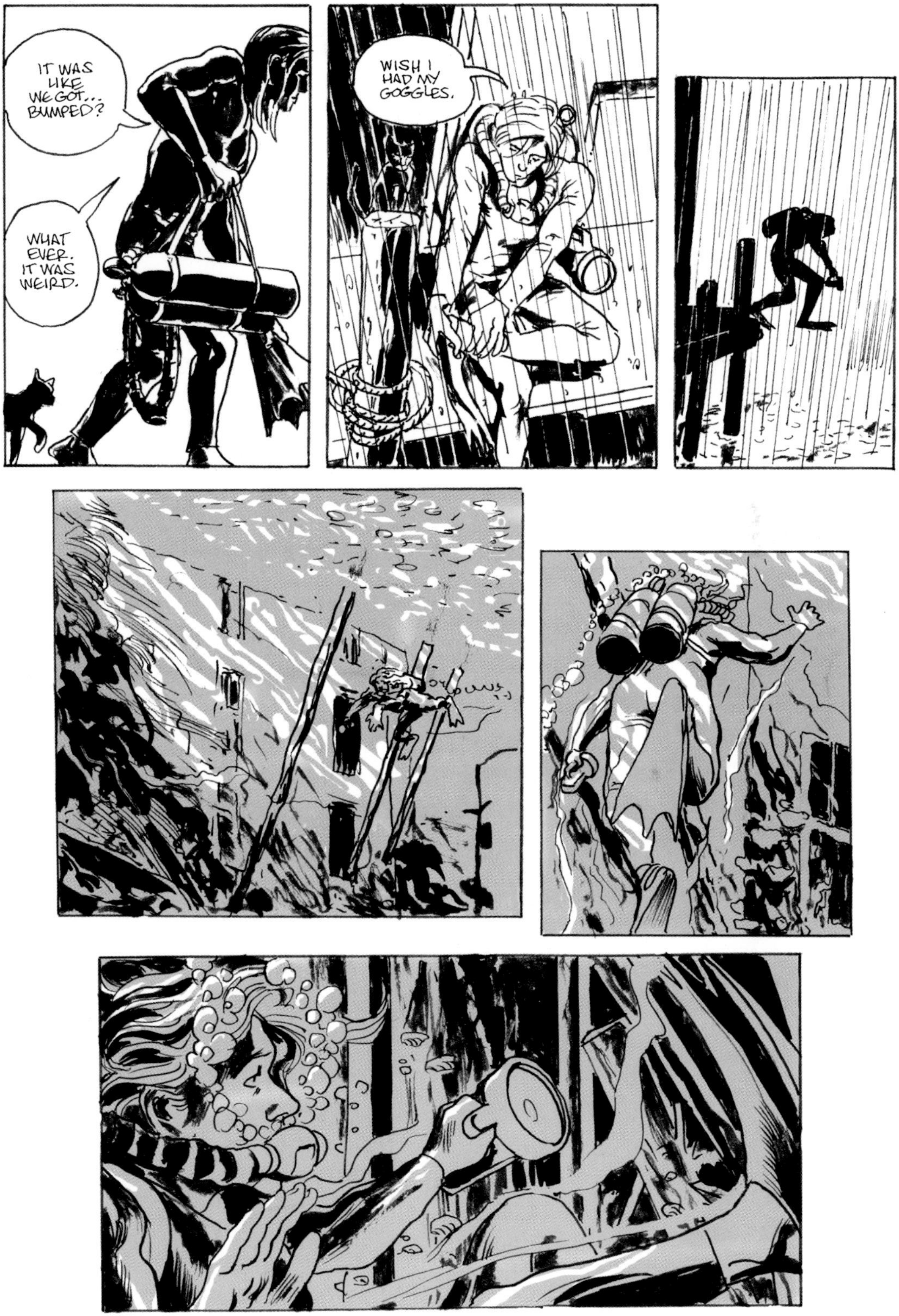
IT WAS LIKE WE GOT... BUMPED?
WHAT EVER. IT WAS WEIRD.
WISH I HAD MY GOGGLES.

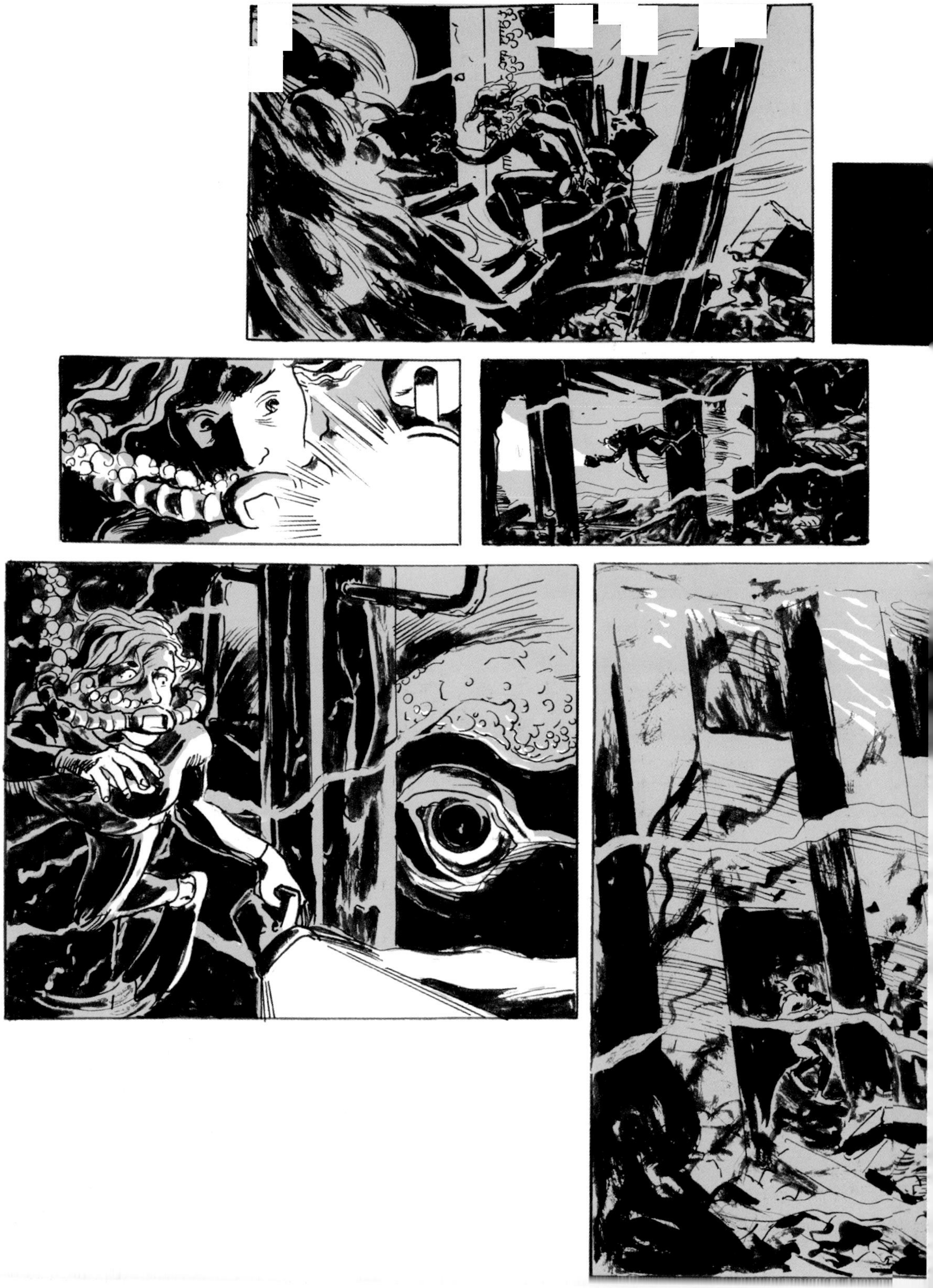

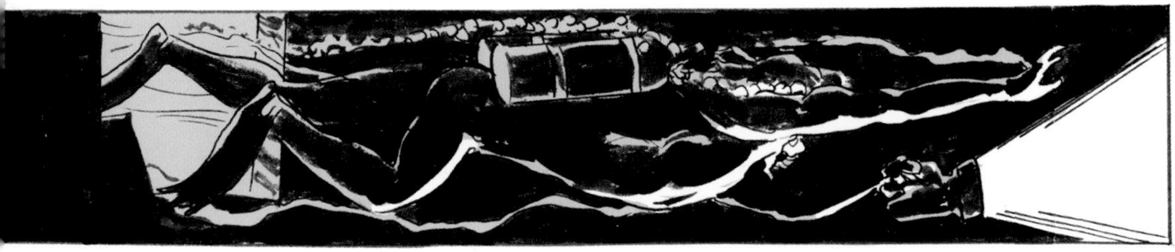

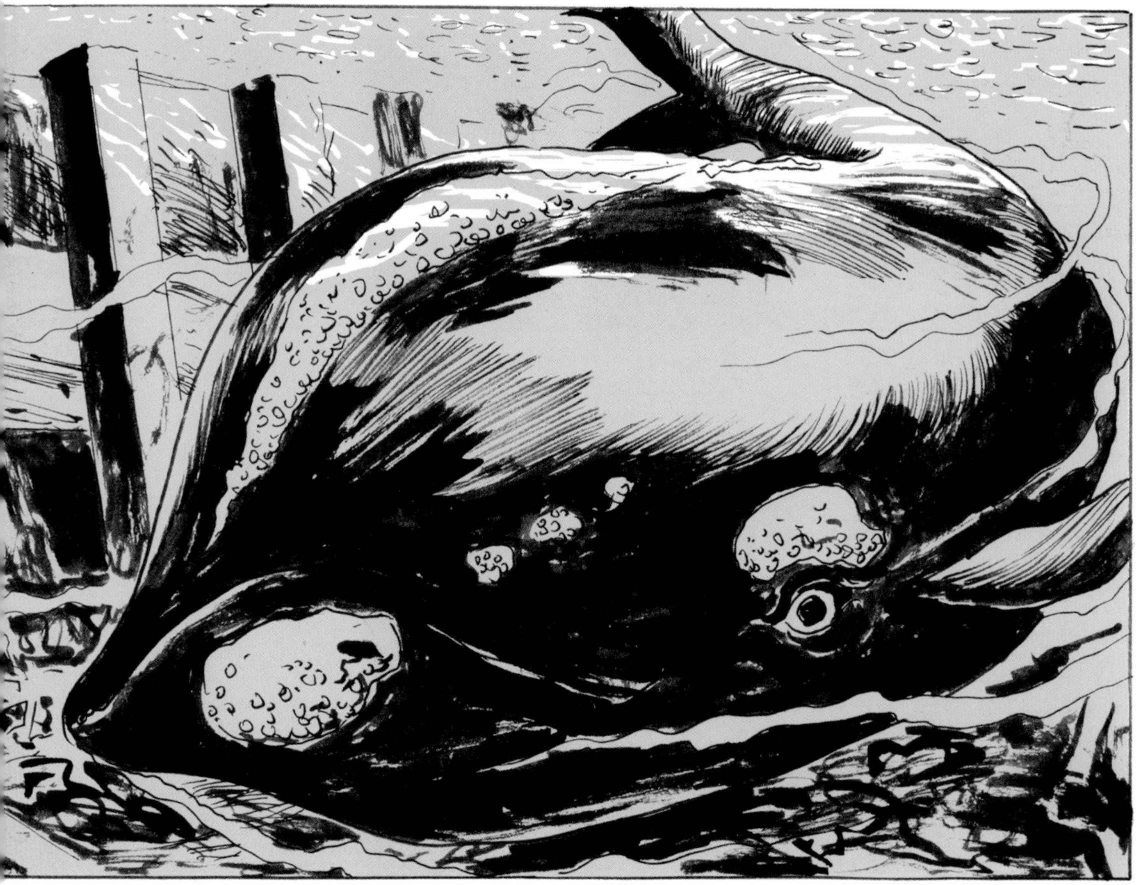

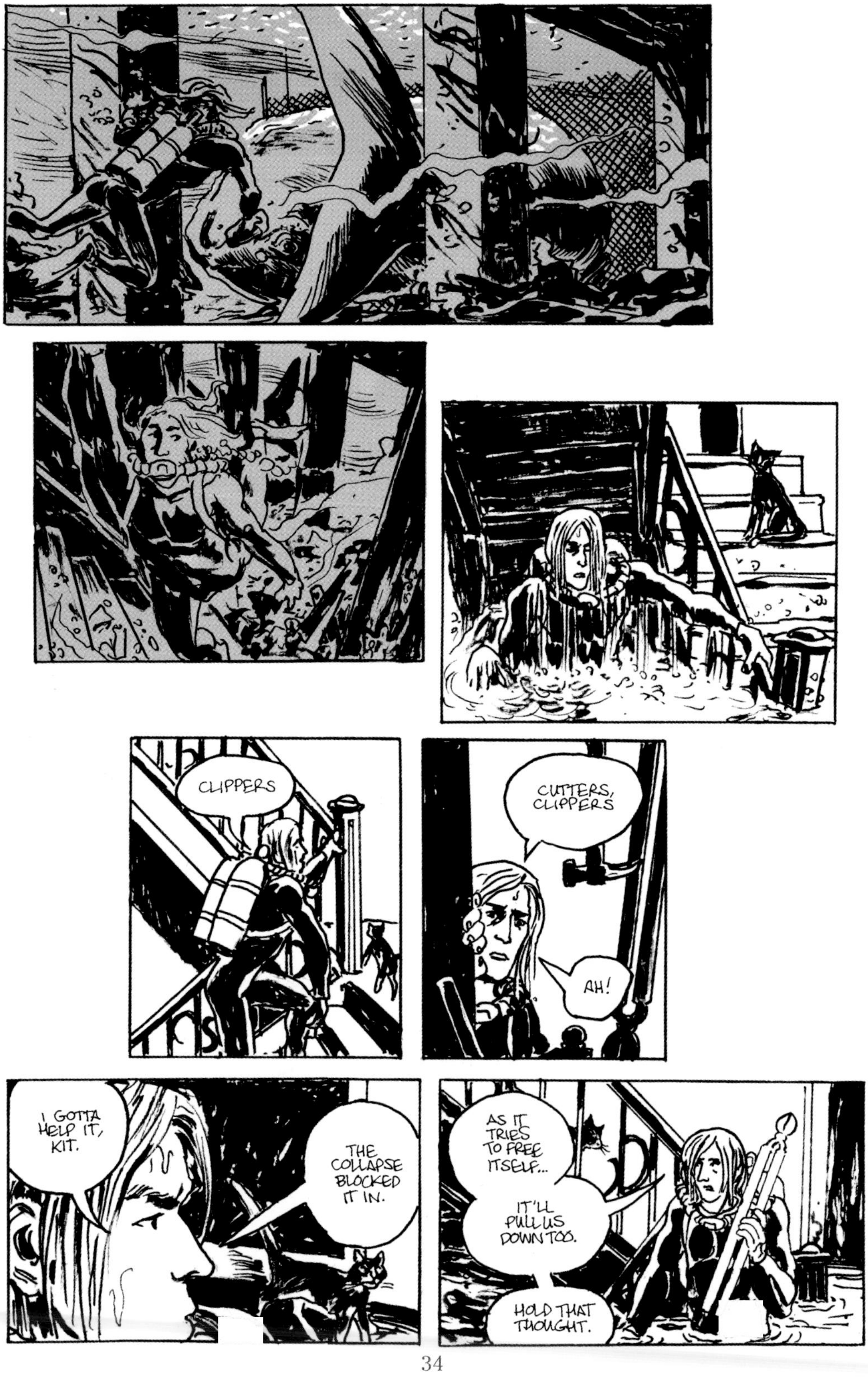
CLIPPERS
CUTTERS, CLIPPERS
AH!
I GOTTA HELP IT, KIT.
THE COLLAPSE BLOCKED IT IN.
AS IT TRIES TO FREE ITSELF...
IT'LL PULL US DOWN TOO.
HOLD THAT THOUGHT.

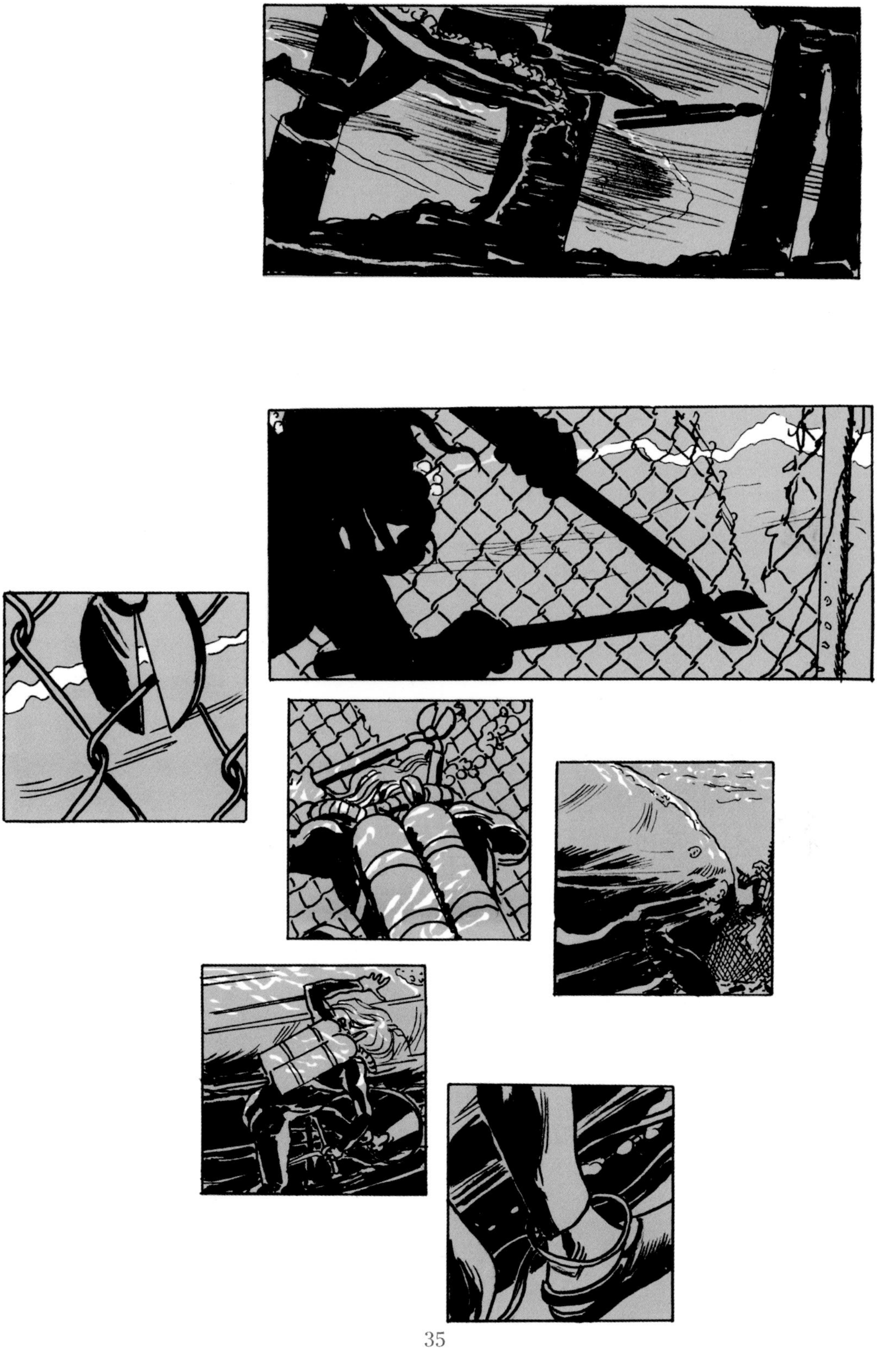

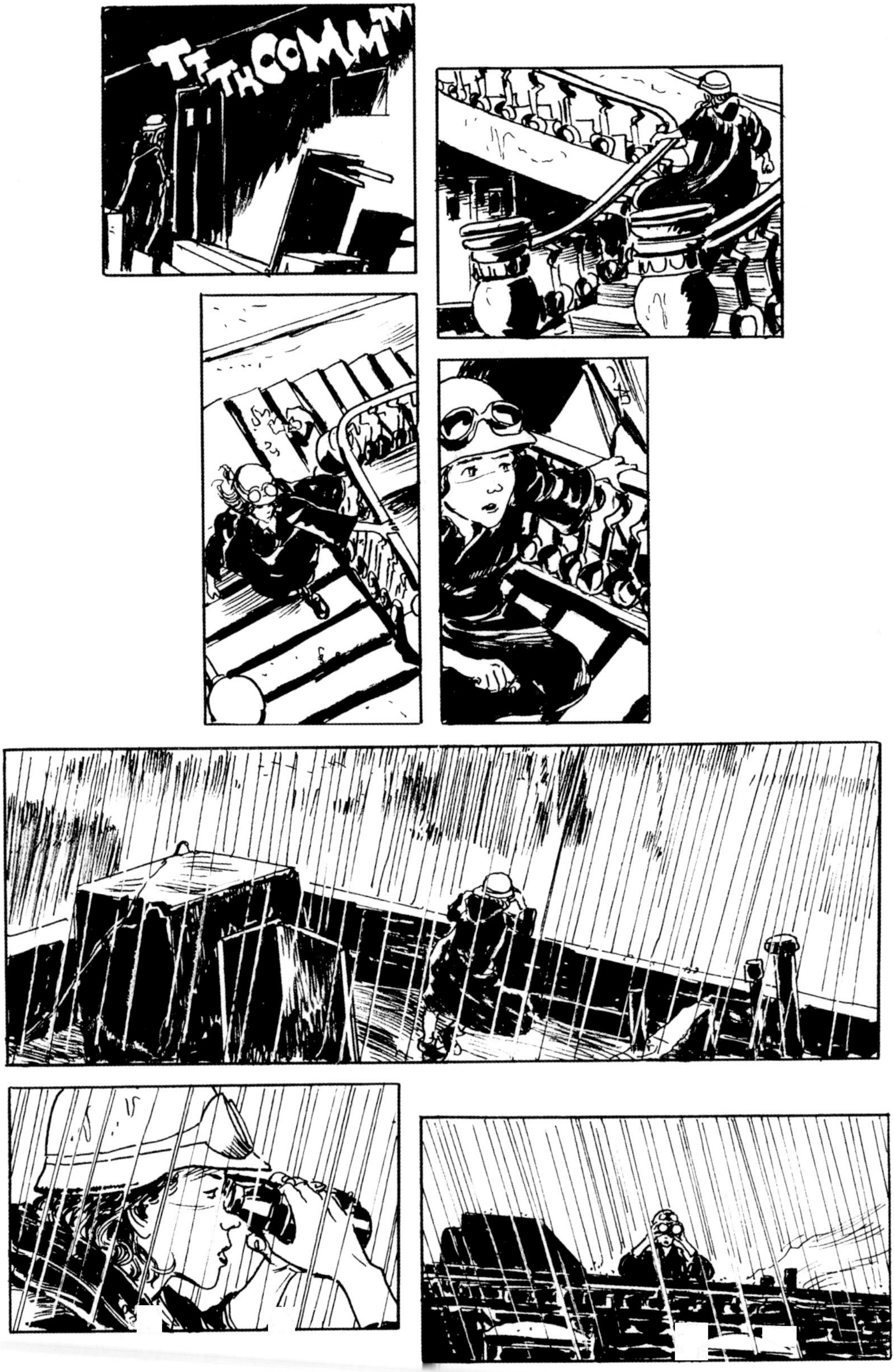
TF TH COMMM

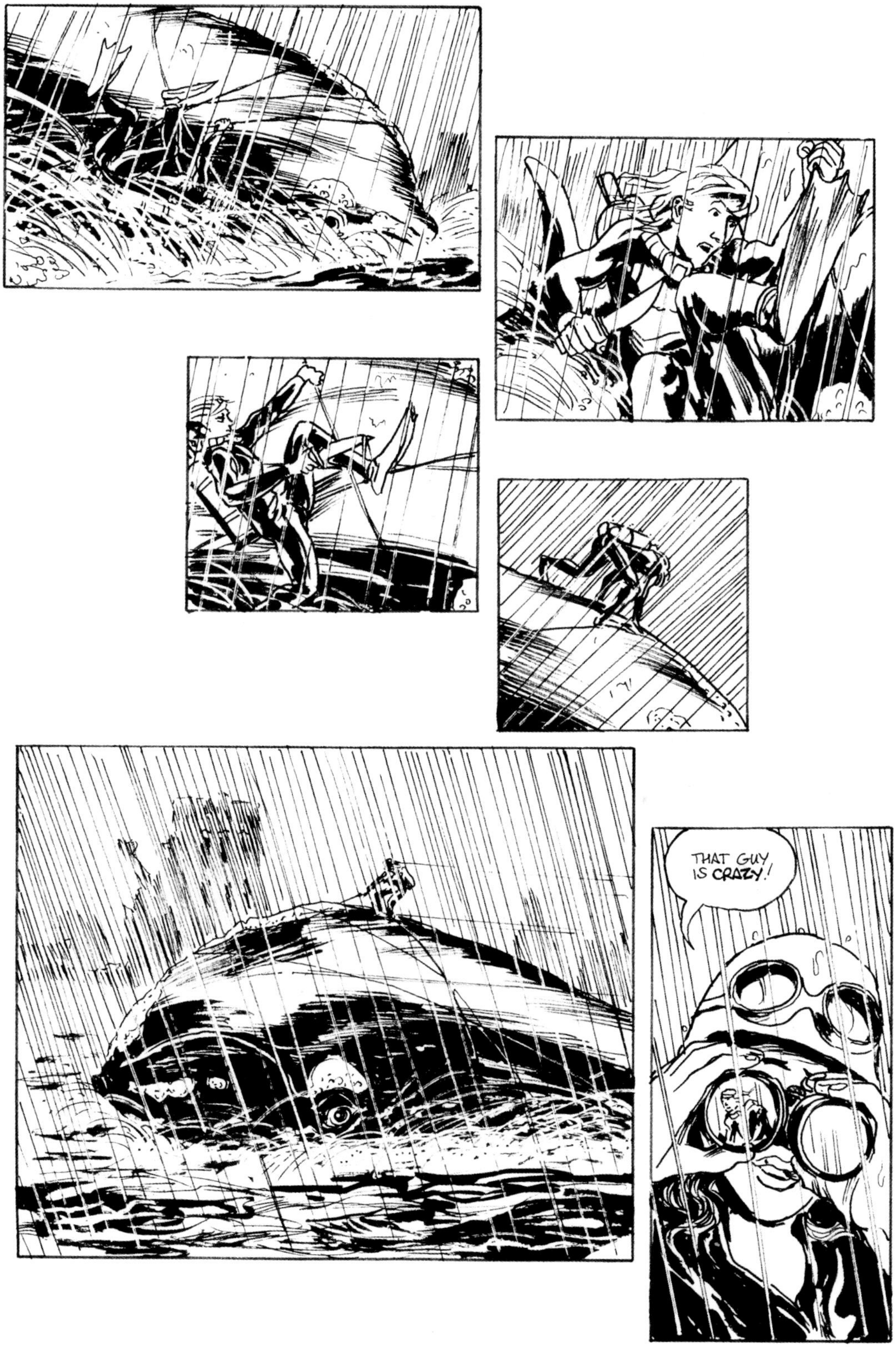
THAT GUY IS CRAZY!

OR,

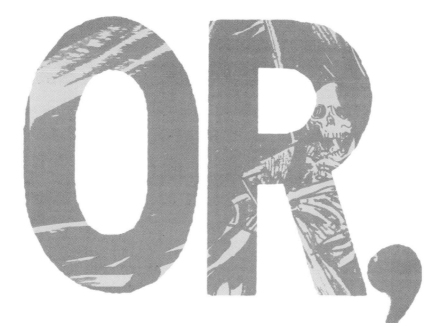

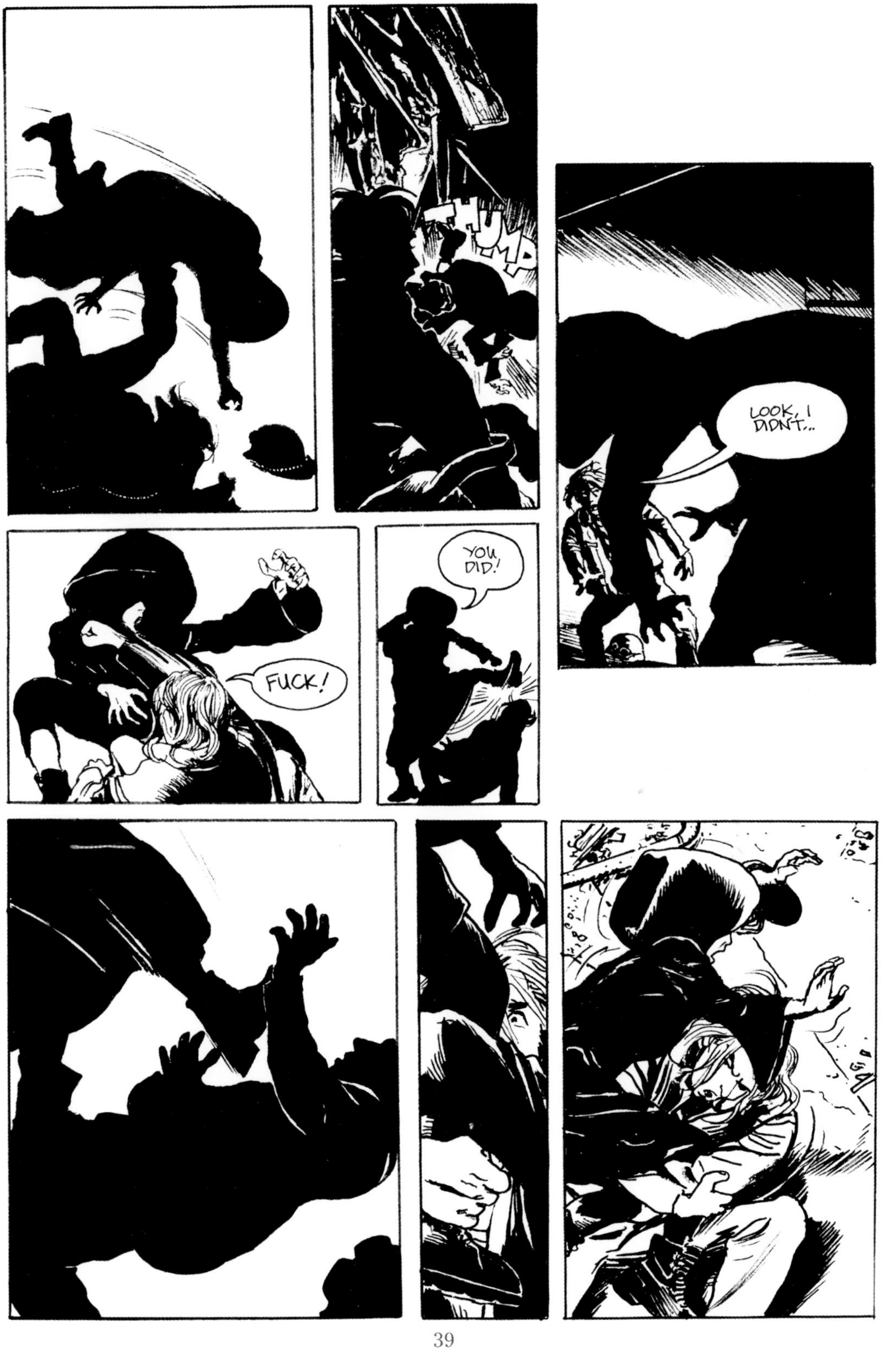
THUMP
LOOK, I DIDN'T...
FUCK!
YOU DID!

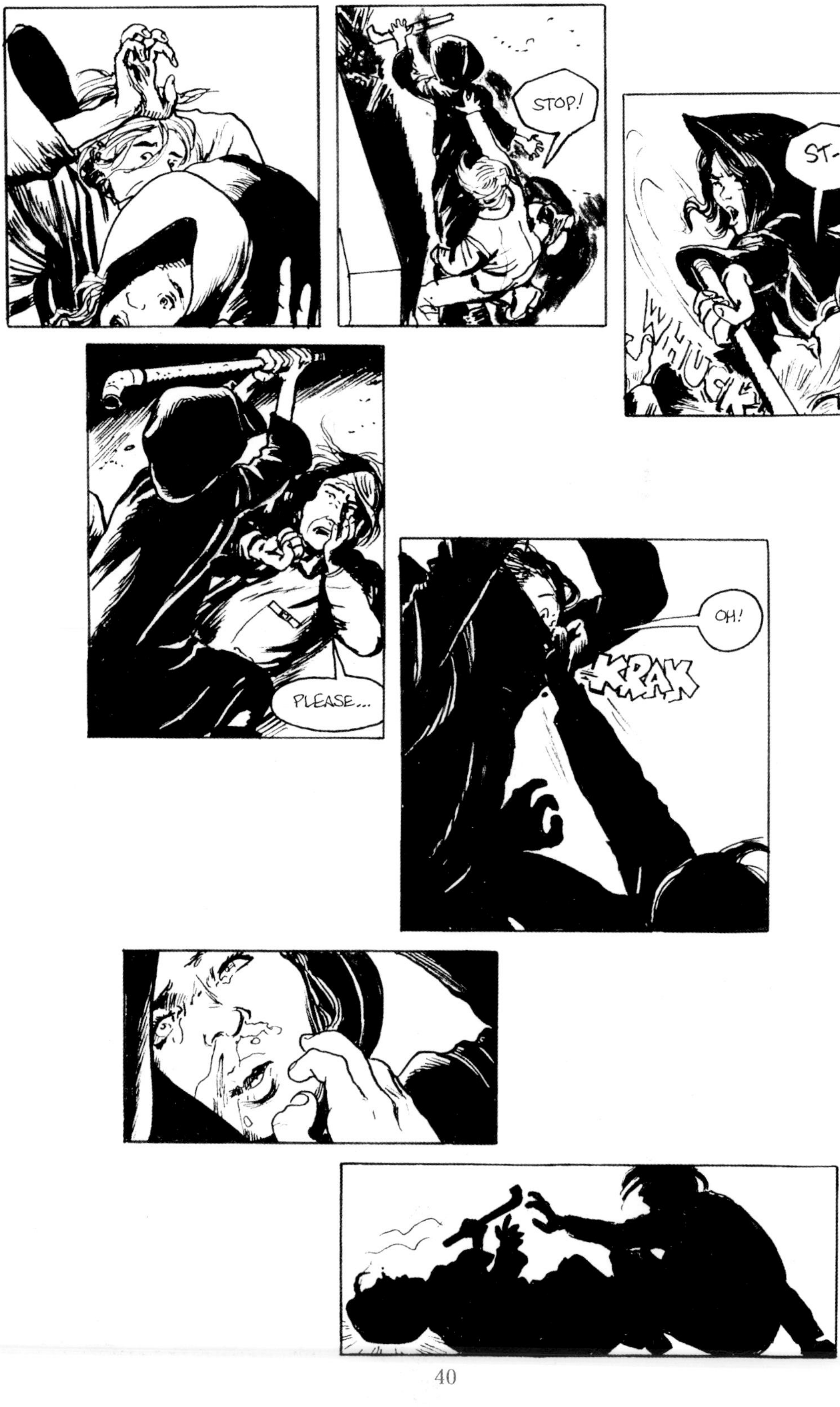
STOP!
ST--
WHUCK
PLEASE...
OH!
KRAK

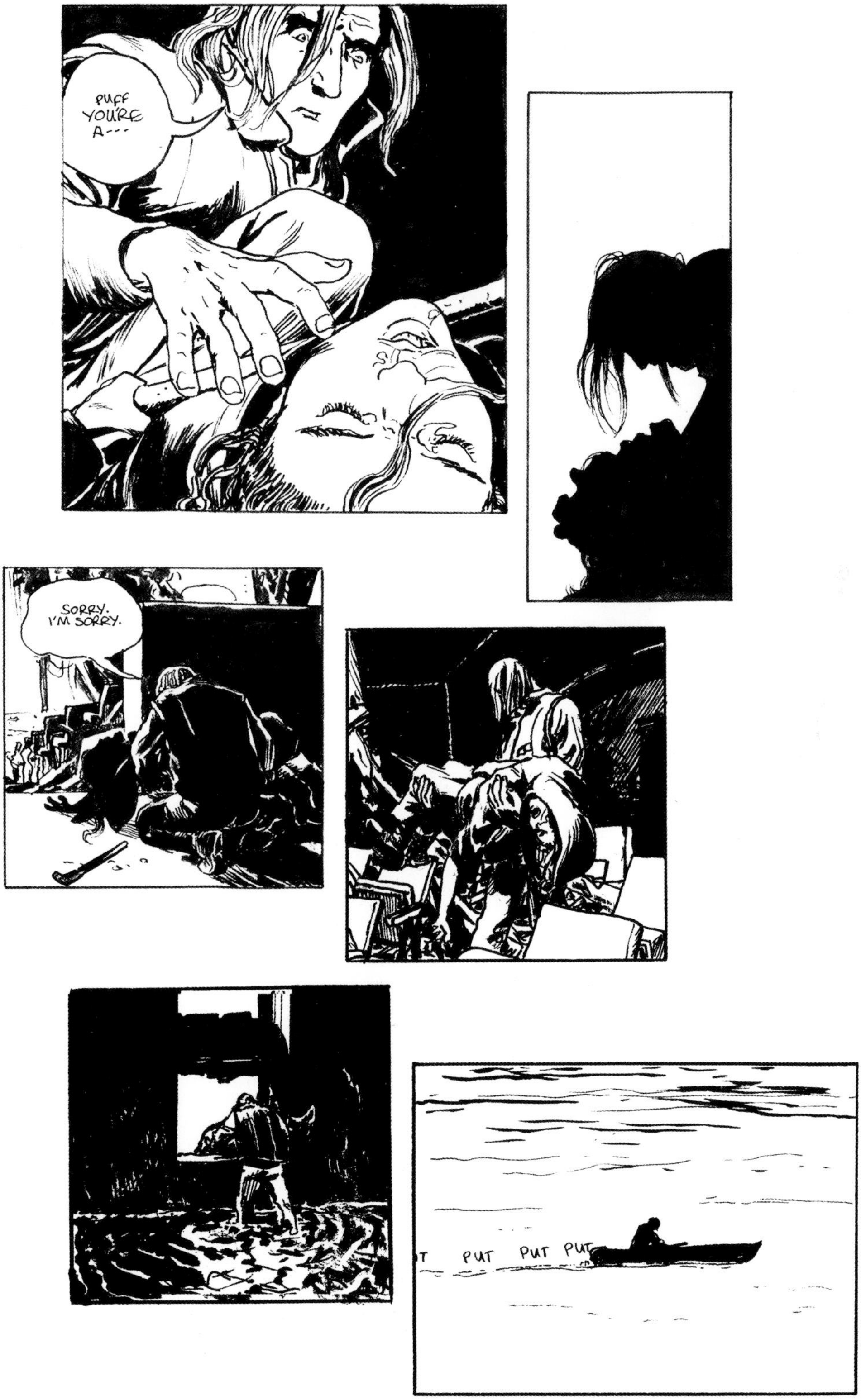
PUFF YOU'RE A---
SORRY. I'M SORRY.
T PUT PUT PUT

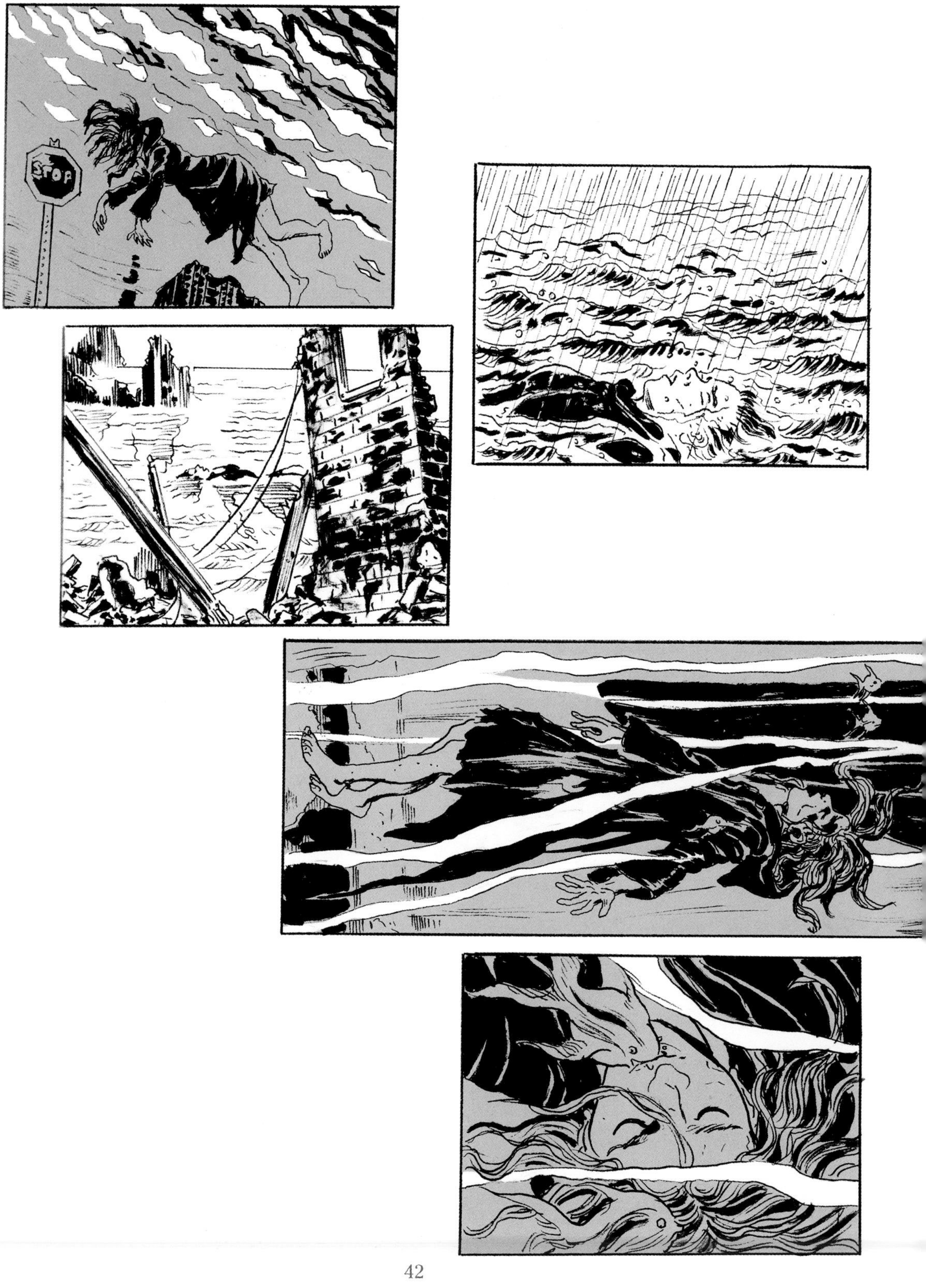
STOP

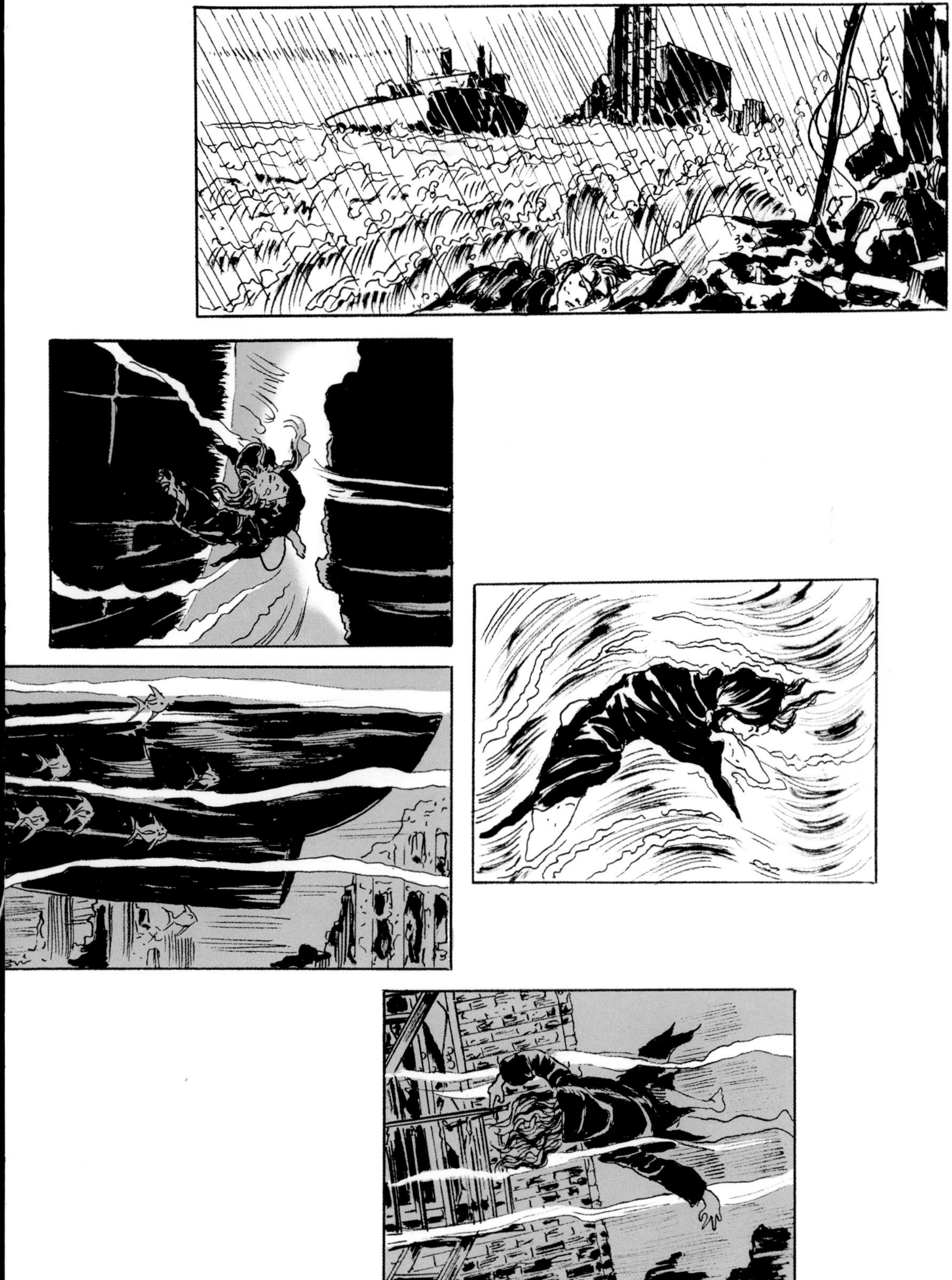

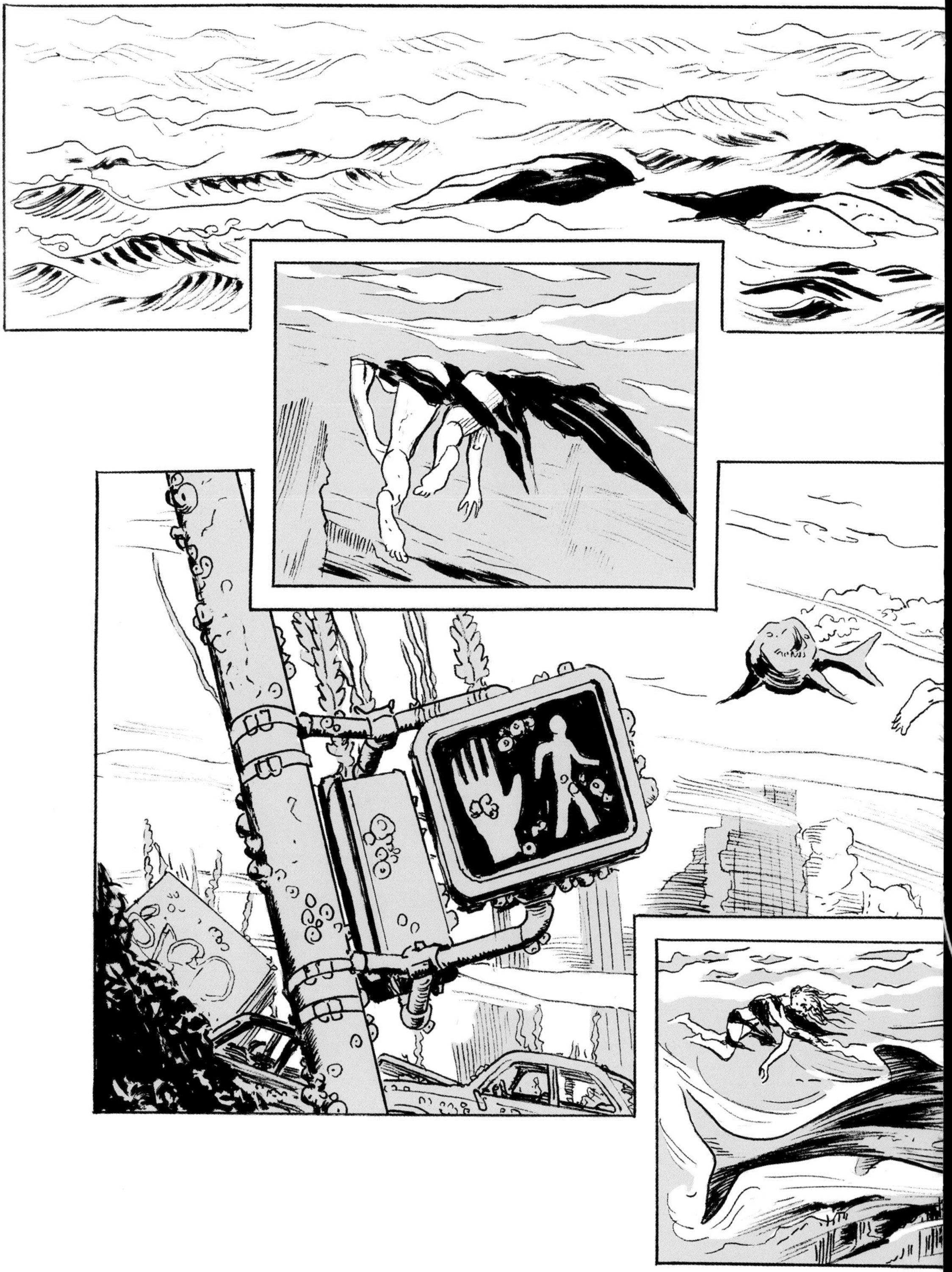

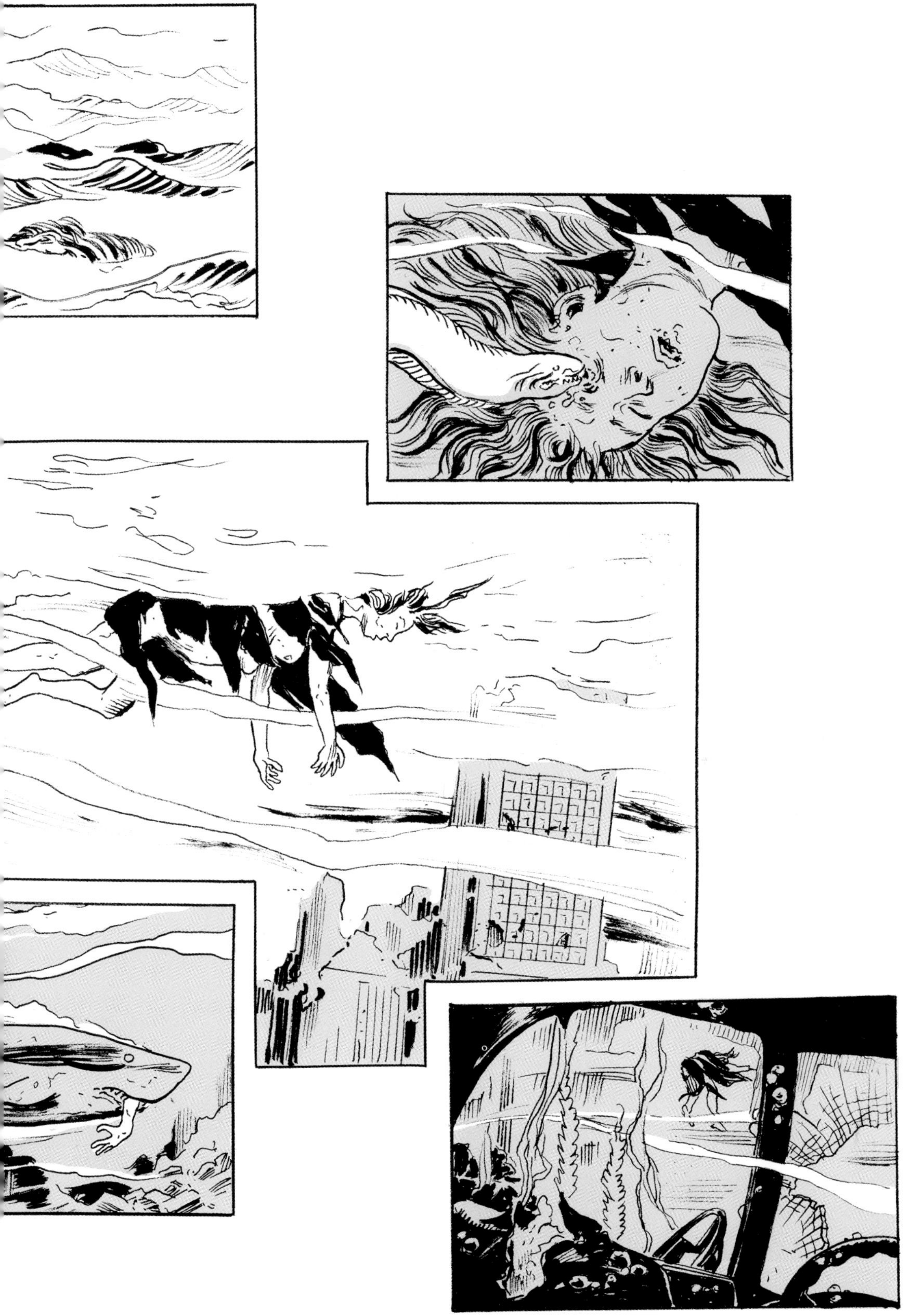

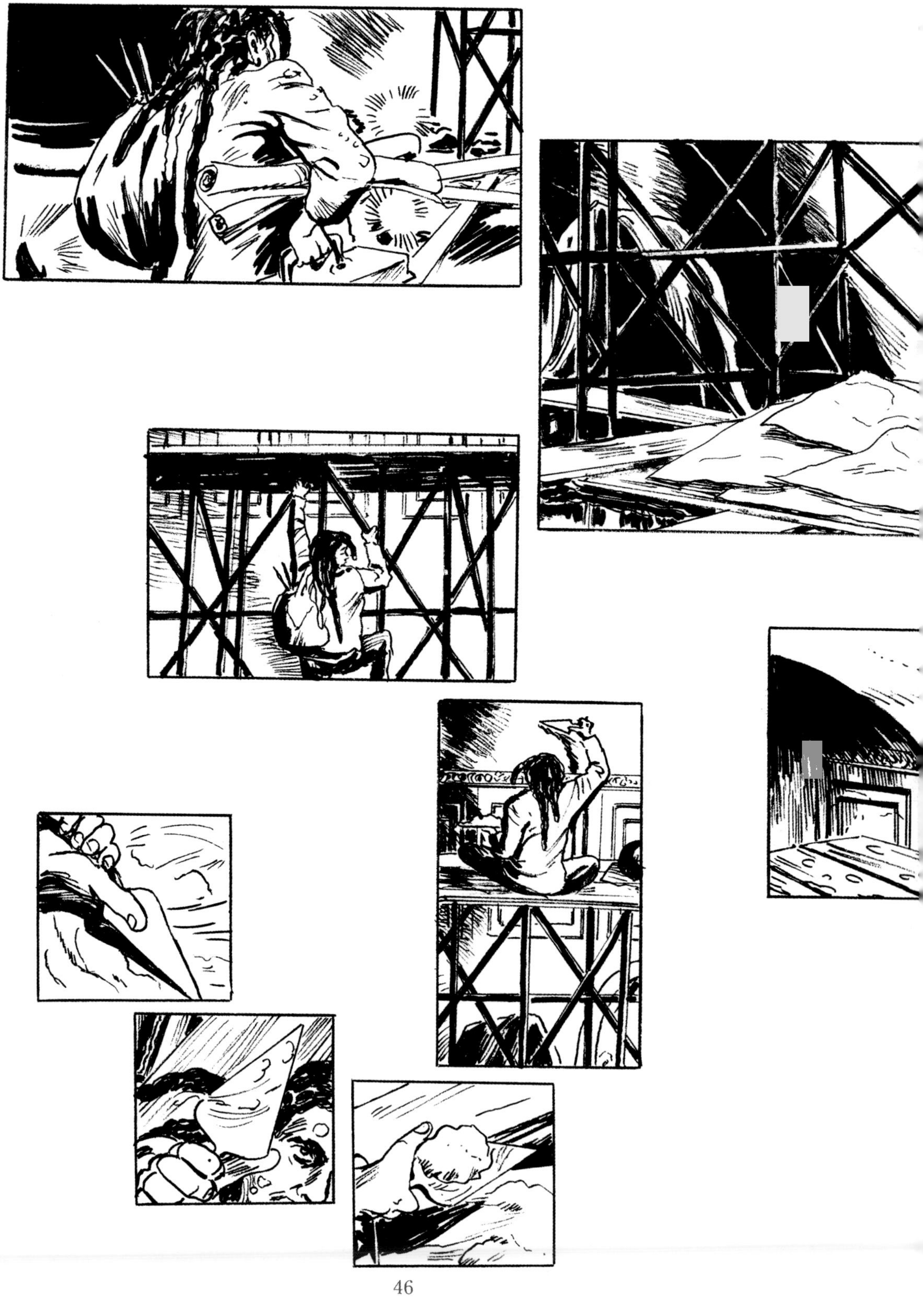

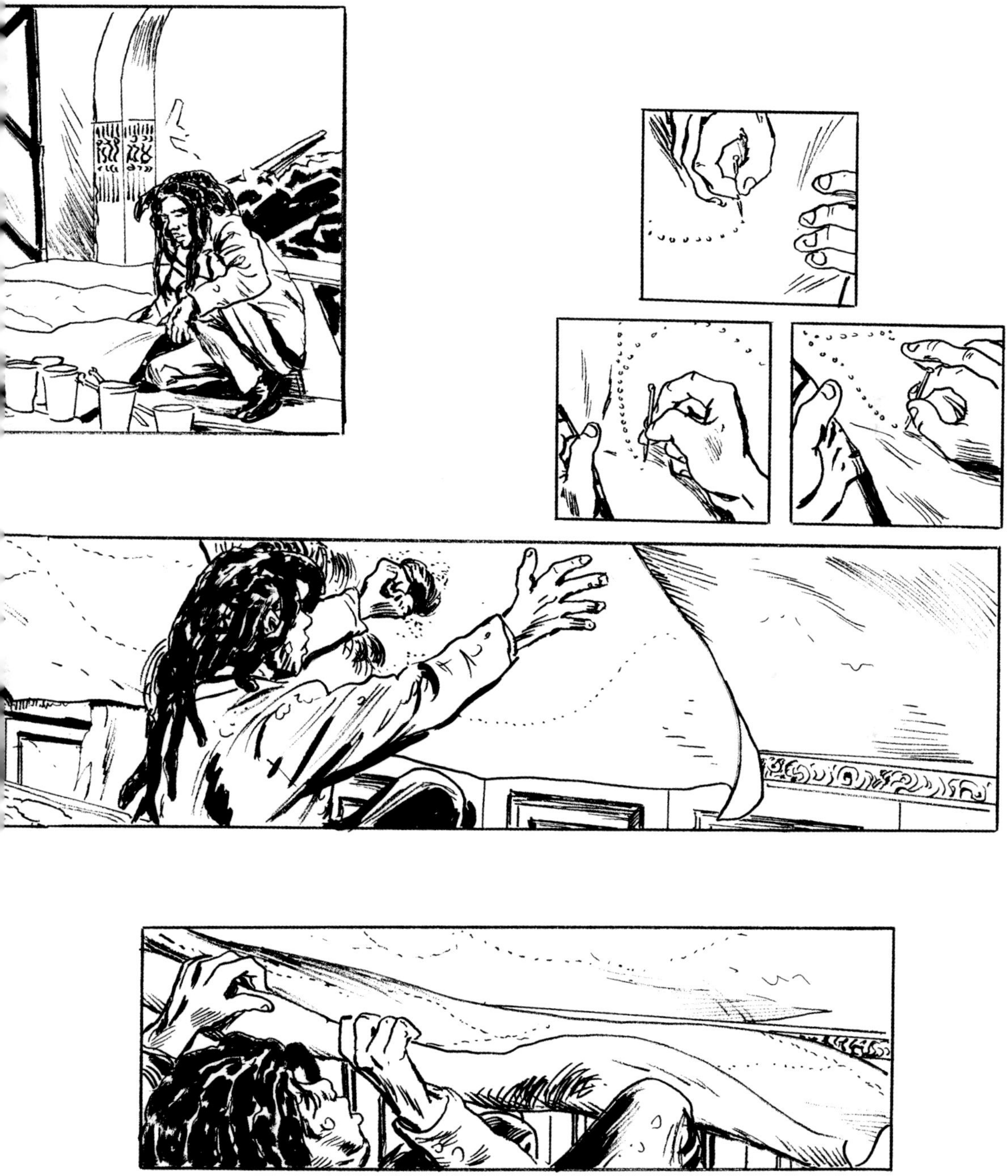

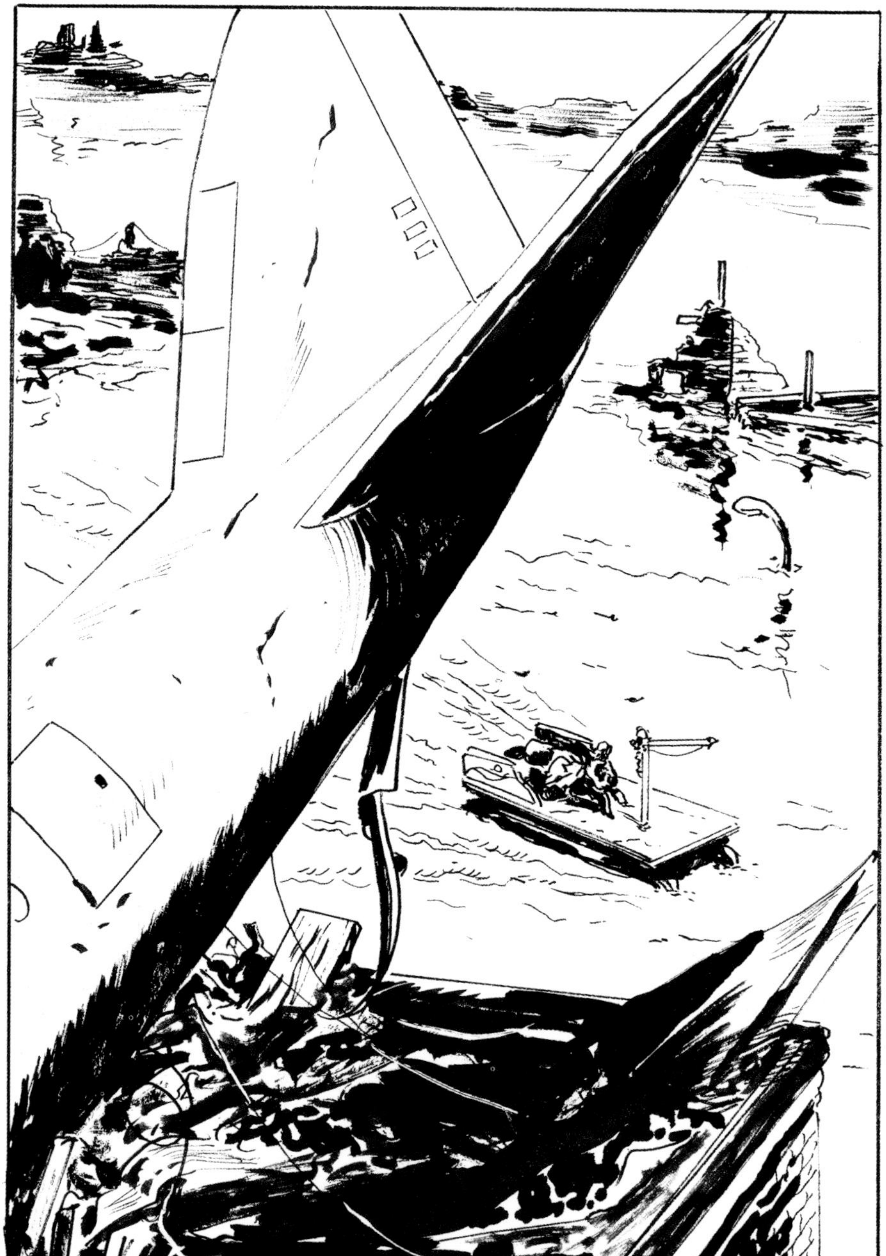

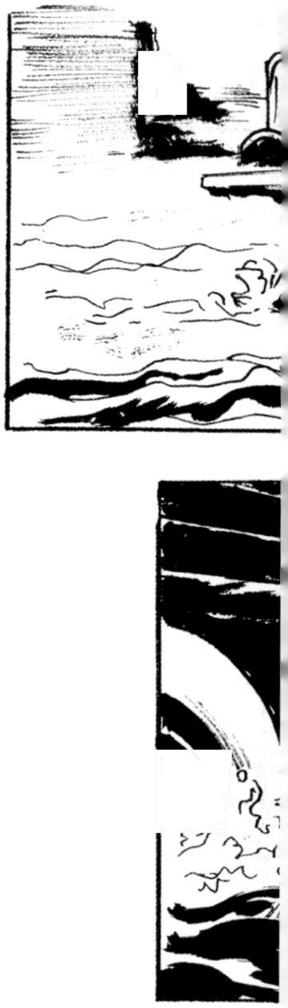

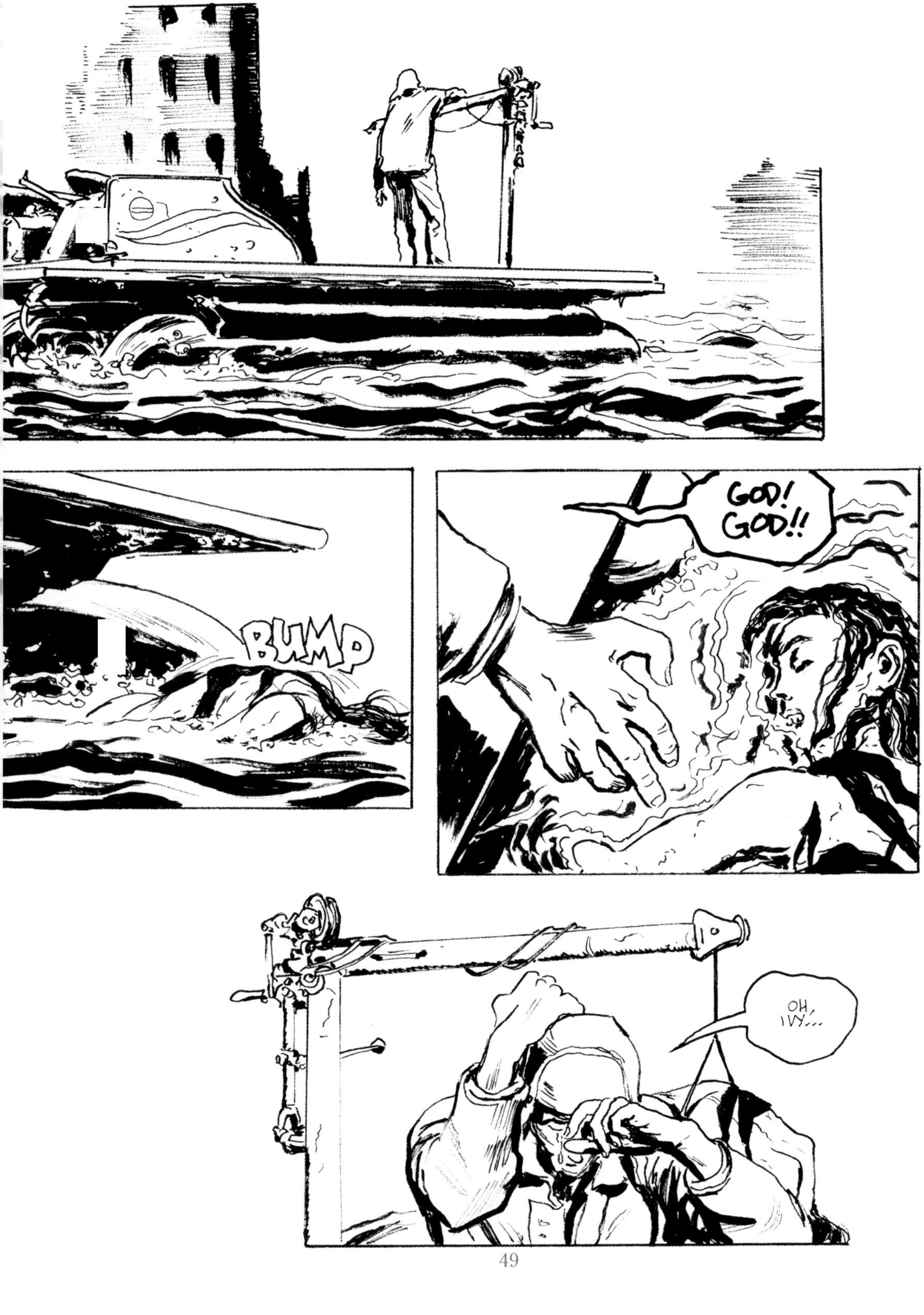
BUMP
GOD! GOD!!
OH, IVY...

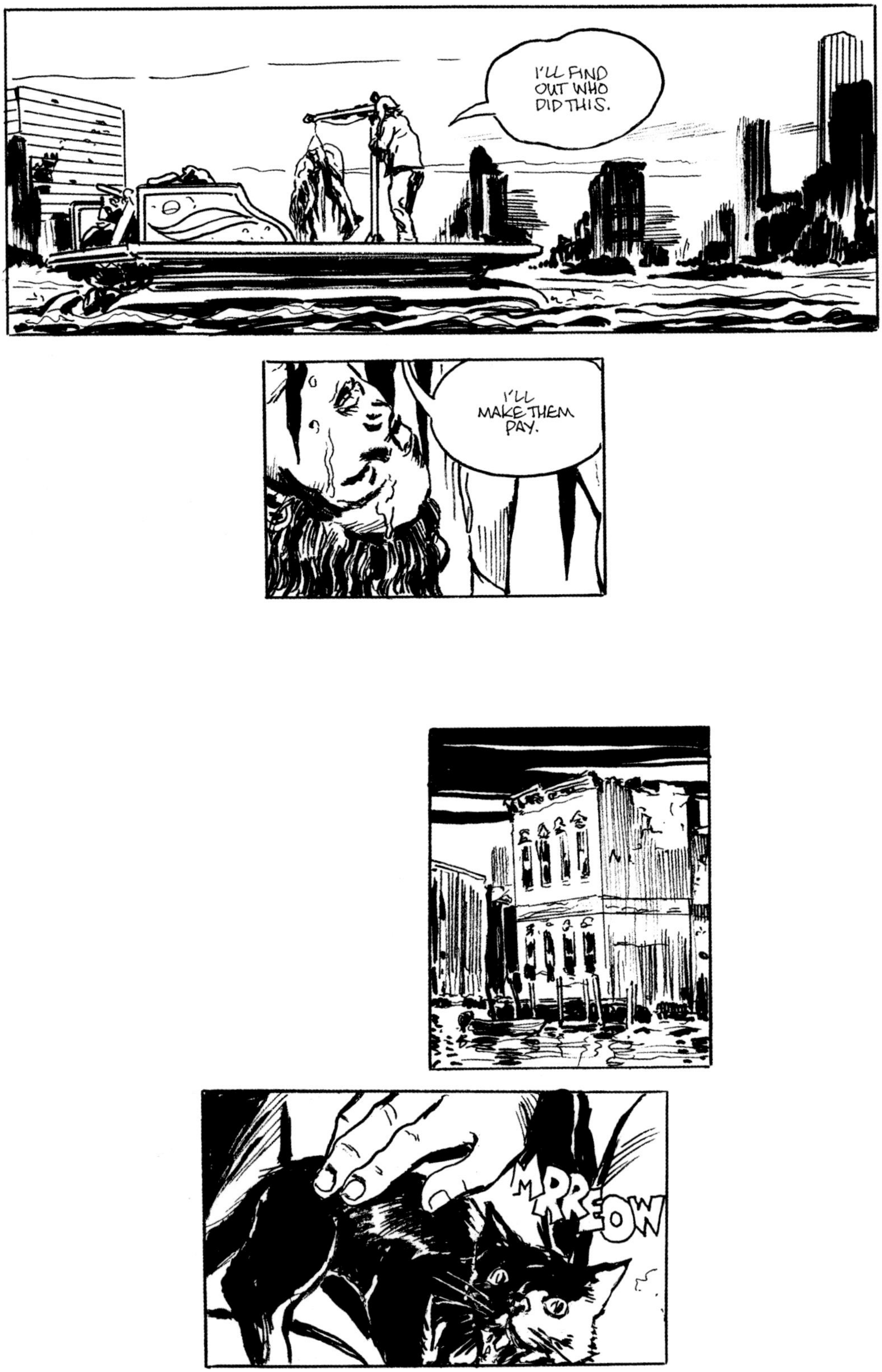
I'LL FIND OUT WHO DID THIS.
I'LL MAKE THEM PAY.
MRREOW

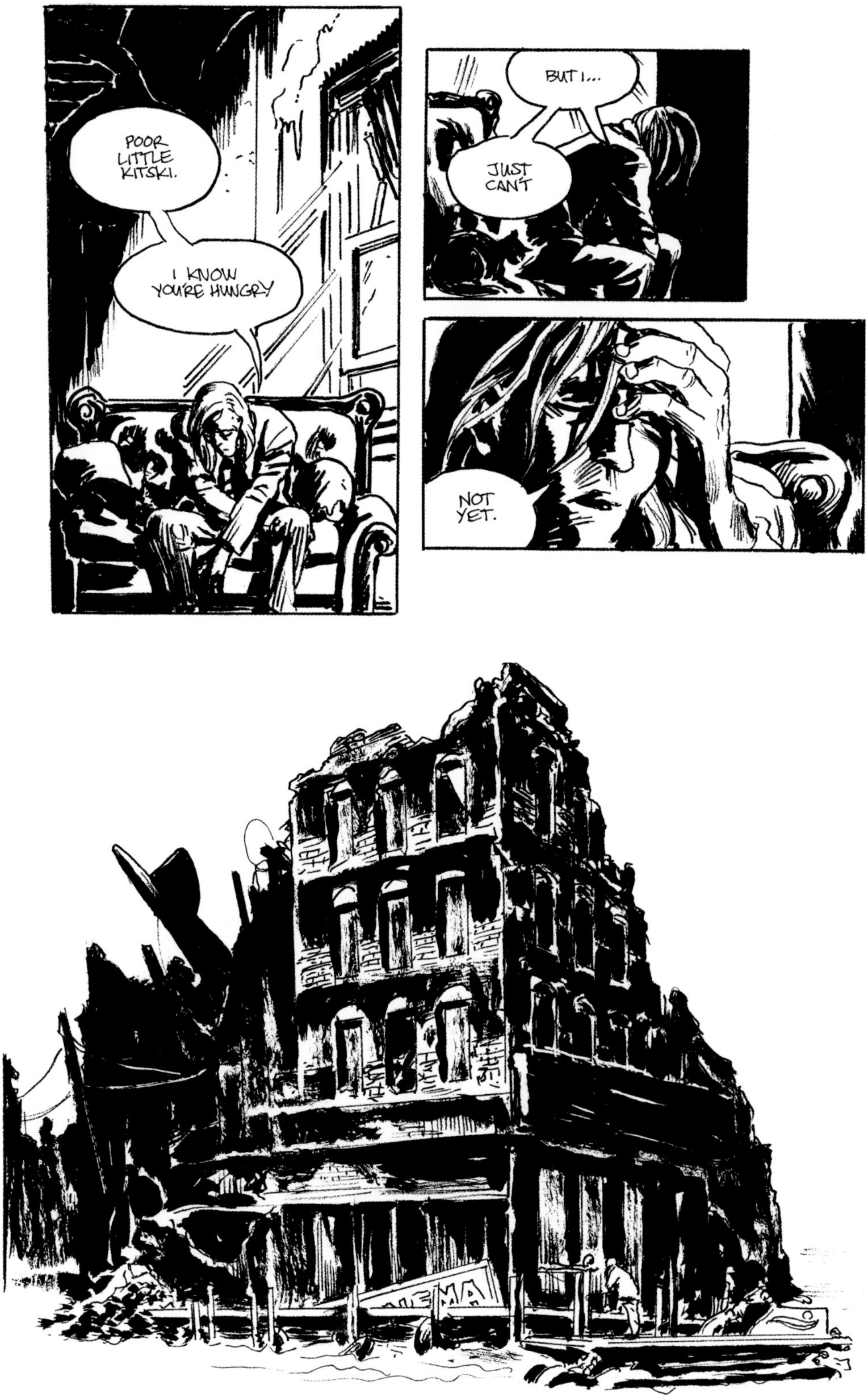
POOR LITTLE KITSKI.
I KNOW YOU'RE HUNGRY
BUT I...
JUST CAN'T
NOT YET.

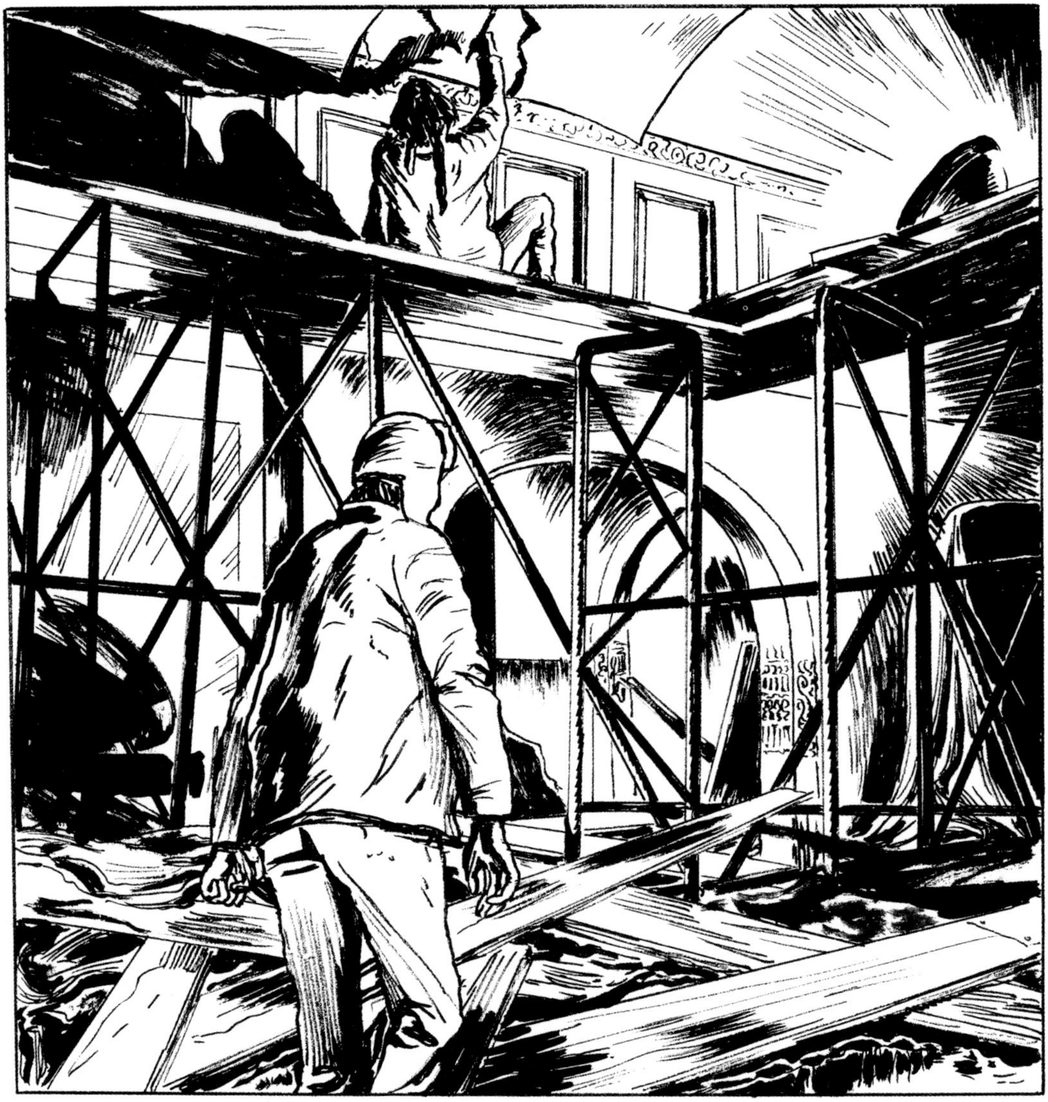

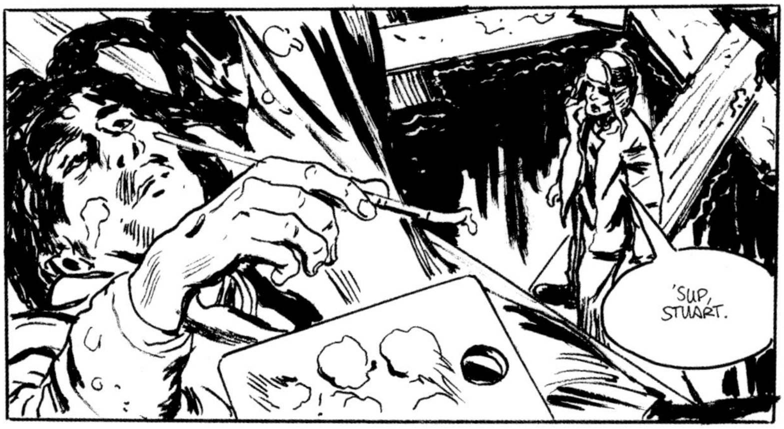
'SUP, STUART.

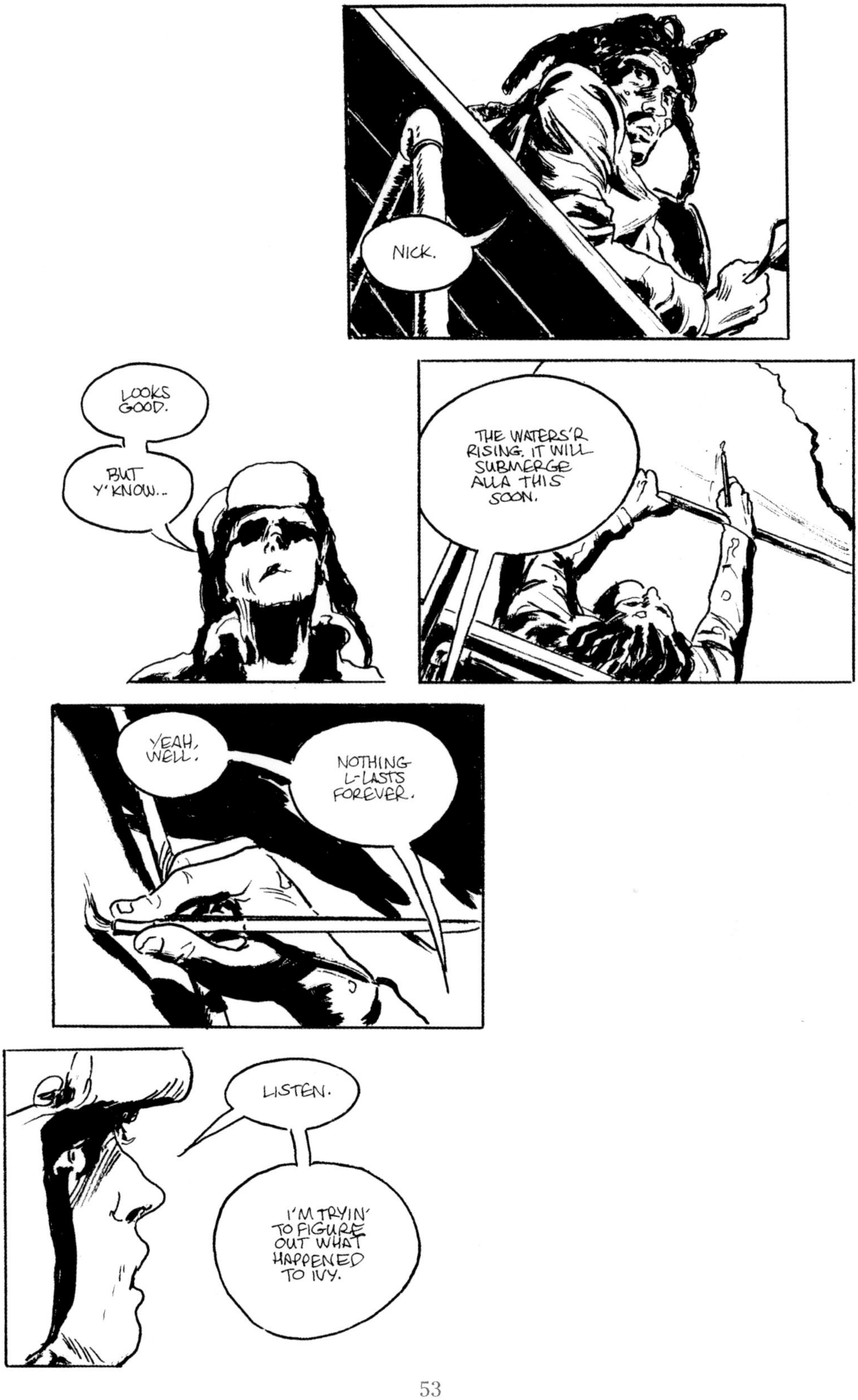
NICK.
LOOKS GOOD.
BUT Y'KNOW...
THE WATERS'R RISING. IT WILL SUBMERGE ALLA THIS SOON.
YEAH, WELL.
NOTHING L-LASTS FOREVER.
LISTEN.
I'M TRYIN' TO FIGURE OUT WHAT HAPPENED TO IVY.

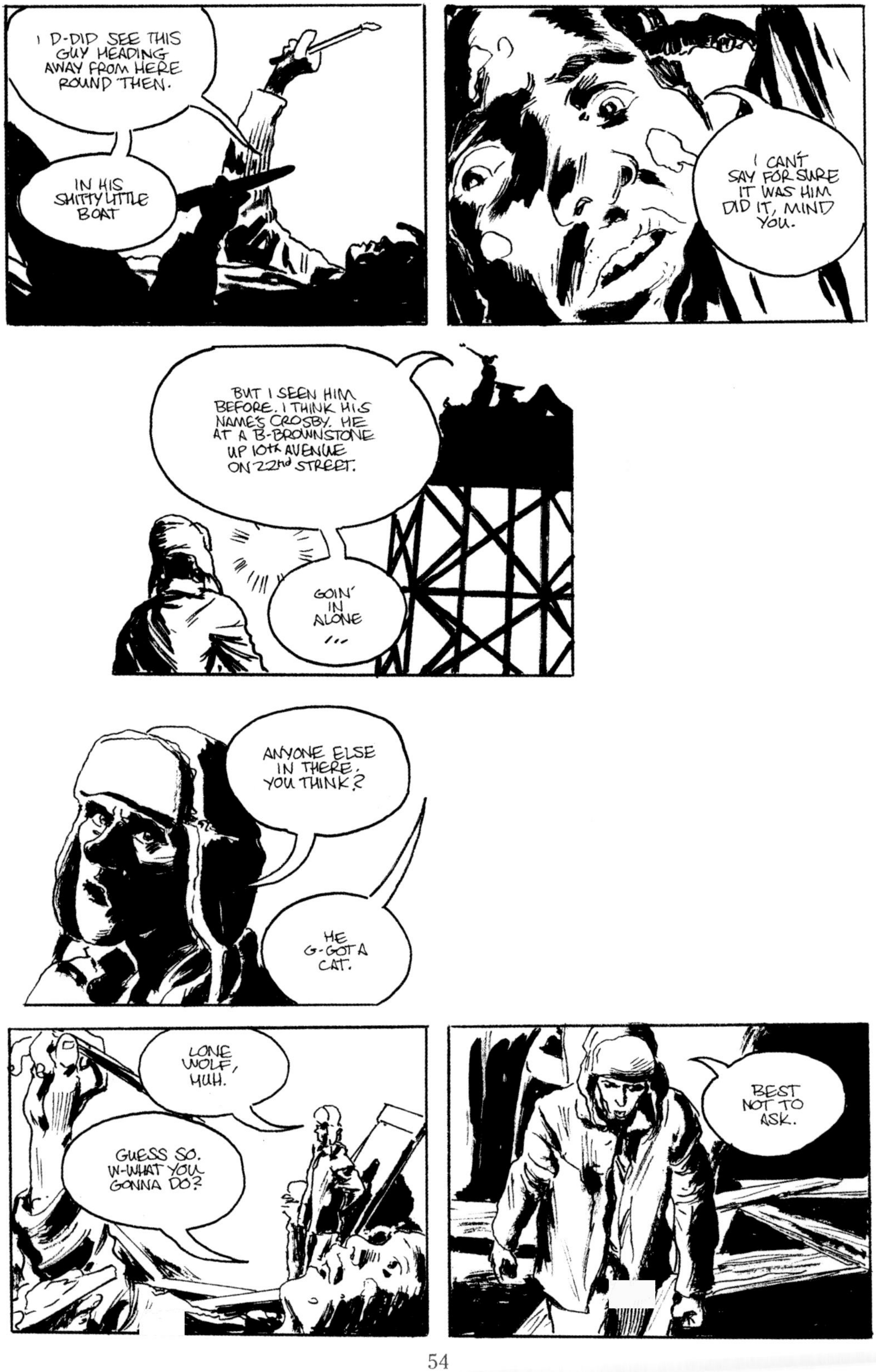
I D-DID SEE THIS GUY HEADING AWAY FROM HERE ROUND THEN.
IN HIS SHITTY LITTLE BOAT
I CAN'T SAY FOR SURE IT WAS HIM DID IT, MIND YOU.
BUT I SEEN HIM BEFORE. I THINK HIS NAME'S CROSBY. HE AT A B-BROWNSTONE UP 10th AVENUE ON 22nd STREET.
GOIN' IN ALONE ...
ANYONE ELSE IN THERE, YOU THINK?
HE G-GOT A CAT.
LONE WOLF, HUH.
GUESS SO. W-WHAT YOU GONNA DO?
BEST NOT TO ASK.

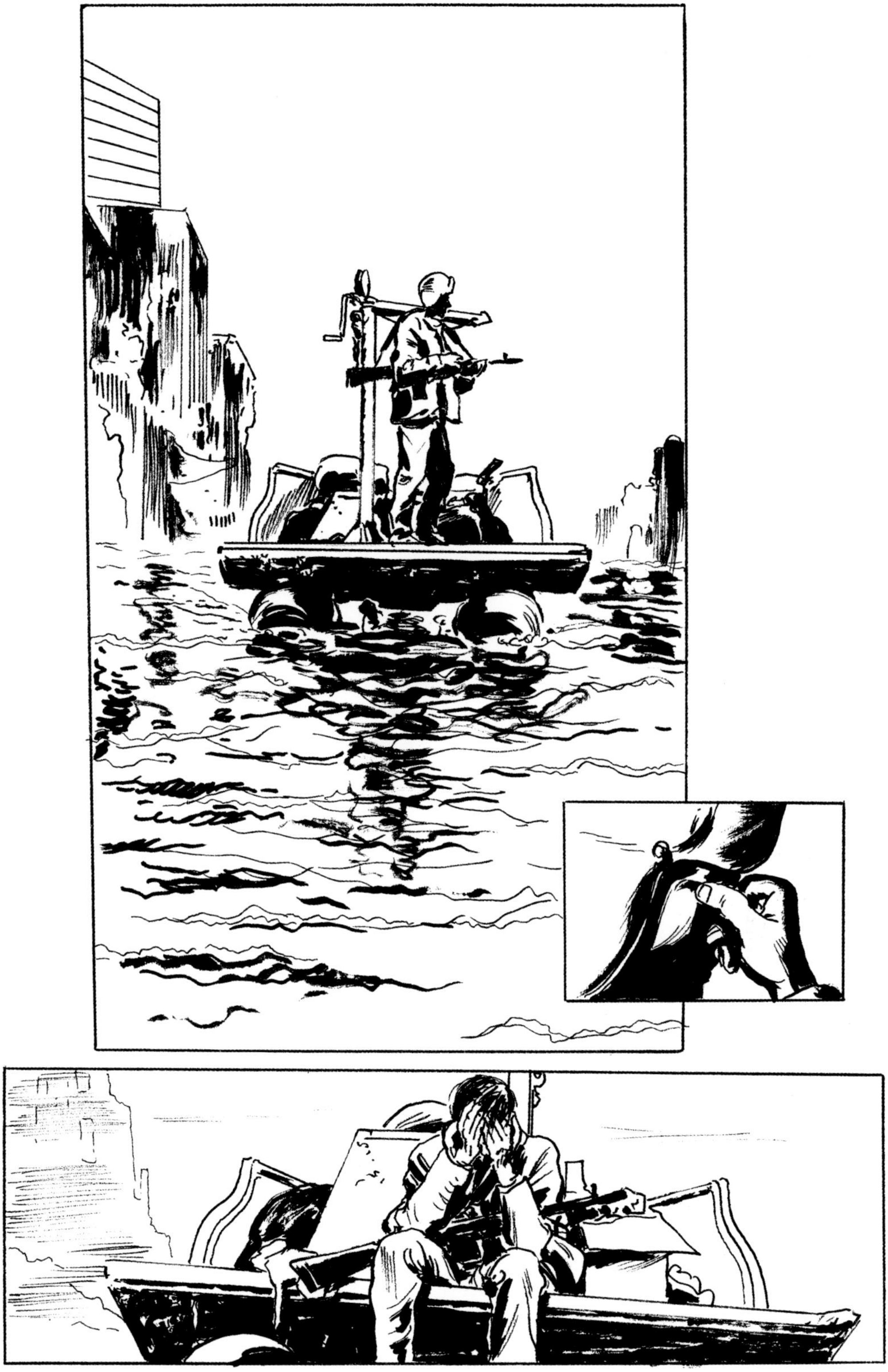

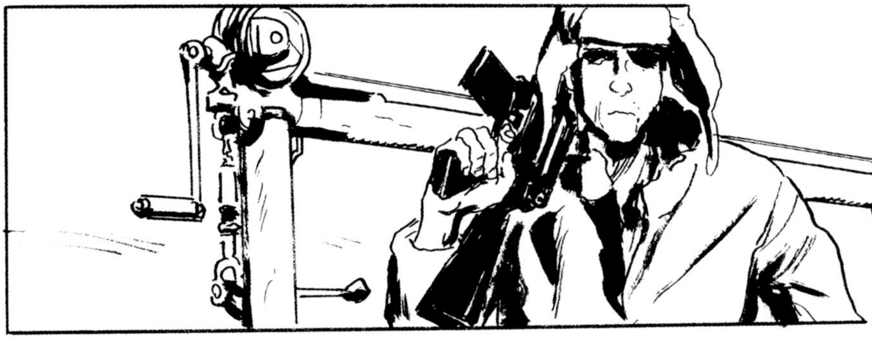

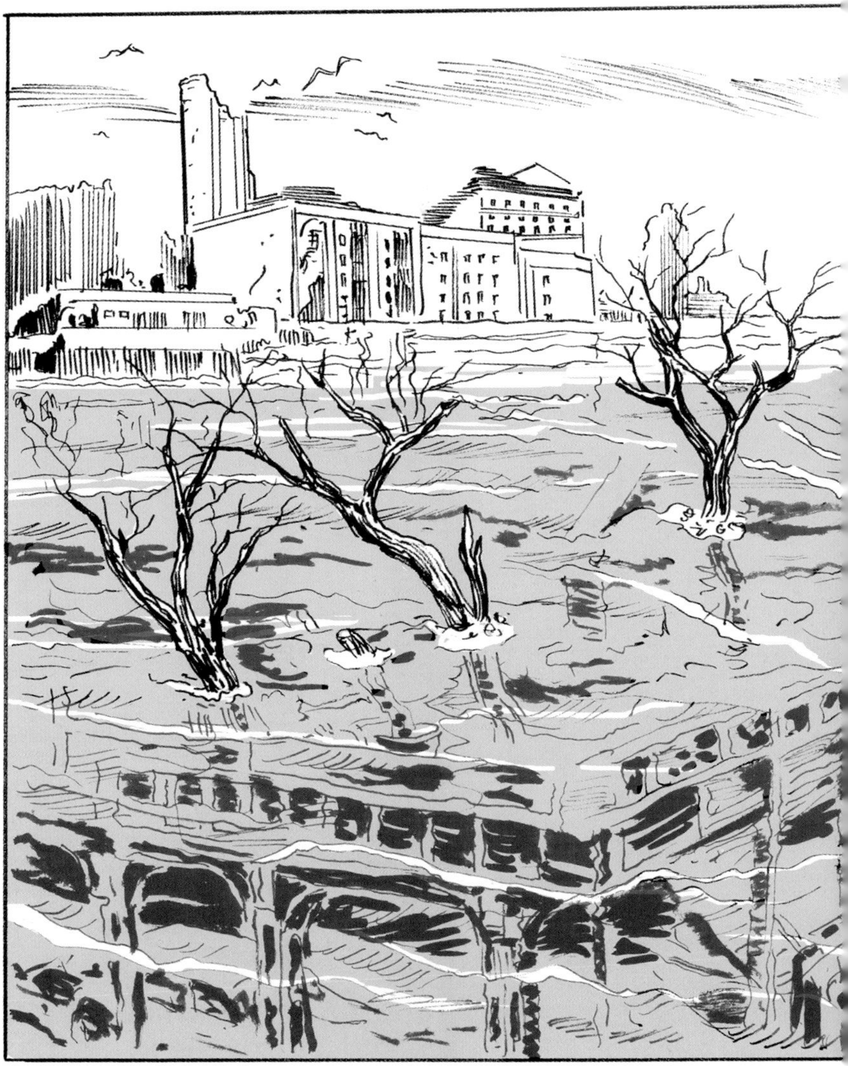

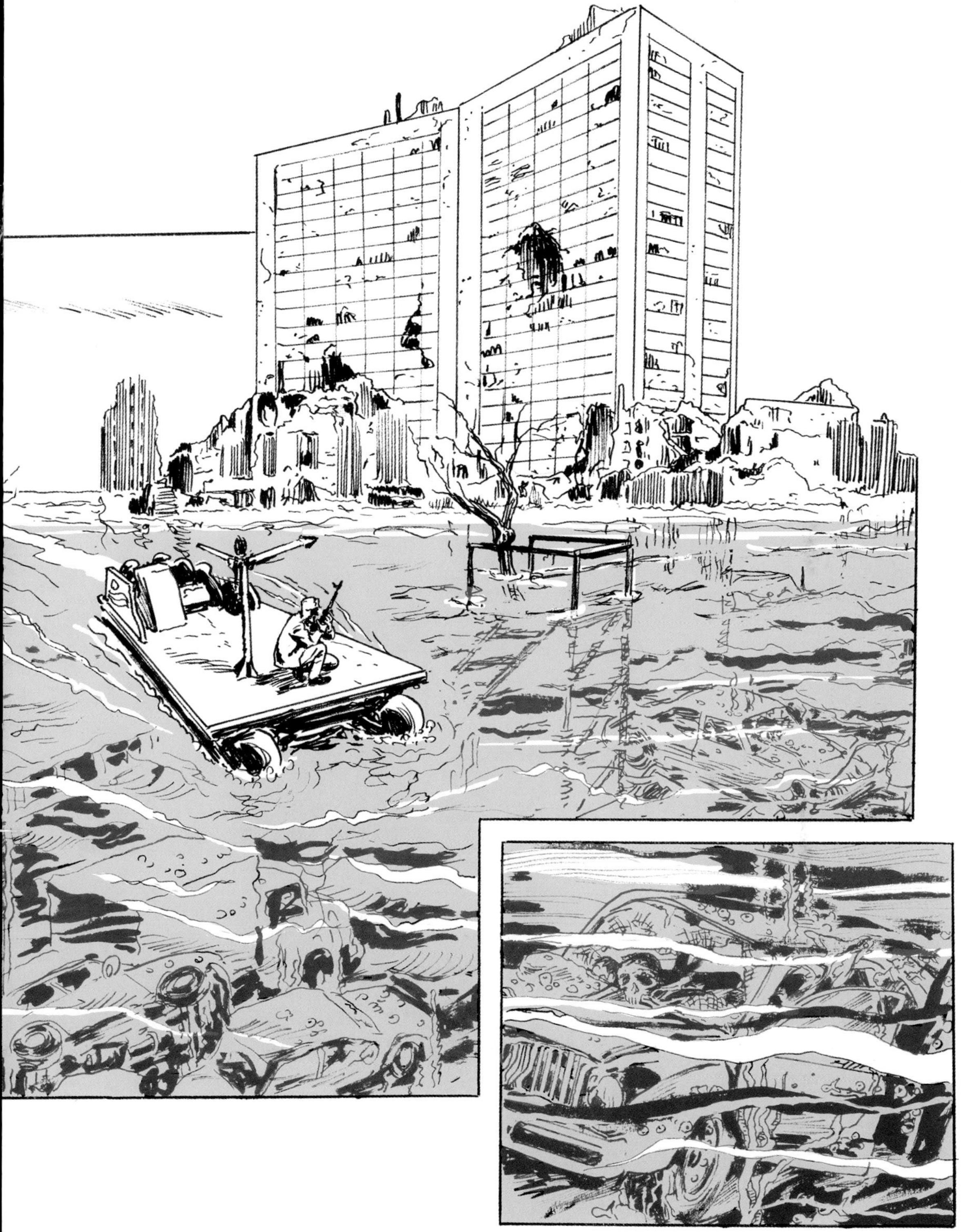

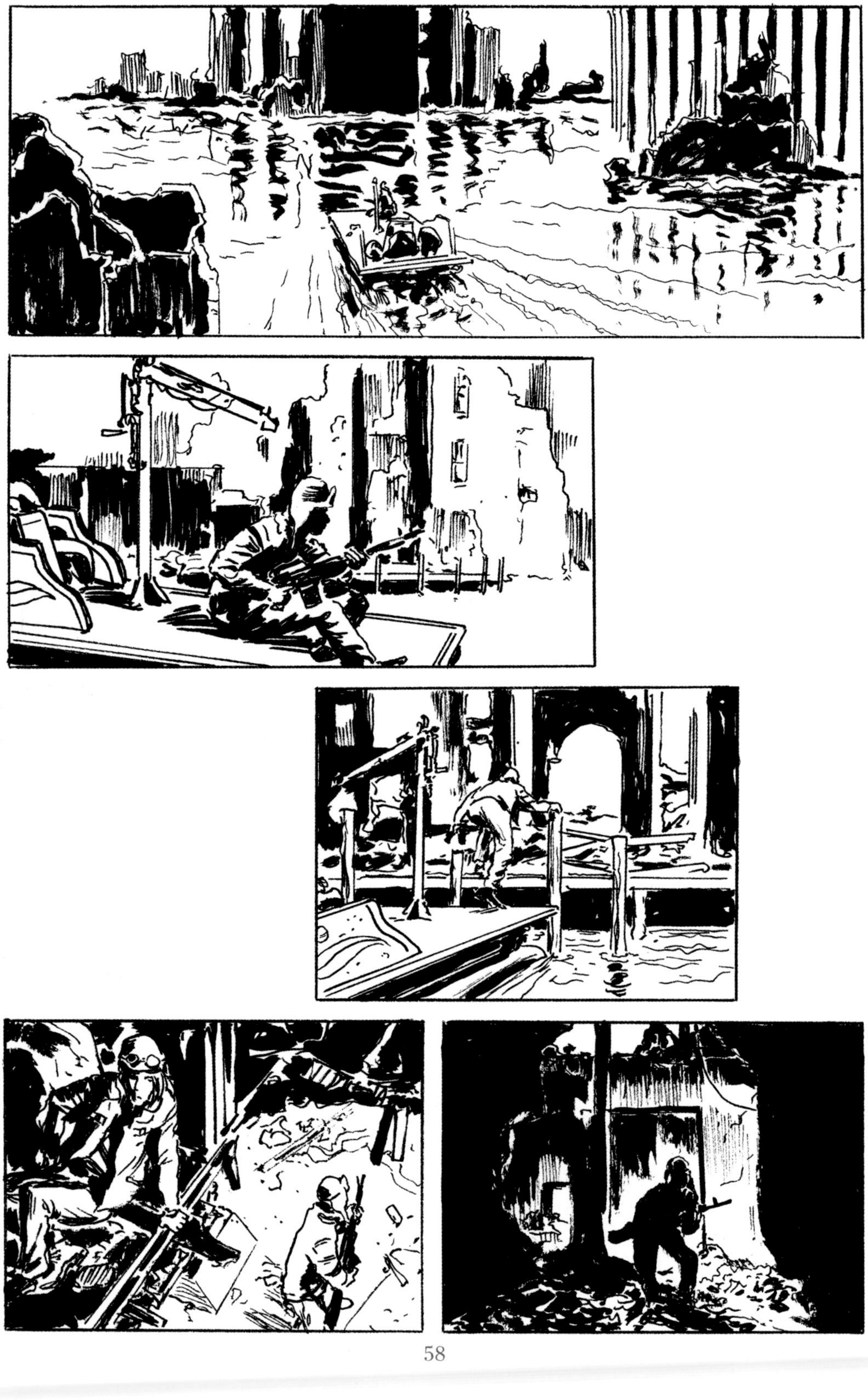

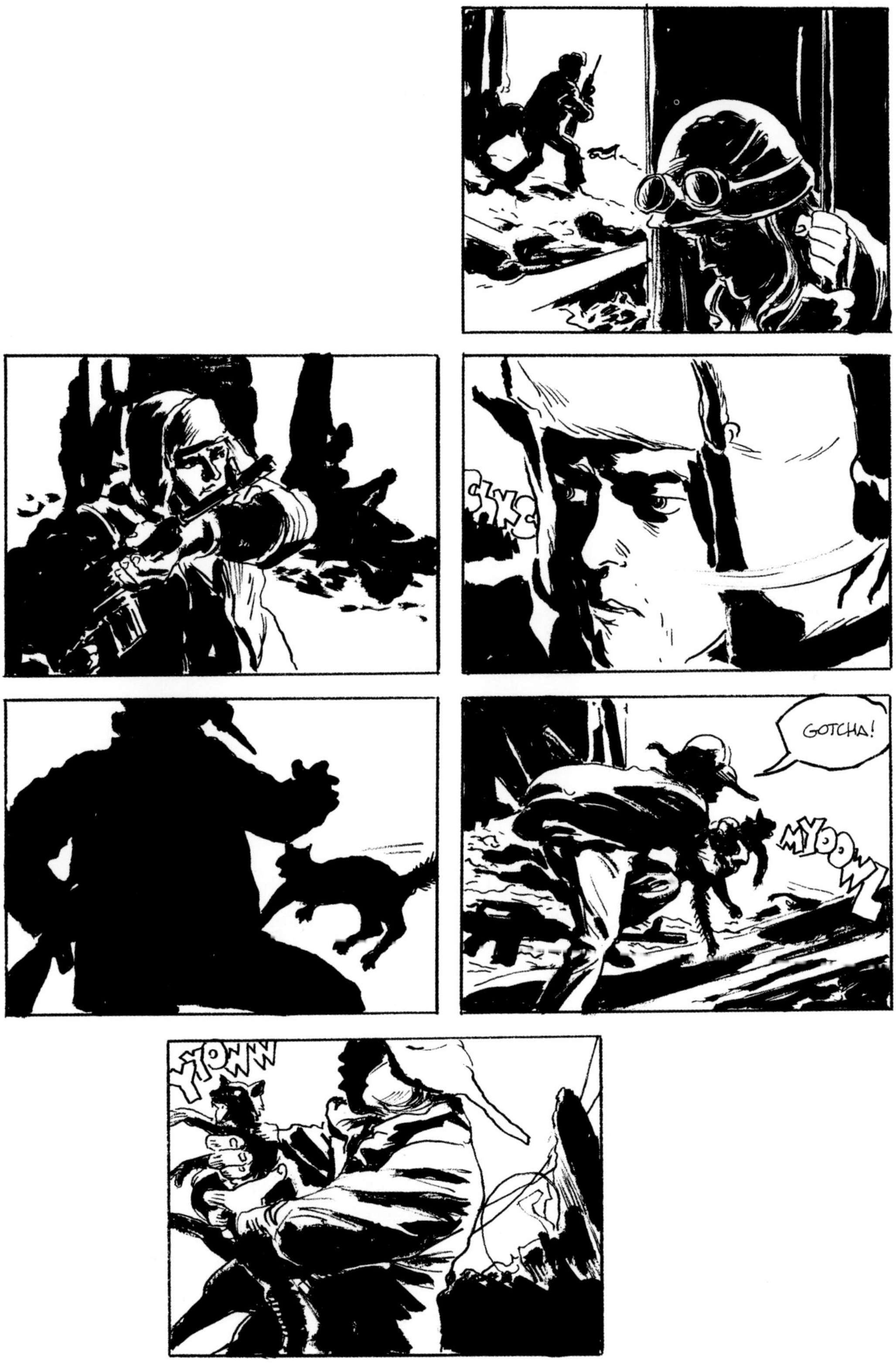
GOTCHA!
MYOOWL
YOWWW

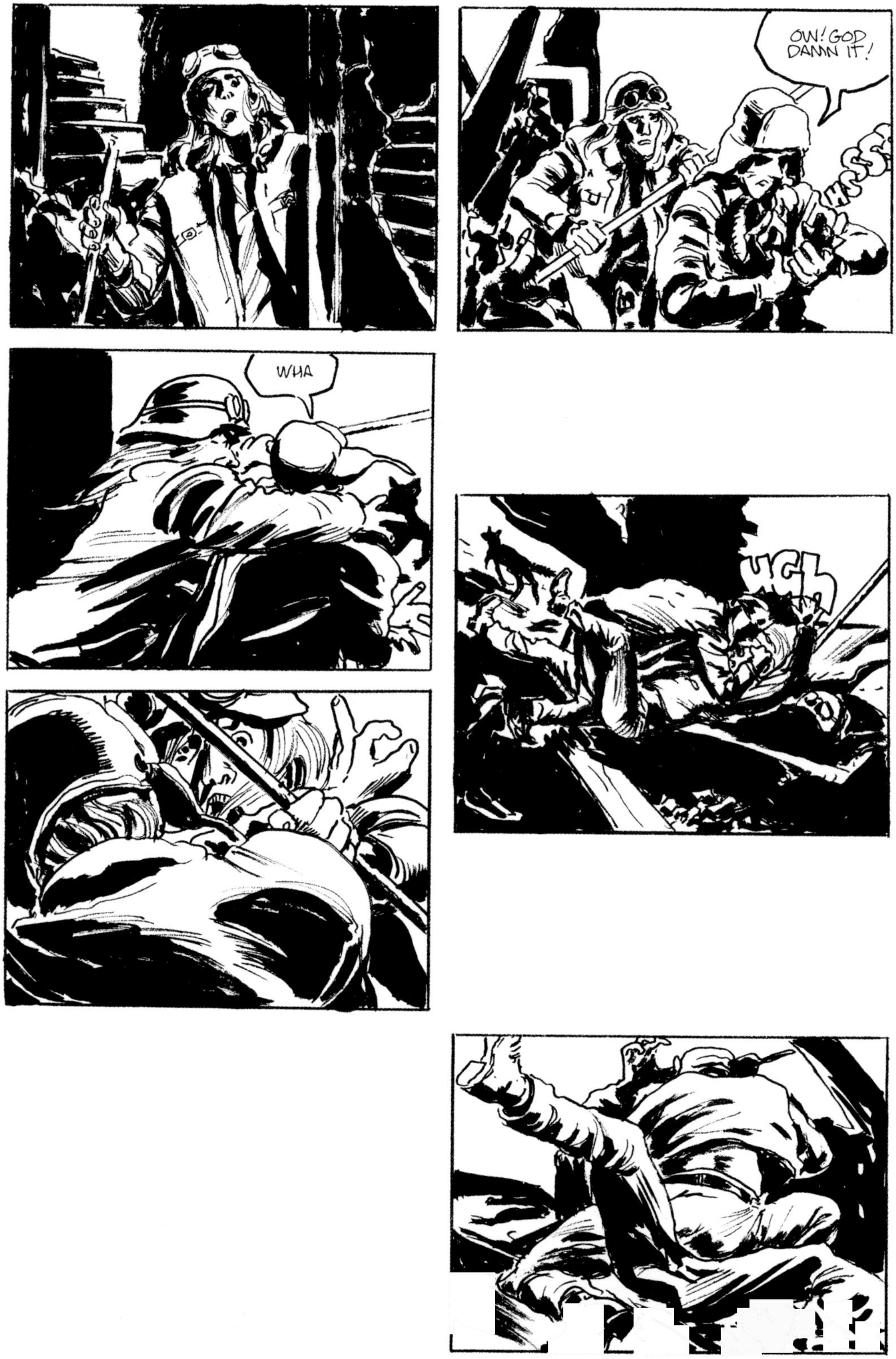
OW! GOD DAMN IT!
WHA

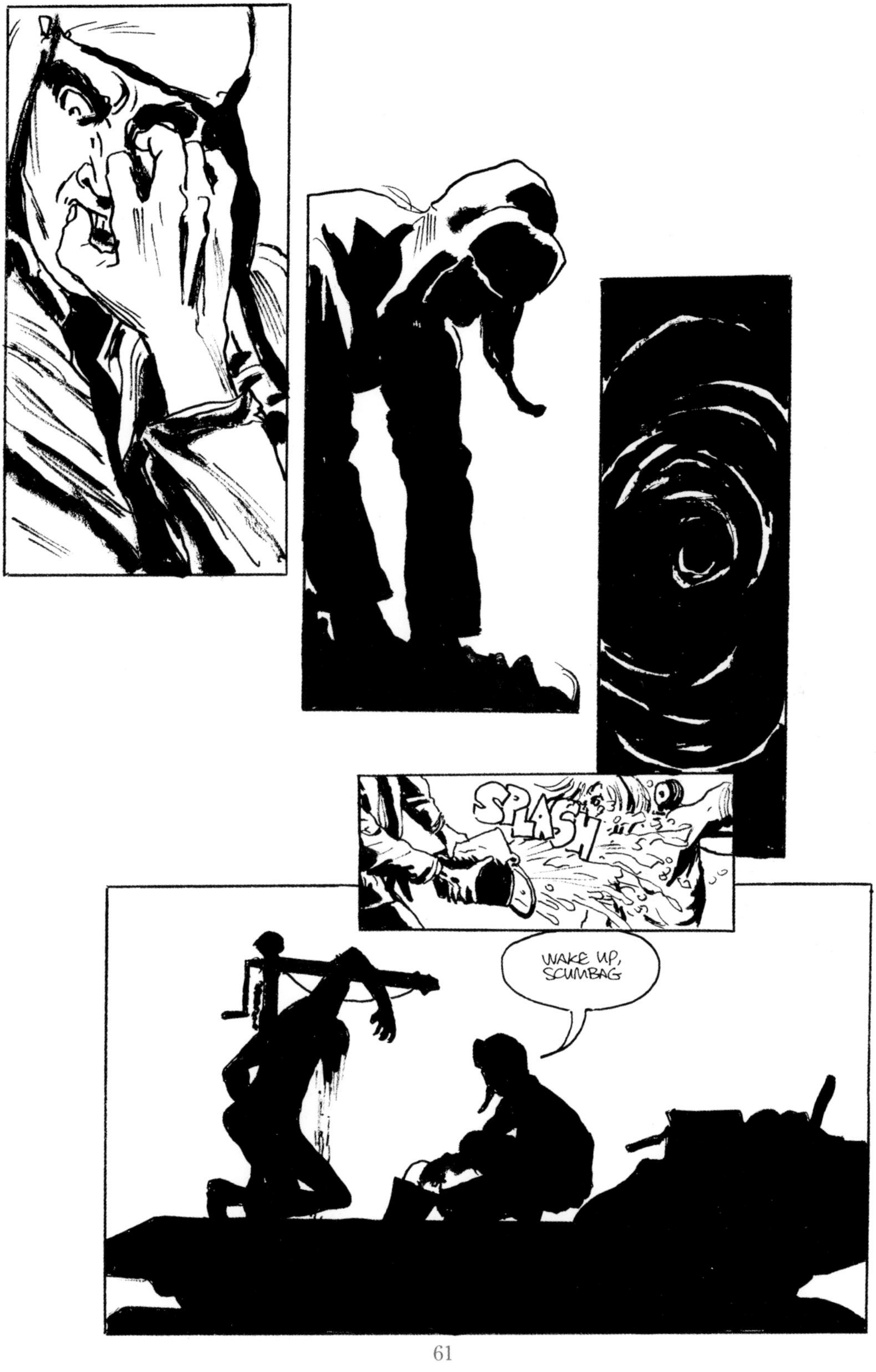
SPLASH
WAKE UP, SCUMBAG

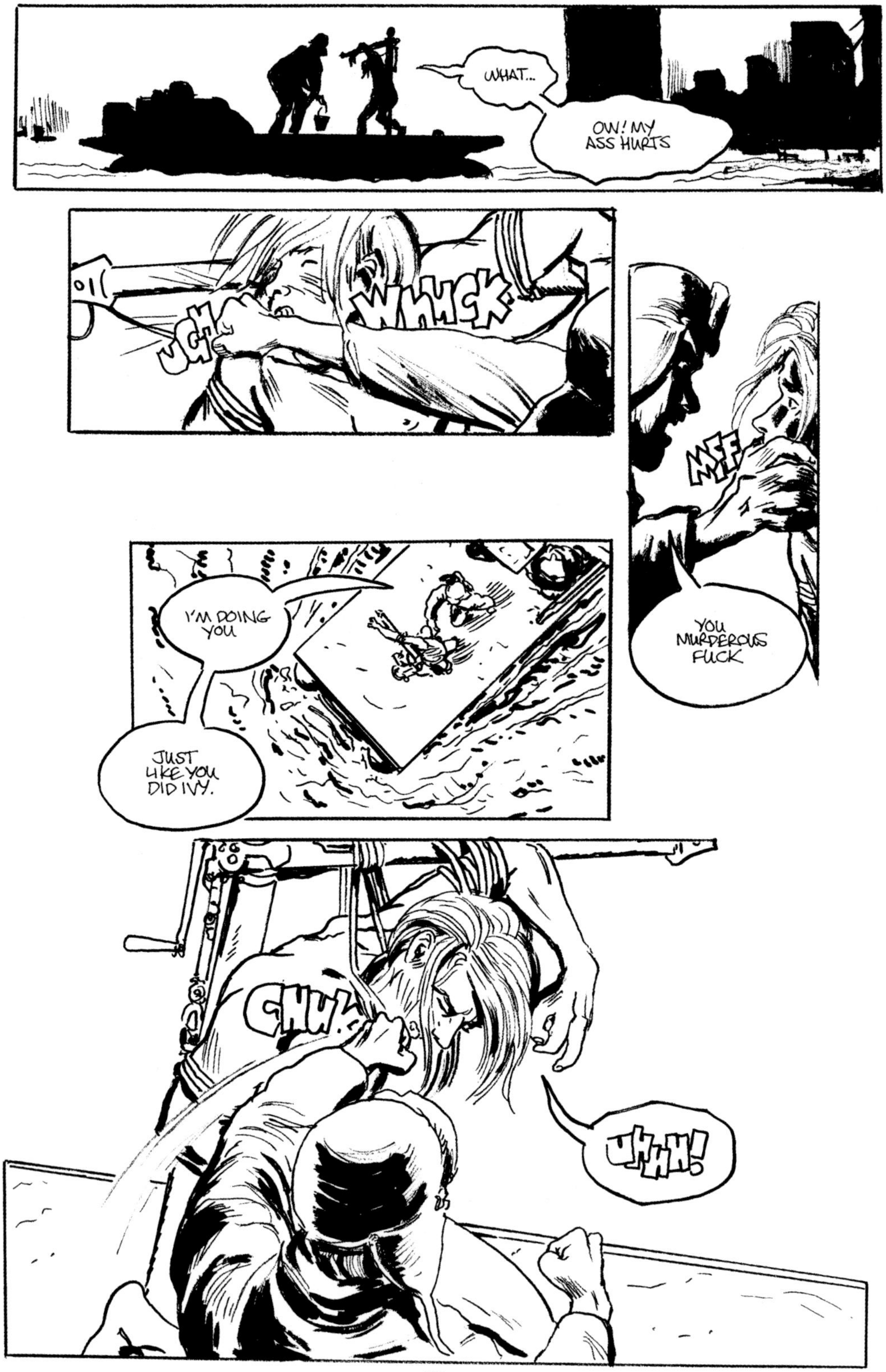
WHAT...
OW! MY ASS HURTS
UGH
WHUCK
MFF
YOU MURDEROUS FUCK
I'M DOING YOU
JUST LIKE YOU DID IVY.
GHUK
UHHH!

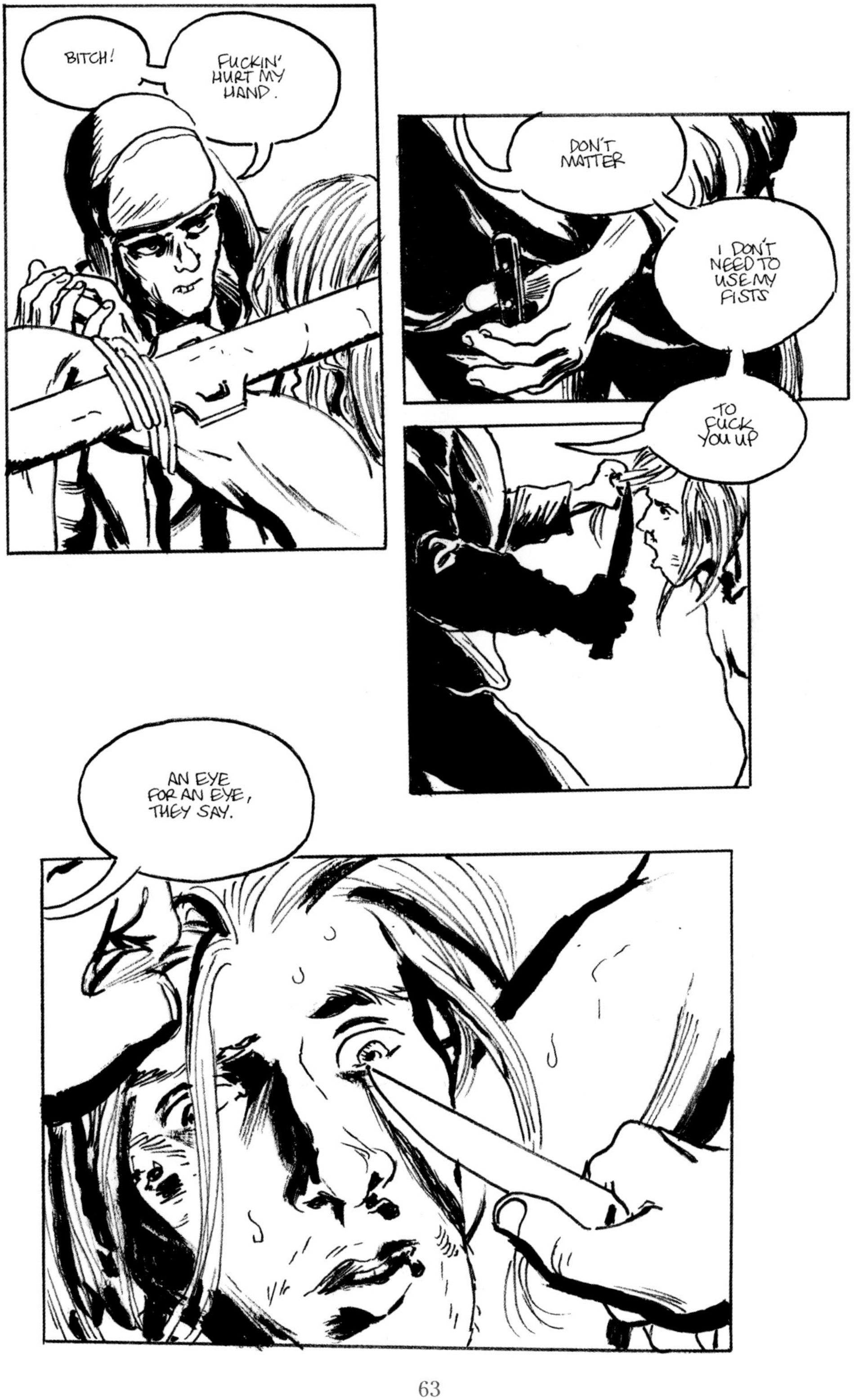
BITCH!
FUCKIN' HURT MY HAND.
DON'T MATTER
I DON'T NEED TO USE MY FISTS
TO FUCK YOU UP
AN EYE FOR AN EYE, THEY SAY.

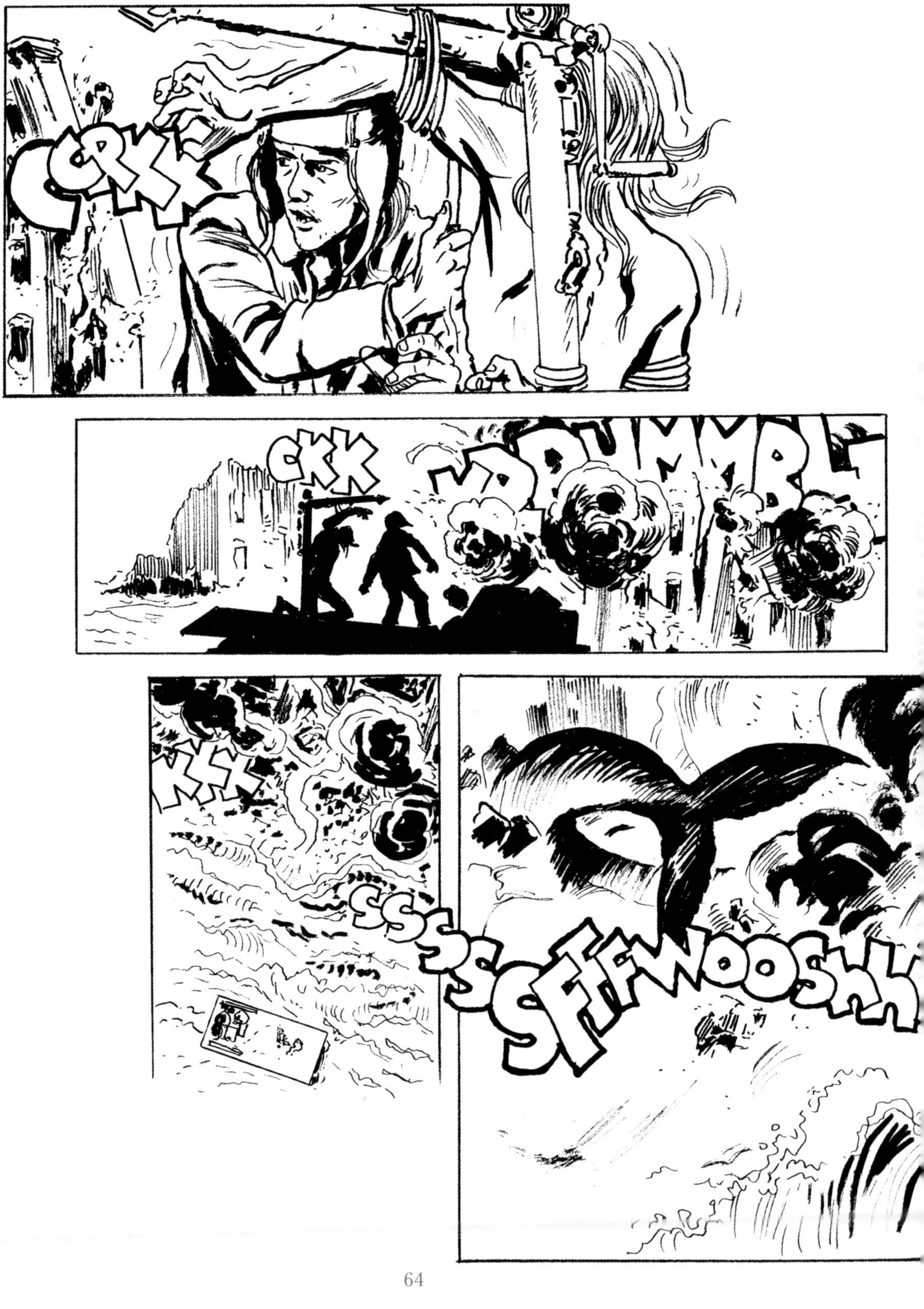
CRKK
CKK
SSSSFFWOOSH

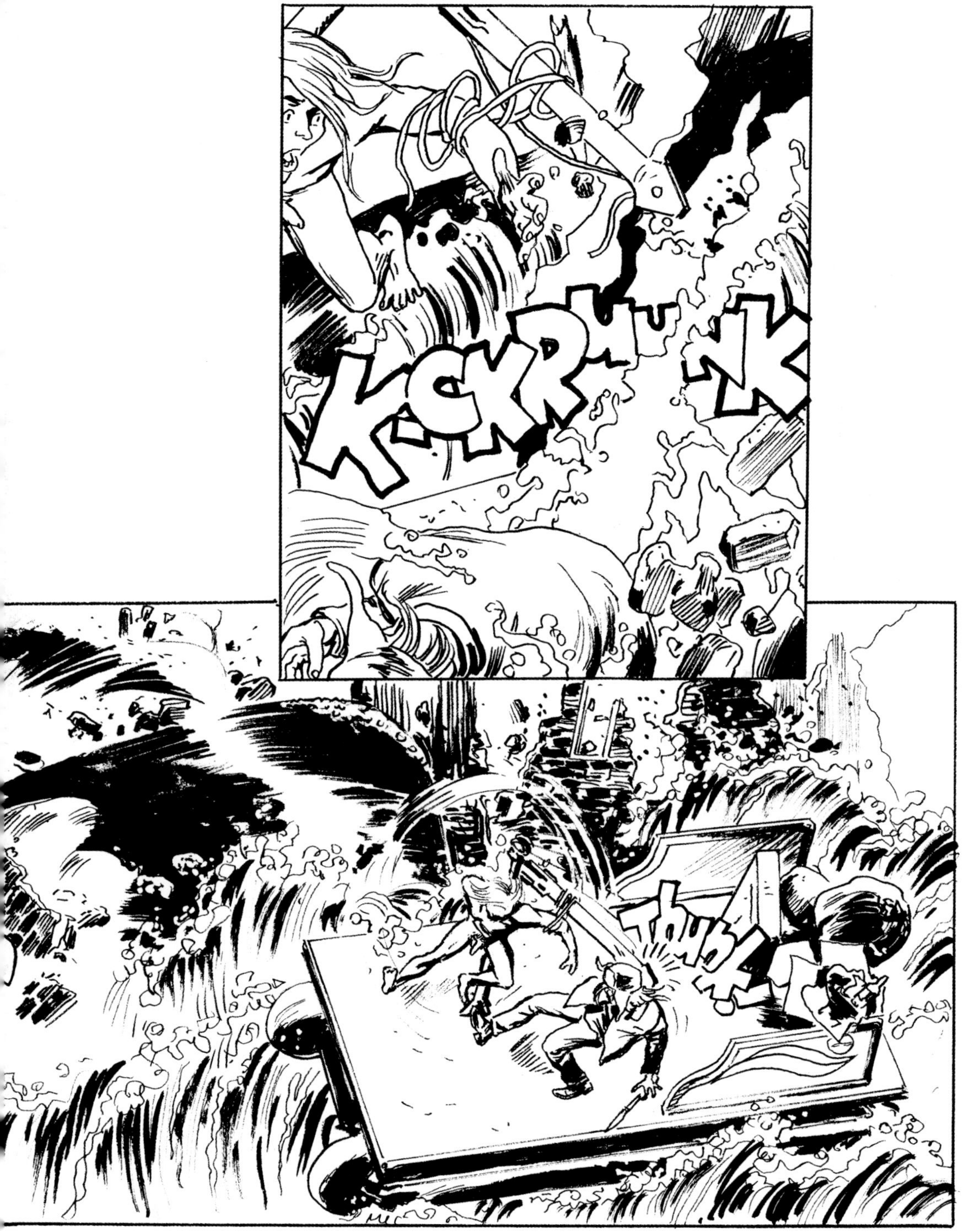
KCKRHUNK
THUDK

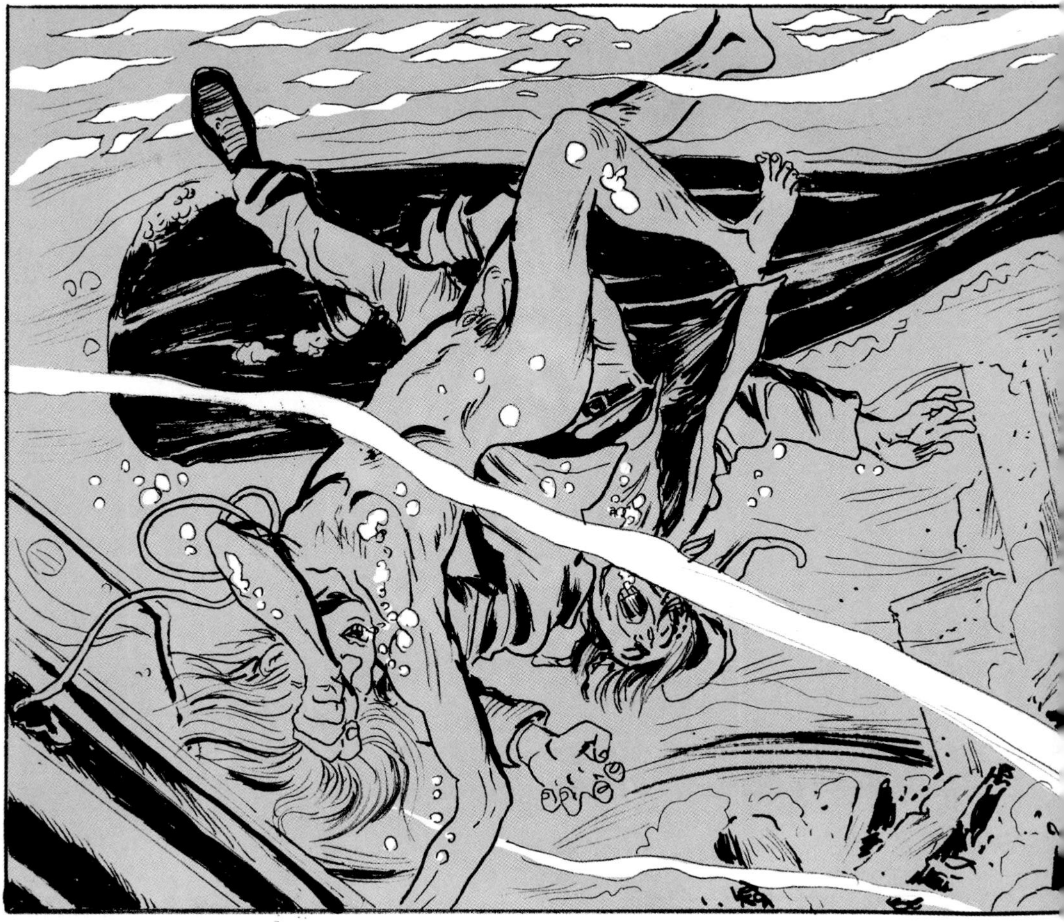

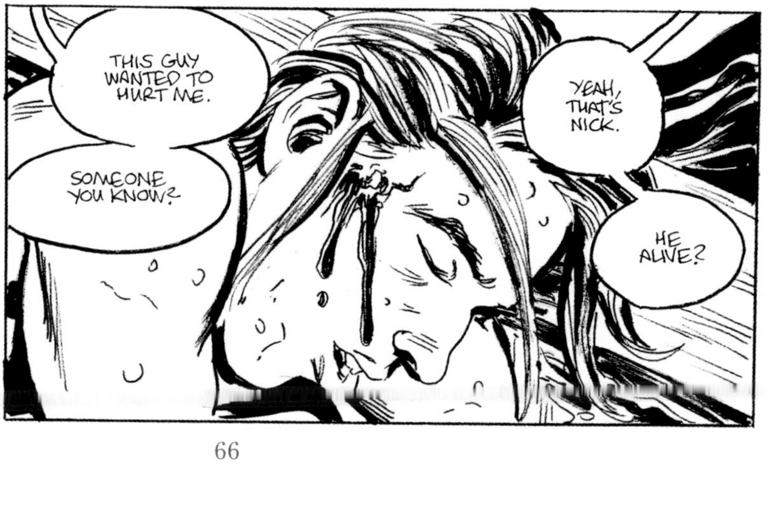
THIS GUY WANTED TO HURT ME.
SOMEONE YOU KNOW?
YEAH, THAT'S NICK.
HE ALIVE?

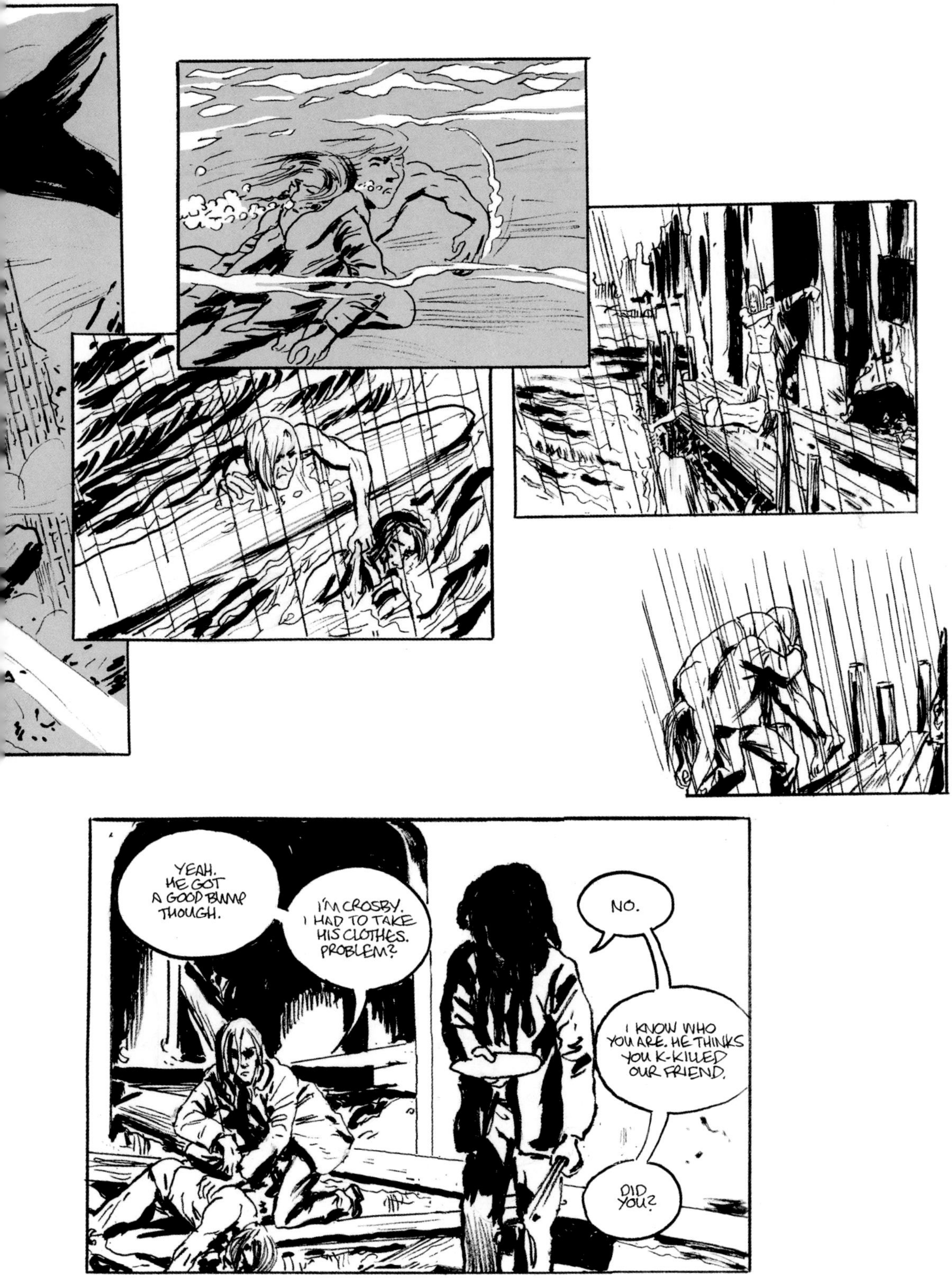

YEAH. HE GOT A GOOD BUMP THOUGH.
I'M CROSBY. I HAD TO TAKE HIS CLOTHES. PROBLEM?
NO.
I KNOW WHO YOU ARE. HE THINKS YOU K-KILLED OUR FRIEND.
DID YOU?

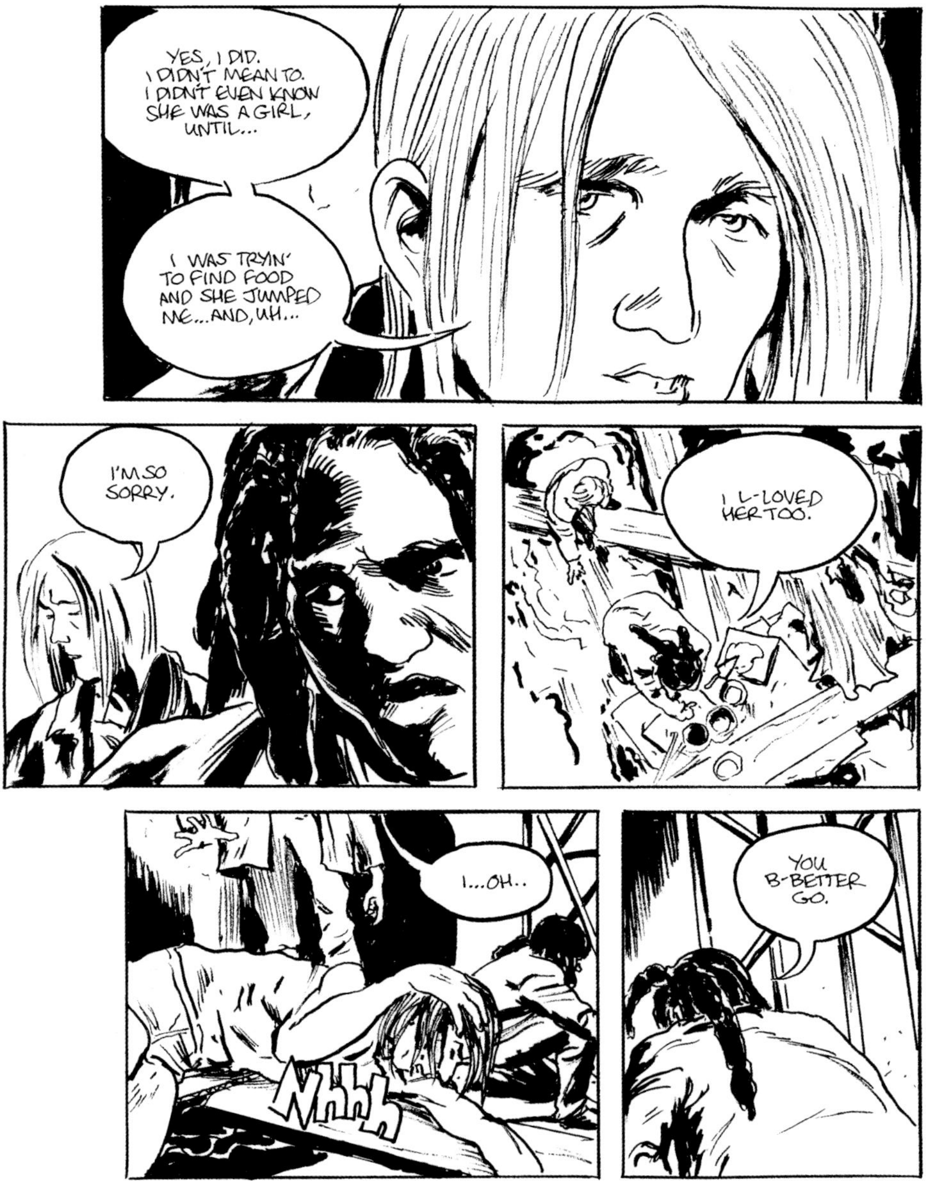
YES, I DID. I DIDN'T MEAN TO. I DIDN'T EVEN KNOW SHE WAS A GIRL, UNTIL...
I WAS TRYIN' TO FIND FOOD AND SHE JUMPED ME... AND, UH...
I'M SO SORRY.
I L-LOVED HER TOO.
I...OH..
Nhhh
YOU B-BETTER GO.

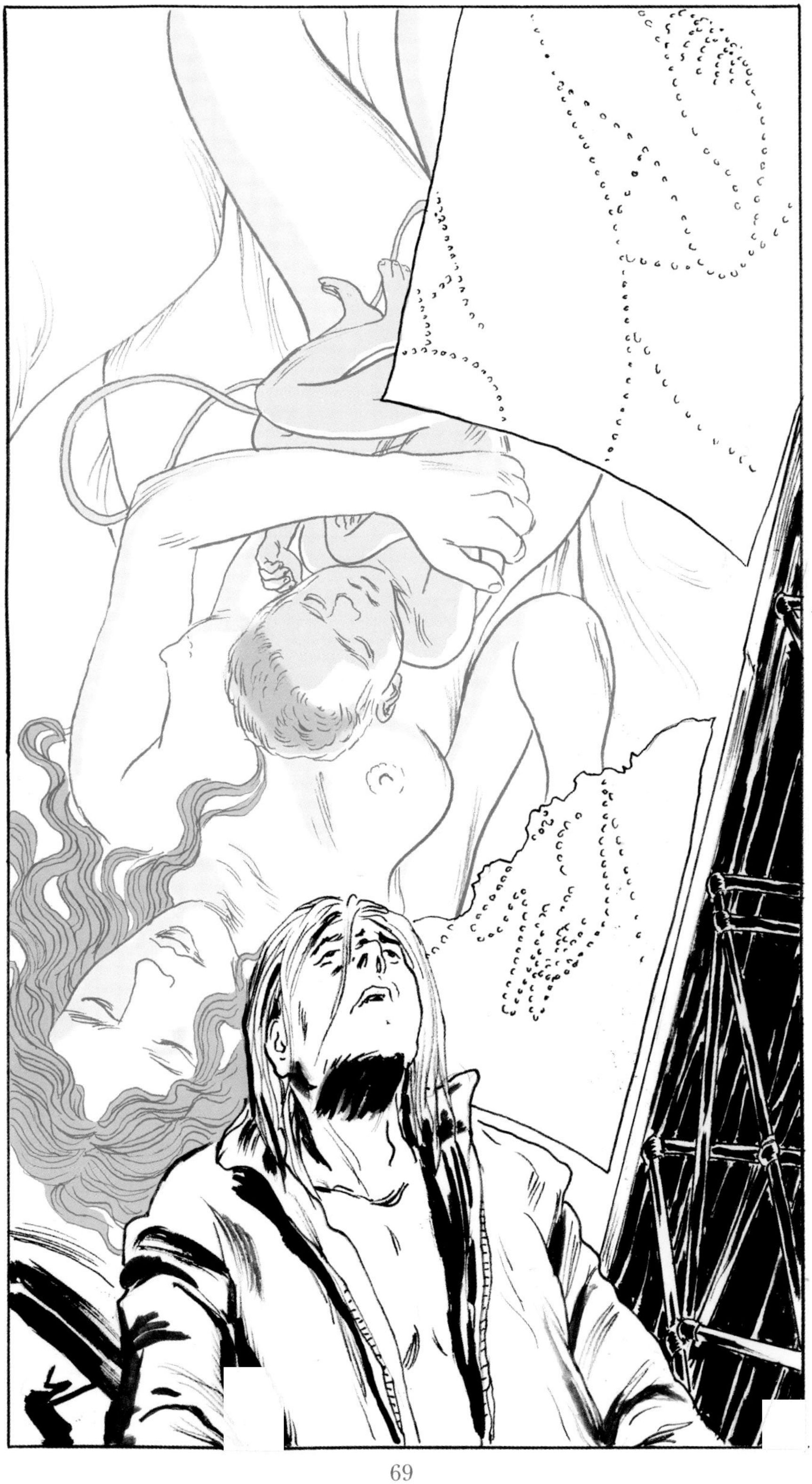

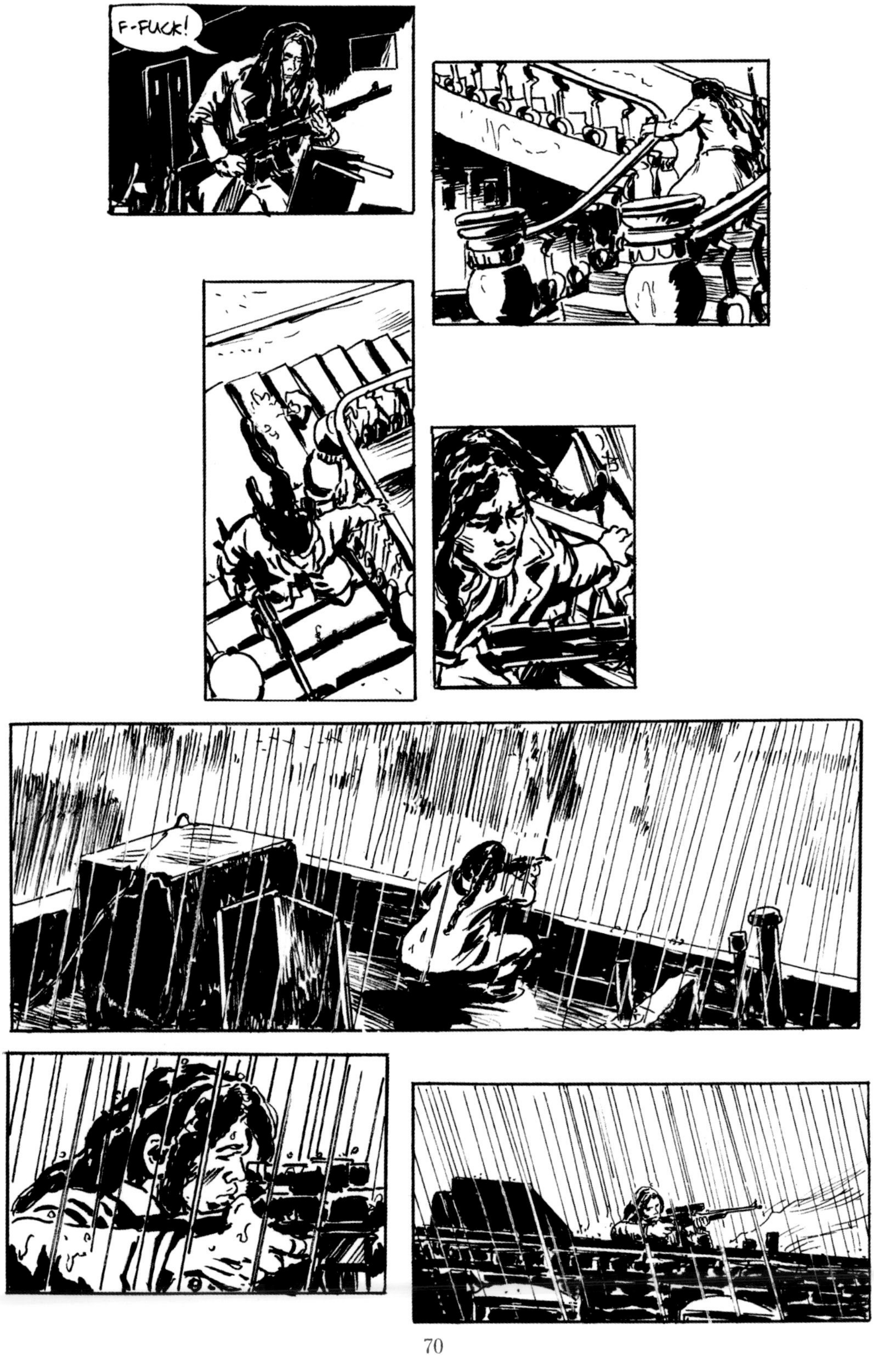
F-FUCK!

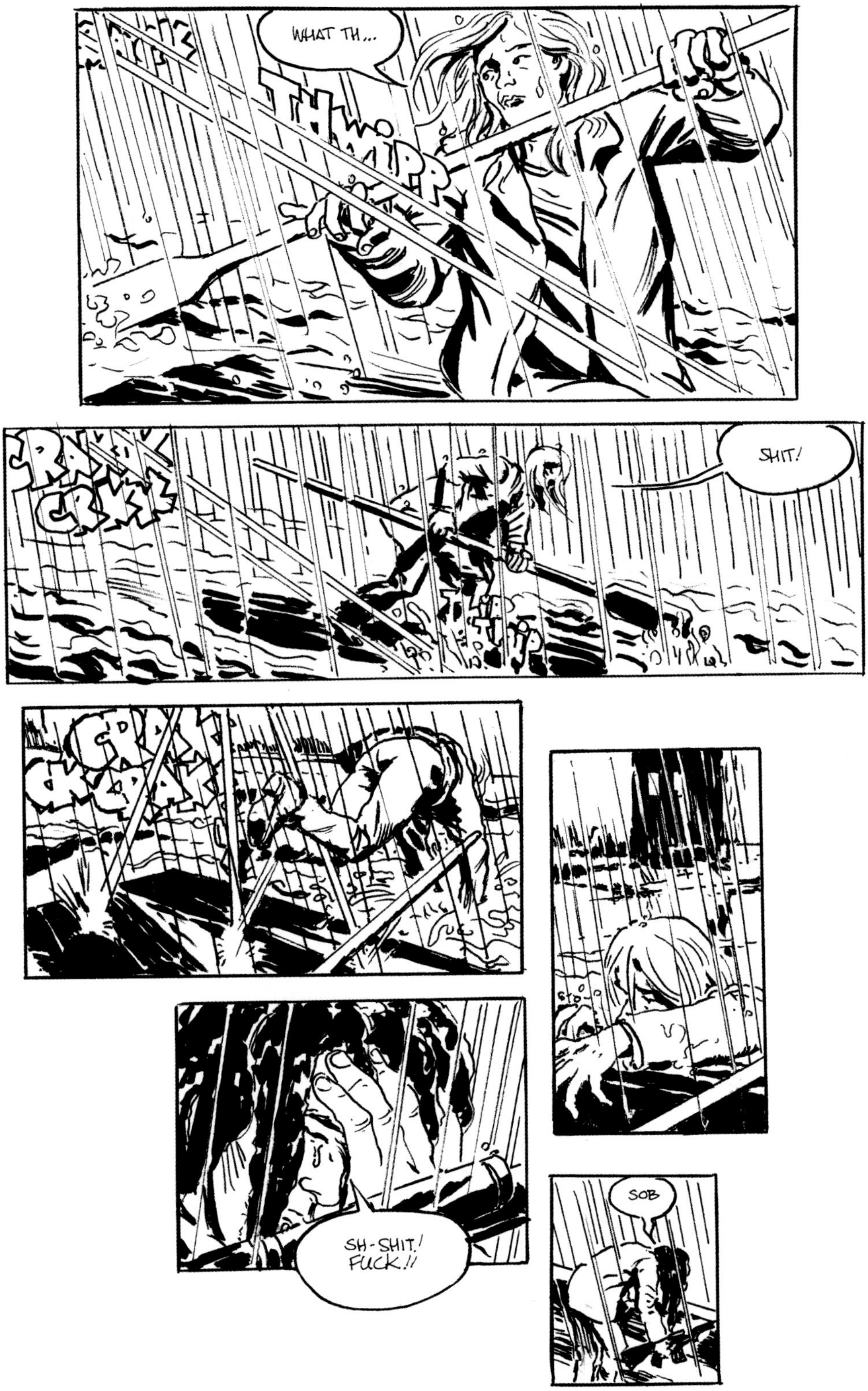
WHAT TH...
SHIT!
SH-SHIT! FUCK!!
SOB

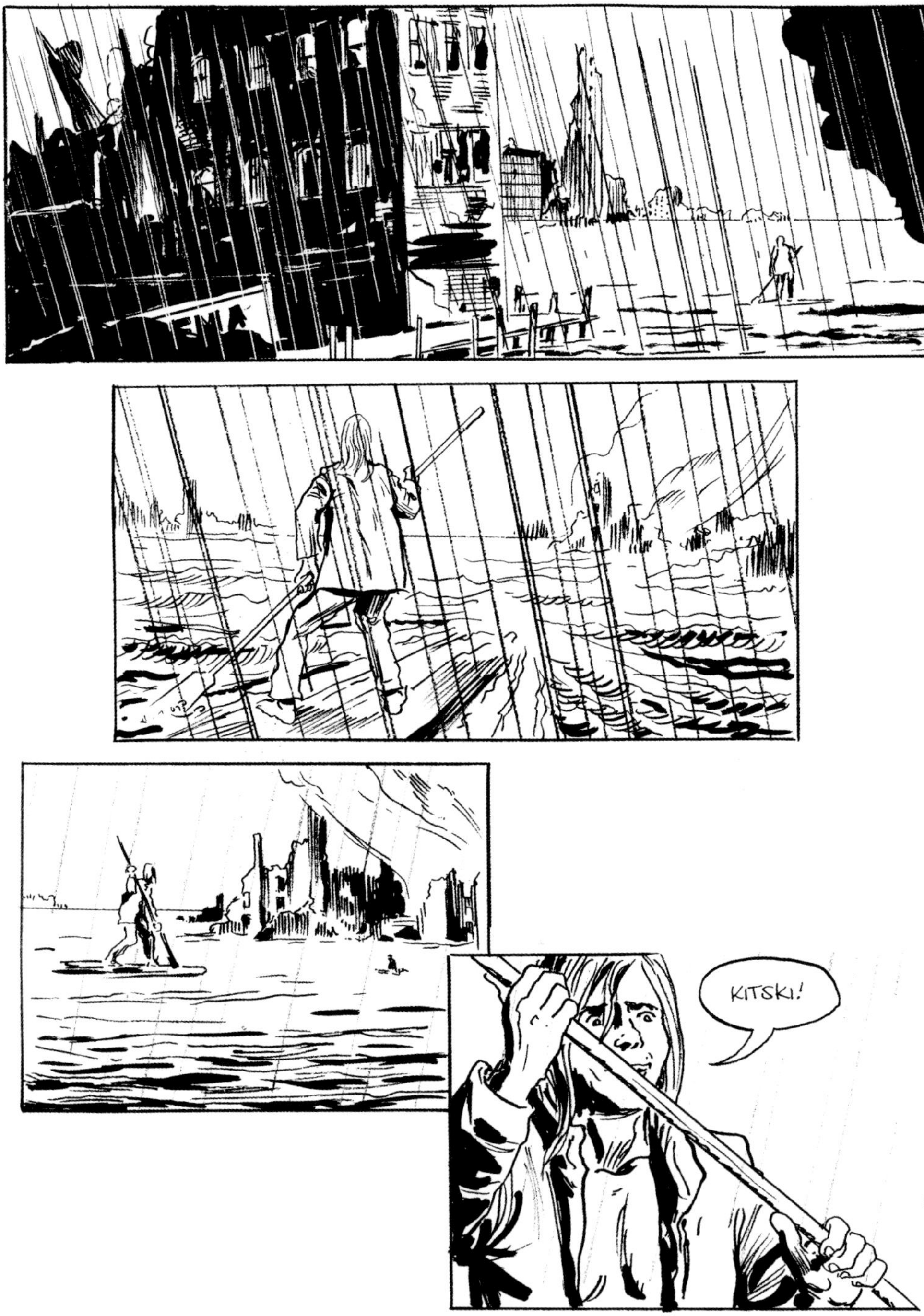
KITSKI!

OR,

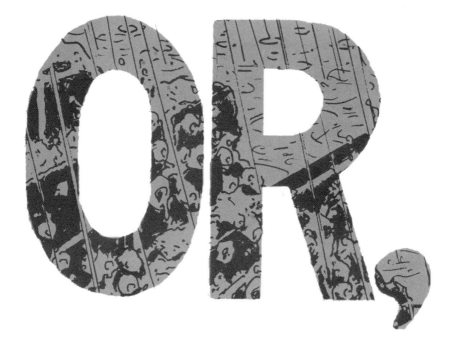

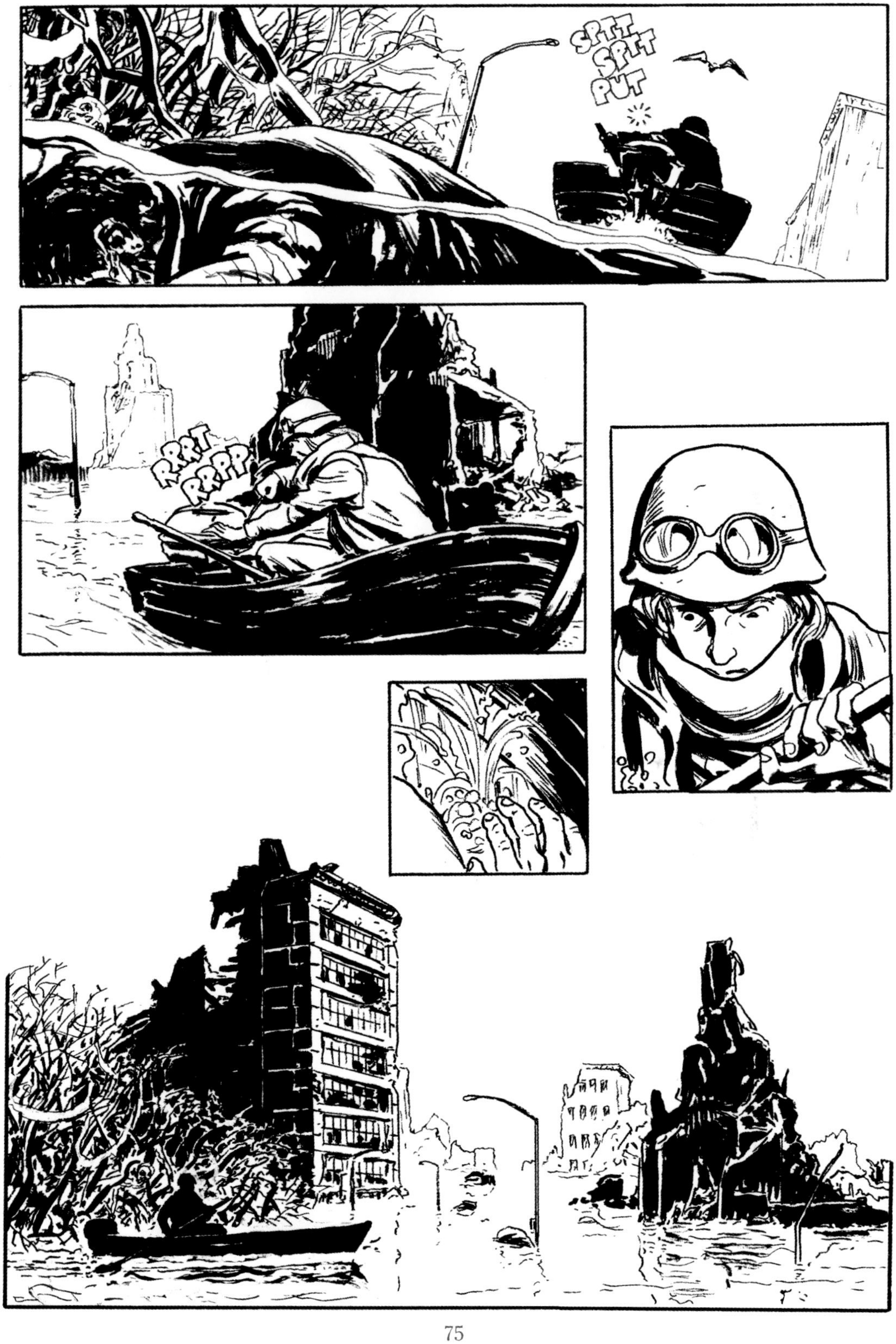
SPTT
SPTT
PUT
RRRT
RRPP

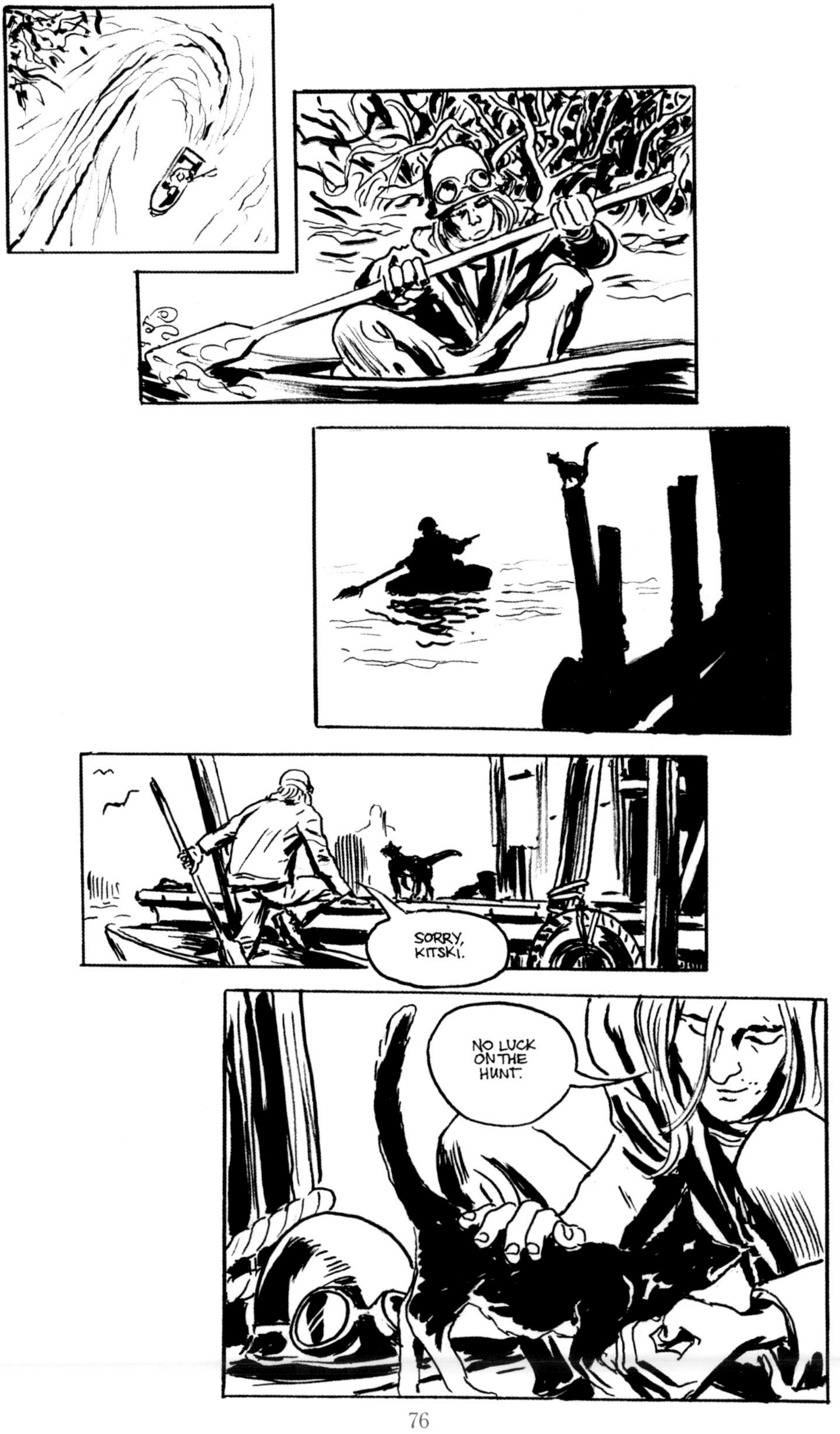
SORRY, KITSKI.
NO LUCK ON THE HUNT.

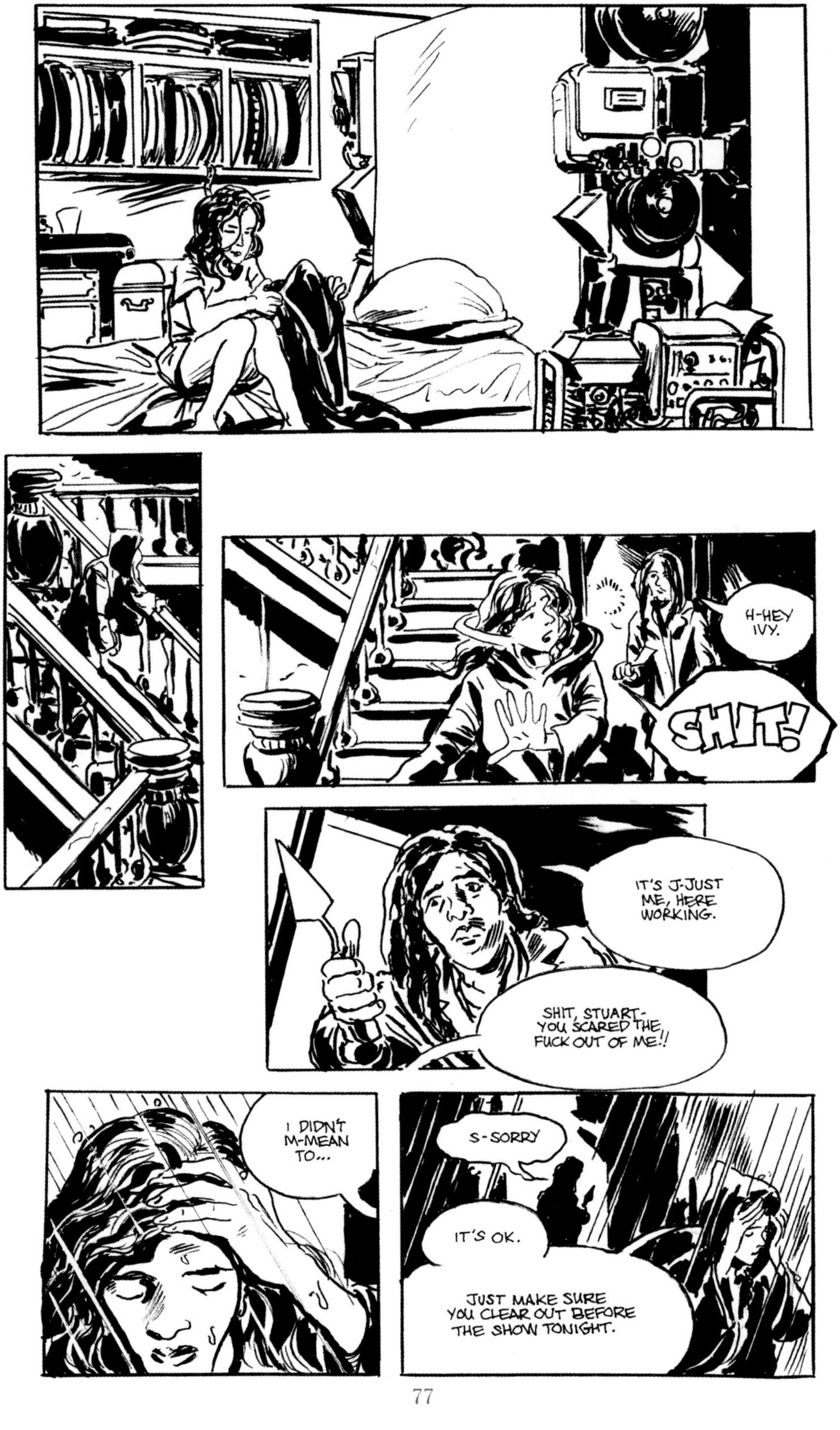
H-HEY IVY.
SHIT!
IT'S J-JUST ME, HERE WORKING.
SHIT, STUART- YOU SCARED THE FUCK OUT OF ME!!
I DIDN'T M-MEAN TO...
S-SORRY
IT'S OK.
JUST MAKE SURE YOU CLEAR OUT BEFORE THE SHOW TONIGHT.

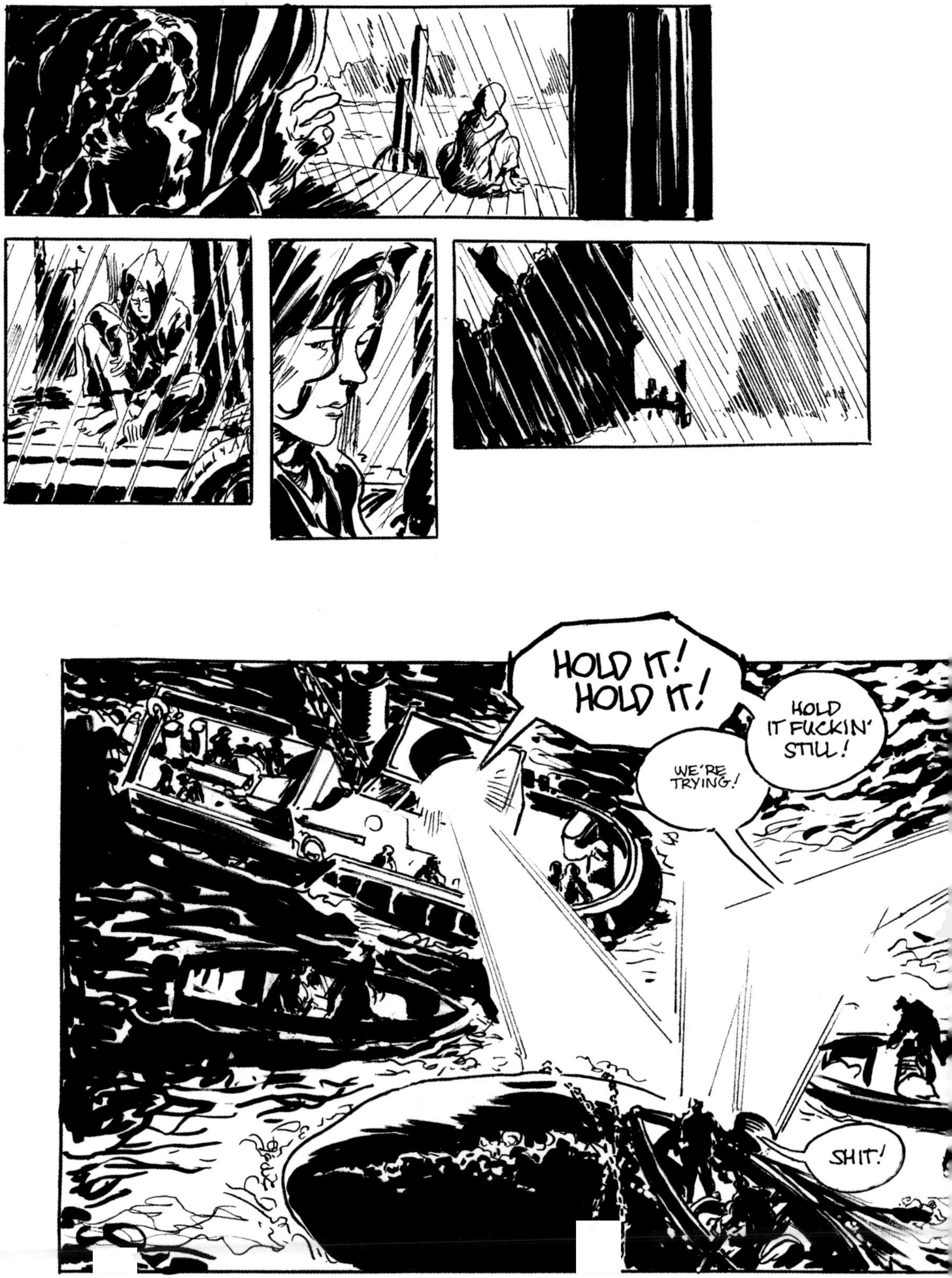
HOLD IT! HOLD IT!
WE'RE TRYING!
HOLD IT FUCKIN' STILL!
SHIT!

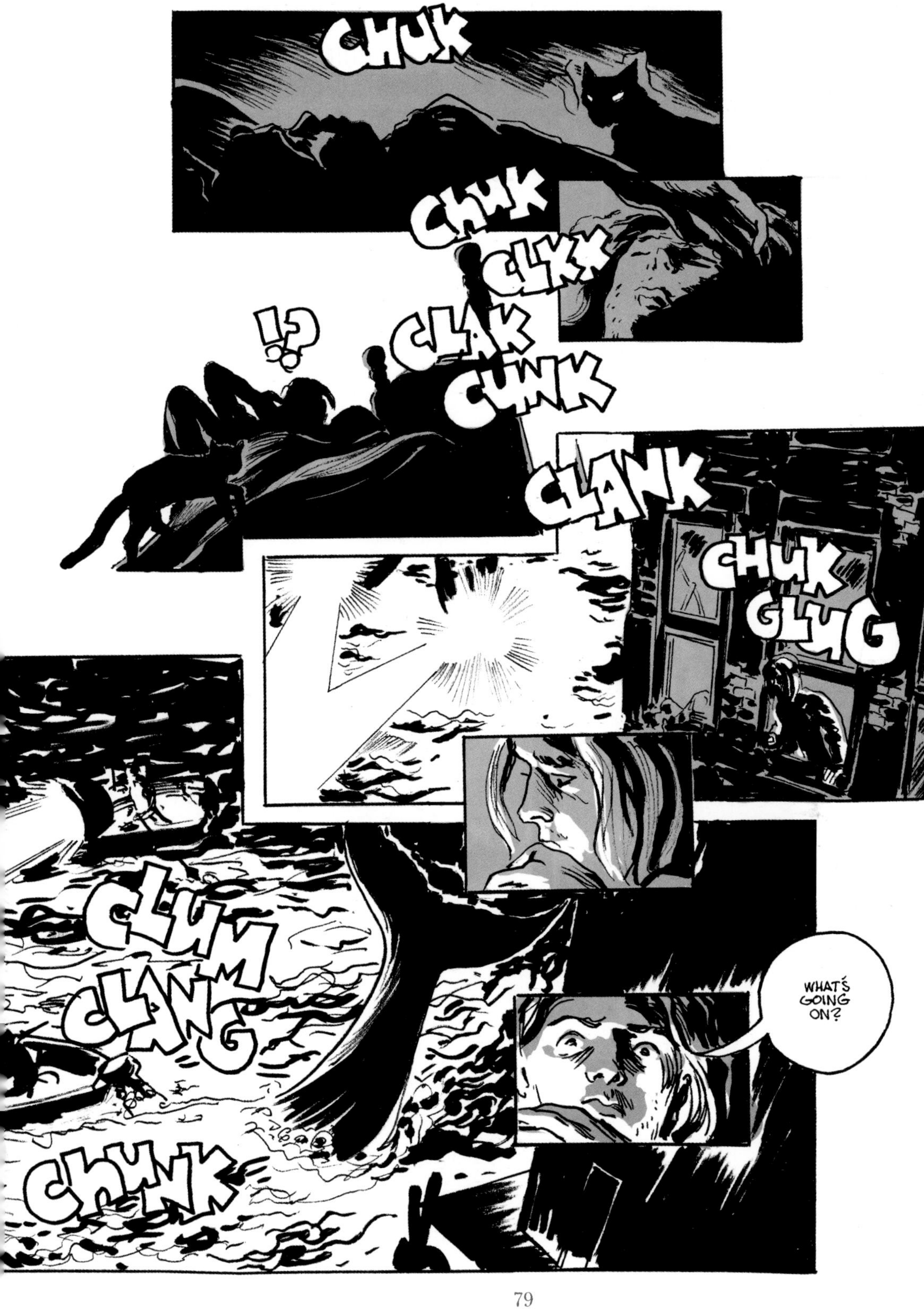
CHUK
CHUK
CLKK
!?
CLAK
CUNK
CLANK
CHUK
GLUG
CLUM
CLANG
CHUNK
WHAT'S GOING ON?

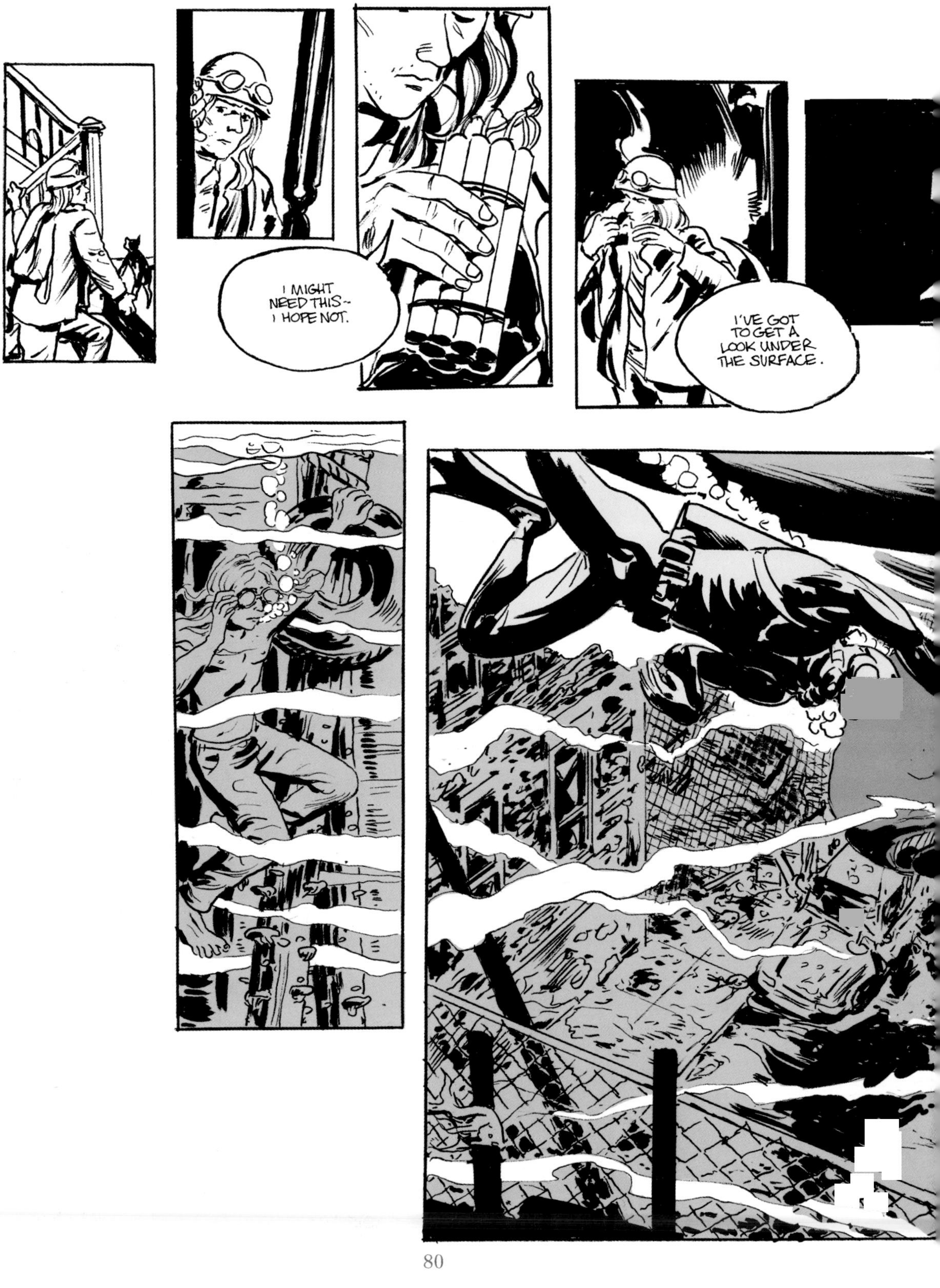
I MIGHT NEED THIS-- I HOPE NOT.
I'VE GOT TO GET A LOOK UNDER THE SURFACE.

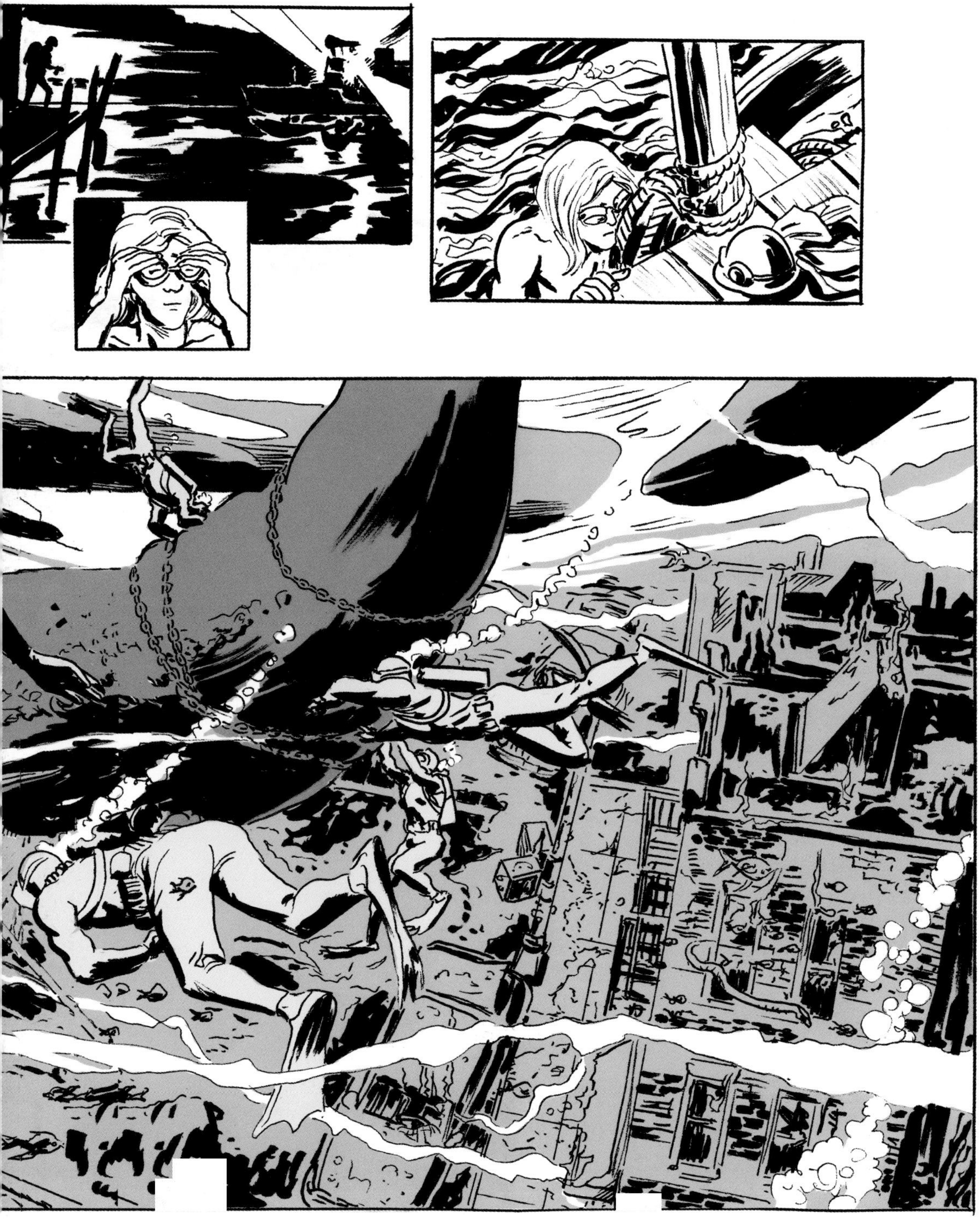

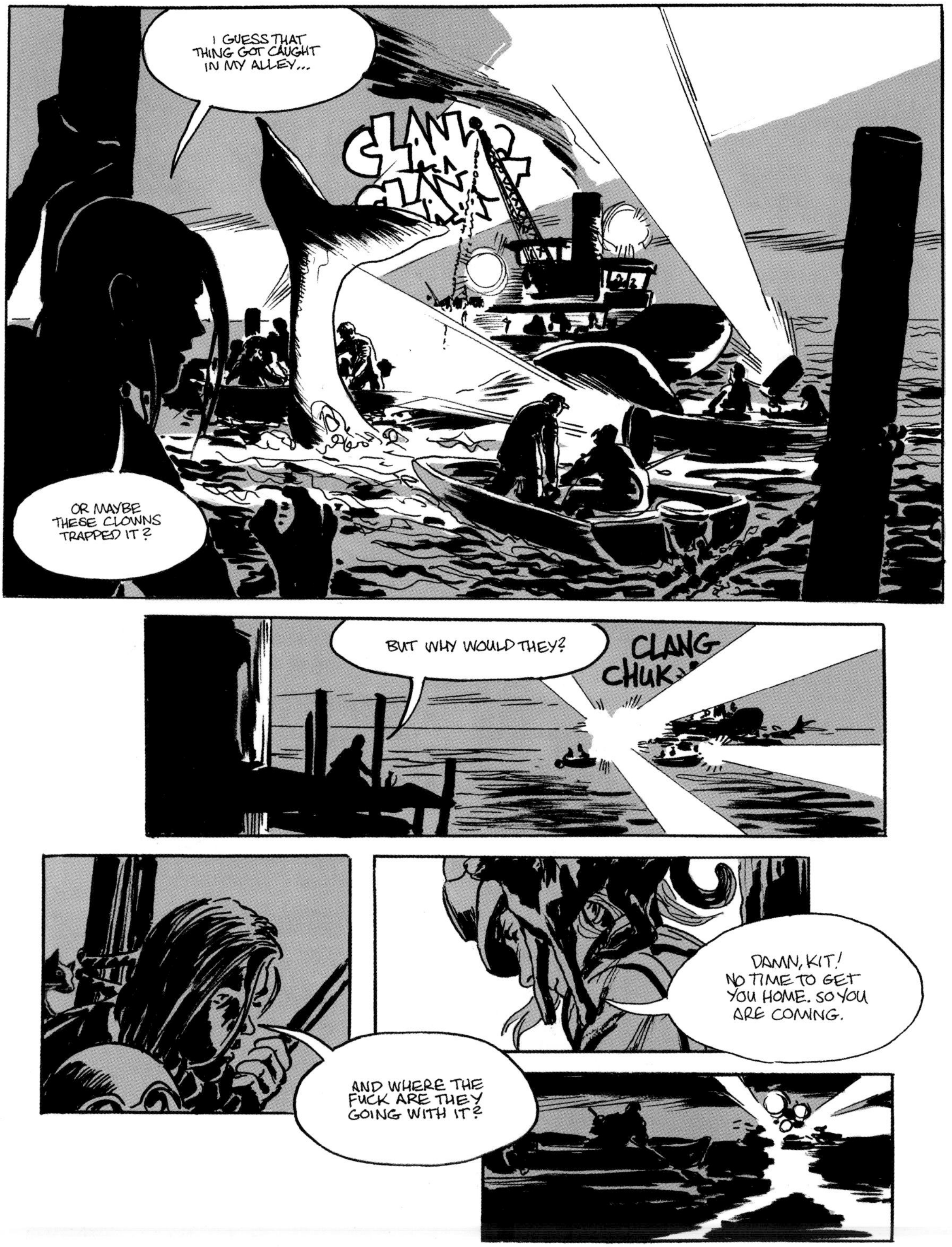
I GUESS THAT THING GOT CAUGHT IN MY ALLEY...
OR MAYBE THESE CLOWNS TRAPPED IT?
BUT WHY WOULD THEY?
CLANG
CHUK
AND WHERE THE FUCK ARE THEY GOING WITH IT?
DAMN, KIT! NO TIME TO GET YOU HOME. SO YOU ARE COMING.

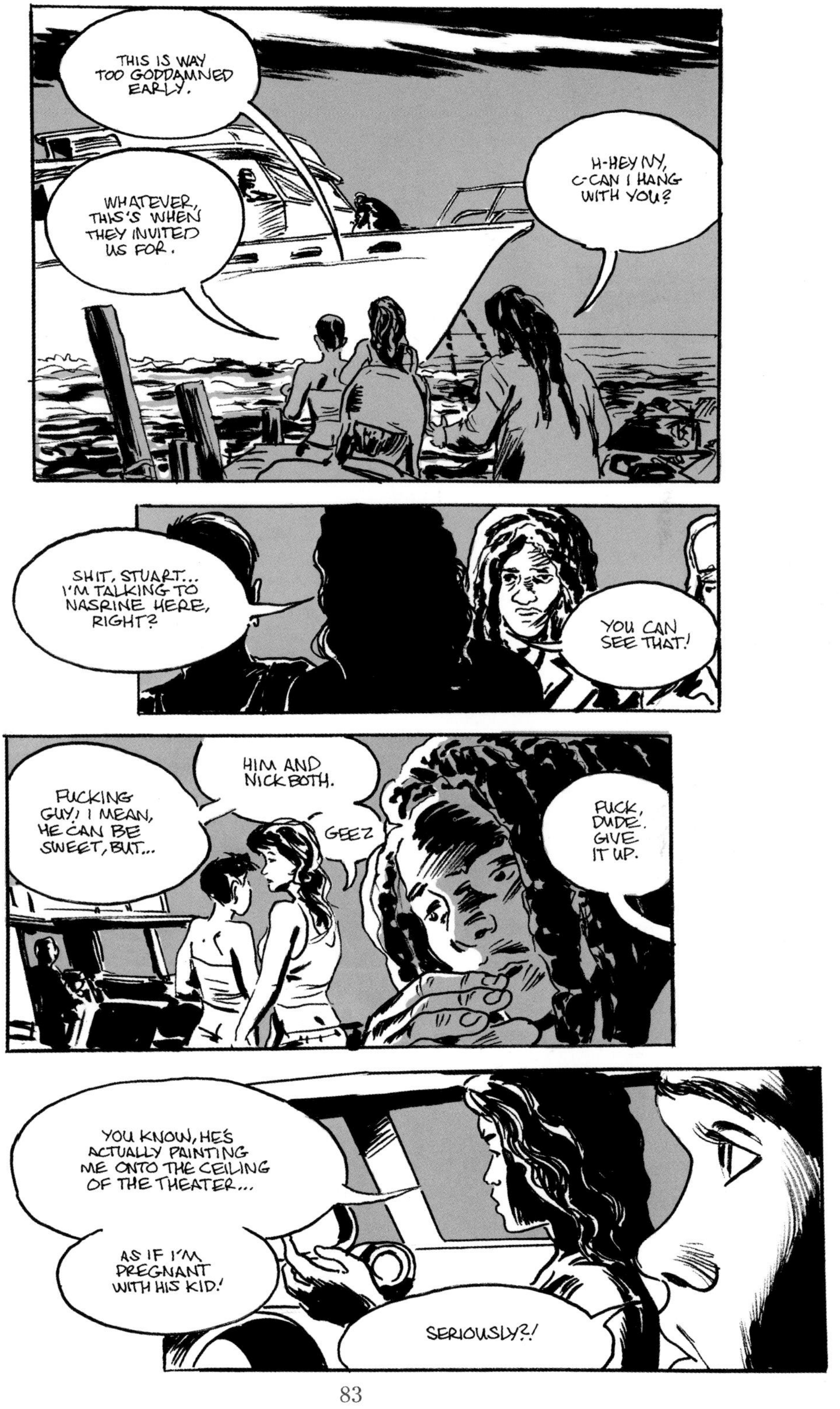
THIS IS WAY TOO GODDAMNED EARLY.
WHATEVER, THIS'S WHEN THEY INVITED US FOR.
H-HEY NY, C-CAN I HANG WITH YOU?
SHIT, STUART... I'M TALKING TO NASRINE HERE, RIGHT?
YOU CAN SEE THAT!
FUCKING GUY, I MEAN, HE CAN BE SWEET, BUT...
HIM AND NICK BOTH.
GEEZ
FUCK, DUDE. GIVE IT UP.
YOU KNOW, HE'S ACTUALLY PAINTING ME ONTO THE CEILING OF THE THEATER...
AS IF I'M PREGNANT WITH HIS KID!
SERIOUSLY?!

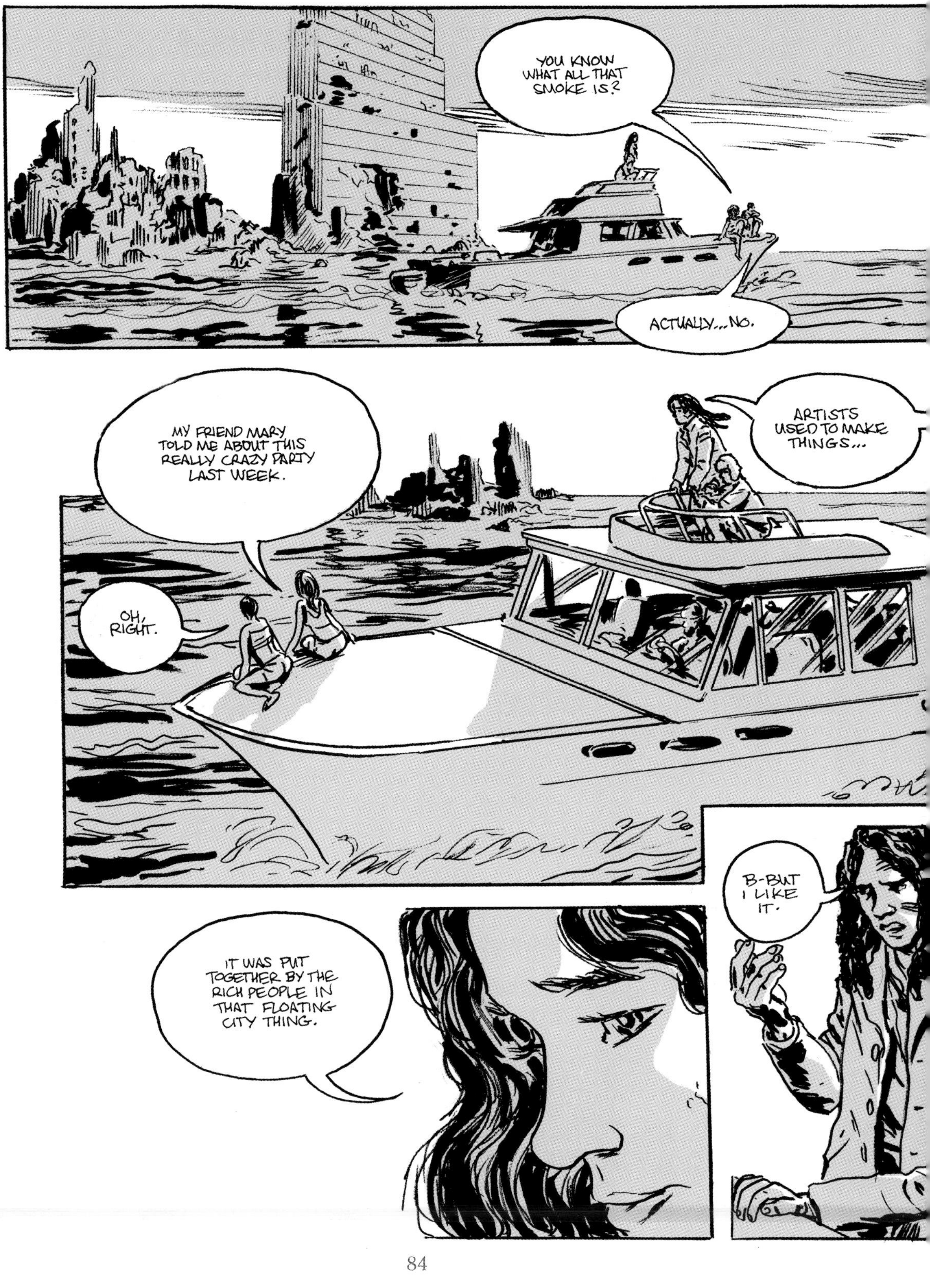

YOU KNOW WHAT ALL THAT SMOKE IS?
ACTUALLY... NO.
MY FRIEND MARY TOLD ME ABOUT THIS REALLY CRAZY PARTY LAST WEEK.
OH, RIGHT.
ARTISTS USED TO MAKE THINGS...
IT WAS PUT TOGETHER BY THE RICH PEOPLE IN THAT FLOATING CITY THING.
B-BUT I LIKE IT.

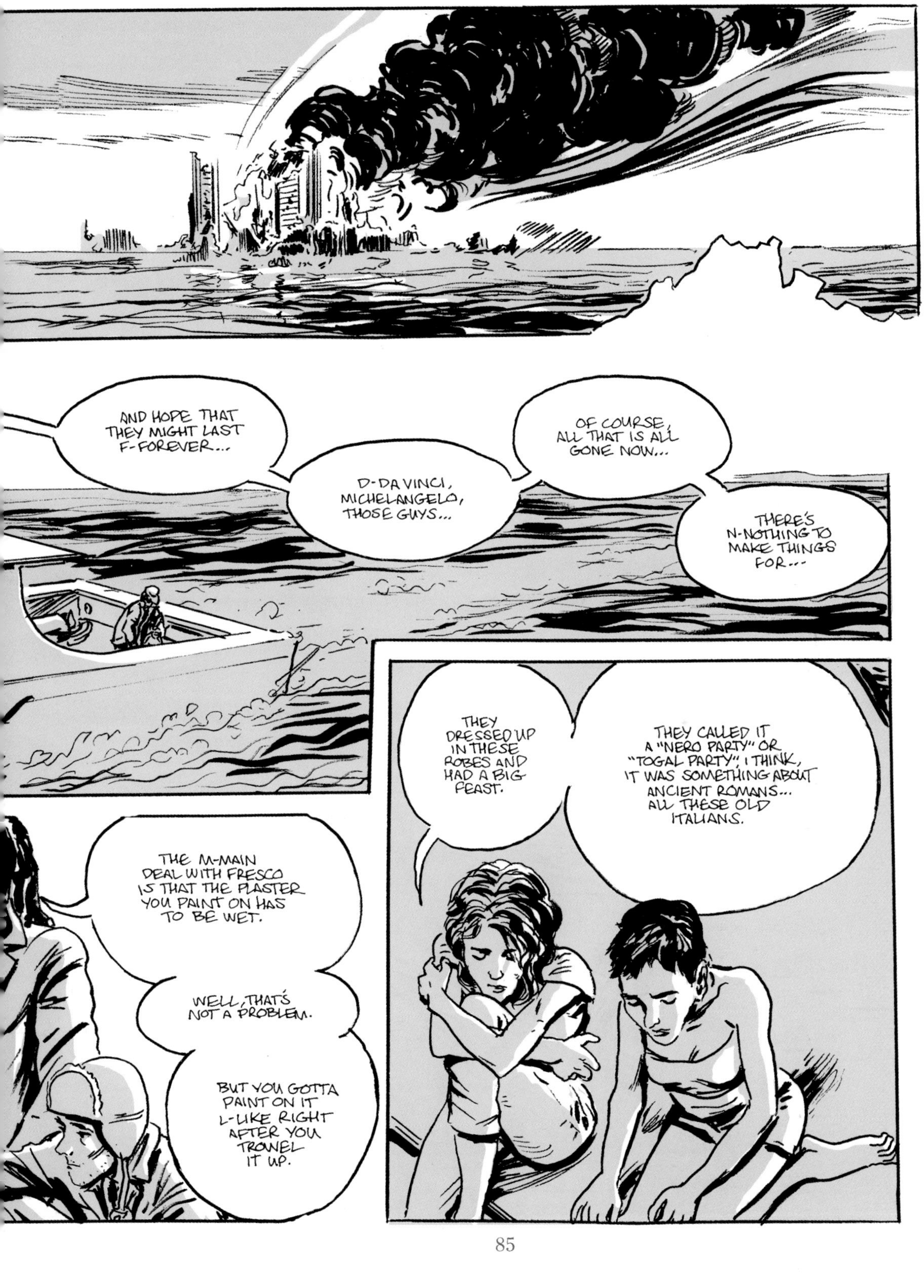
AND HOPE THAT THEY MIGHT LAST F-FOREVER...
D-DA VINCI, MICHELANGELO, THOSE GUYS...
OF COURSE, ALL THAT IS ALL GONE NOW...
THERE'S N-NOTHING TO MAKE THINGS FOR...
THEY DRESSED UP IN THESE ROBES AND HAD A BIG FEAST.
THEY CALLED IT A "NERO PARTY" OR "TOGAL PARTY", I THINK, IT WAS SOMETHING ABOUT ANCIENT ROMANS... ALL THESE OLD ITALIANS.
THE M-MAIN DEAL WITH FRESCO IS THAT THE PLASTER YOU PAINT ON HAS TO BE WET.
WELL, THAT'S NOT A PROBLEM.
BUT YOU GOTTA PAINT ON IT L-LIKE RIGHT AFTER YOU TROWEL IT UP.

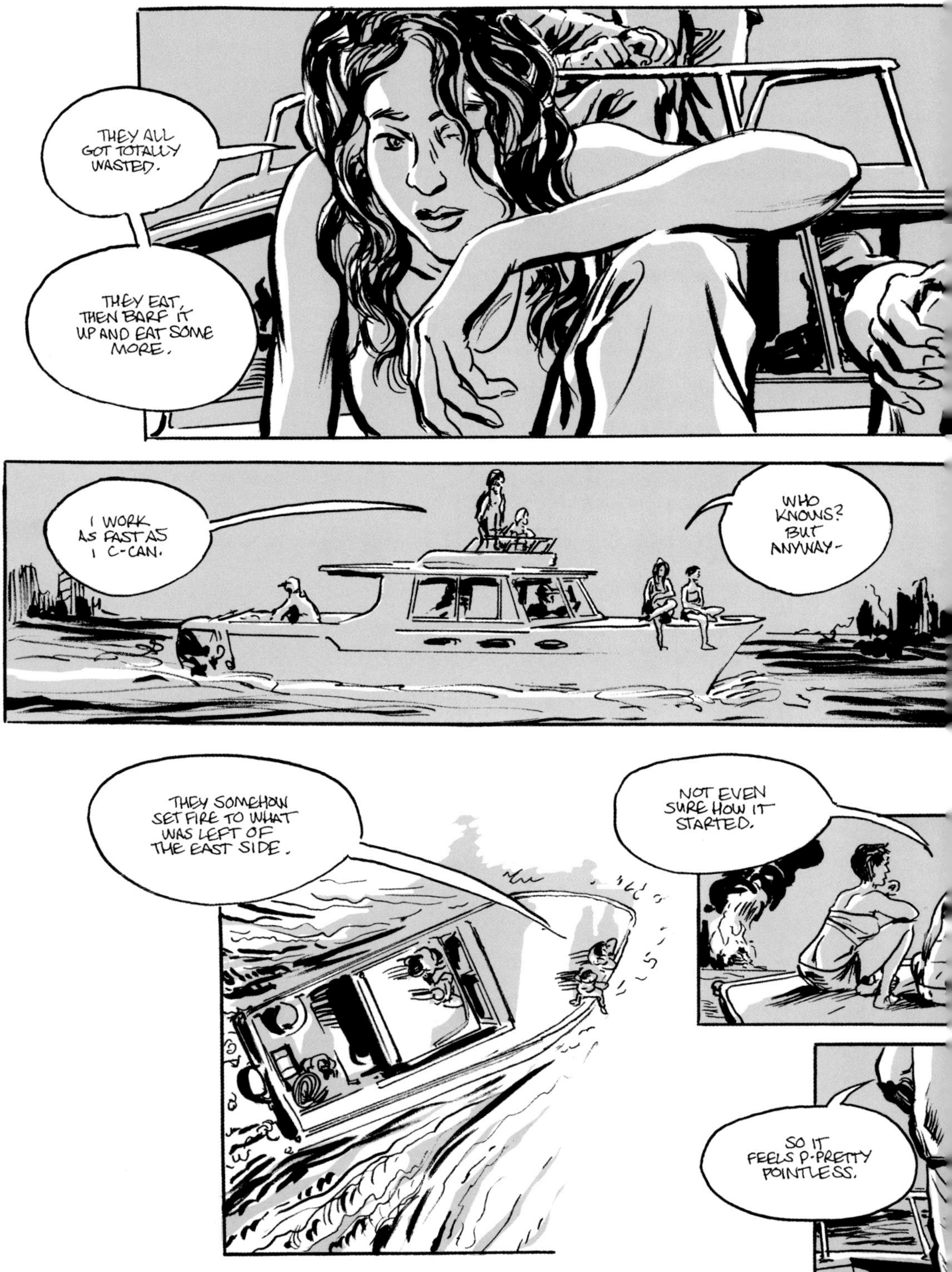
THEY ALL GOT TOTALLY WASTED.
THEY EAT, THEN BARF IT UP AND EAT SOME MORE.
I WORK AS FAST AS I C-CAN.
WHO KNOWS? BUT ANYWAY-
THEY SOMEHOW SET FIRE TO WHAT WAS LEFT OF THE EAST SIDE.
NOT EVEN SURE HOW IT STARTED.
SO IT FEELS P-PRETTY POINTLESS.

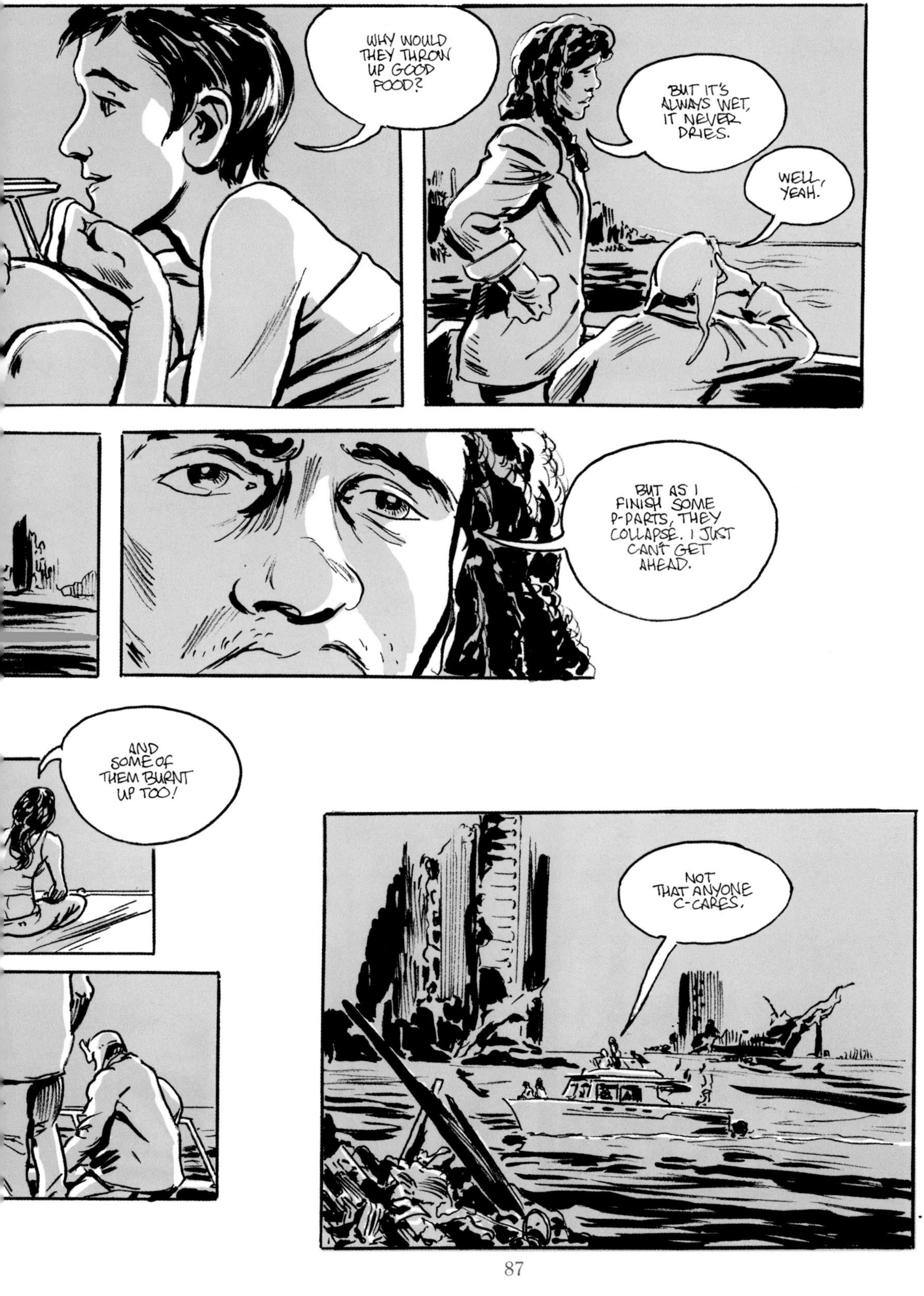
WHY WOULD THEY THROW UP GOOD FOOD?
BUT IT'S ALWAYS WET, IT NEVER DRIES.
WELL, YEAH.
BUT AS I FINISH SOME P-PARTS, THEY COLLAPSE. I JUST CAN'T GET AHEAD.
AND SOME OF THEM BURNT UP TOO!
NOT THAT ANYONE C-CARES.

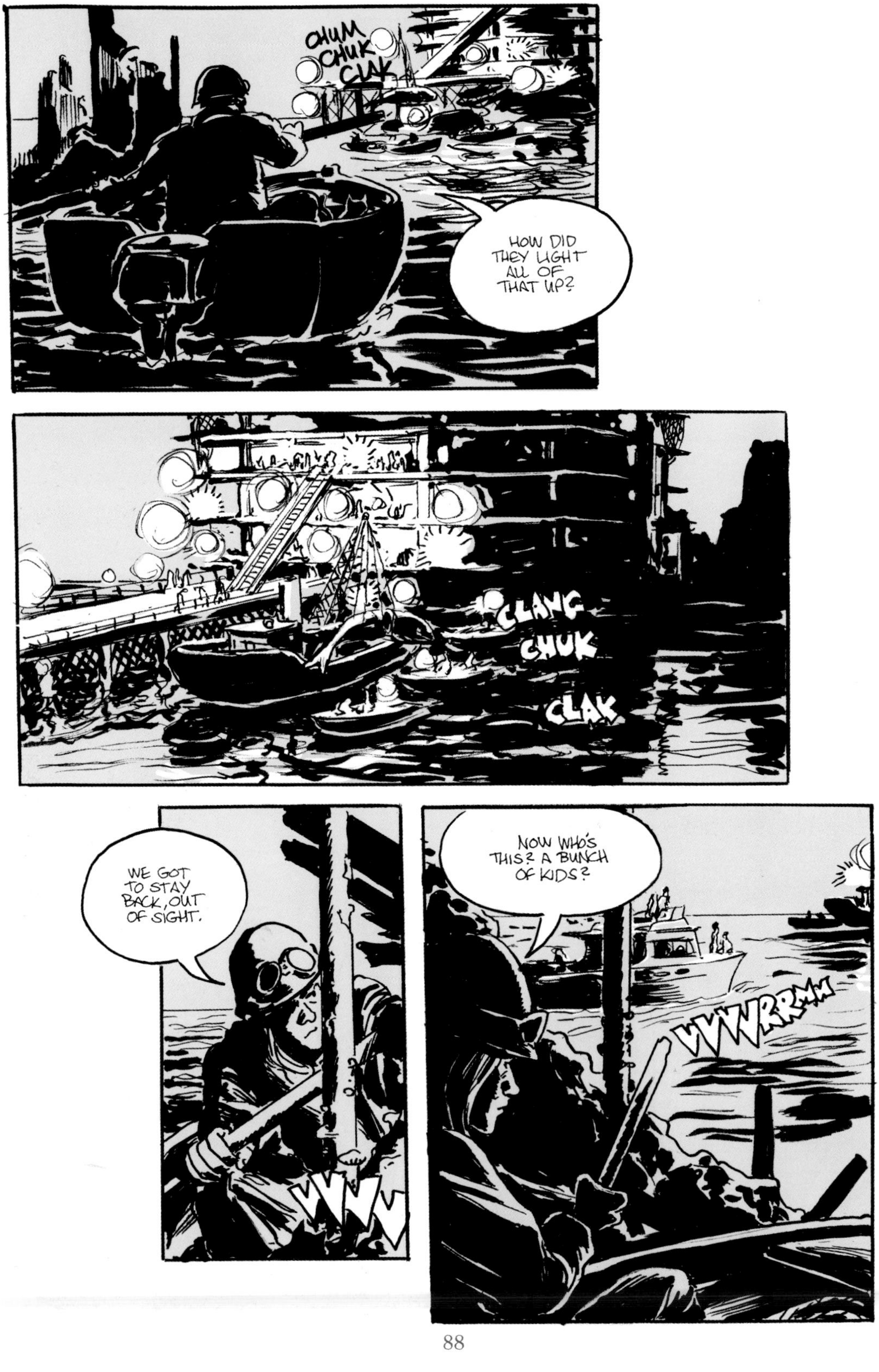
CHUM CHUK CLAK
HOW DID THEY LIGHT ALL OF THAT UP?
CLANG CHUK CLAK
WE GOT TO STAY BACK, OUT OF SIGHT.
VVVV
NOW WHO'S THIS? A BUNCH OF KIDS?
VVVVRRMM

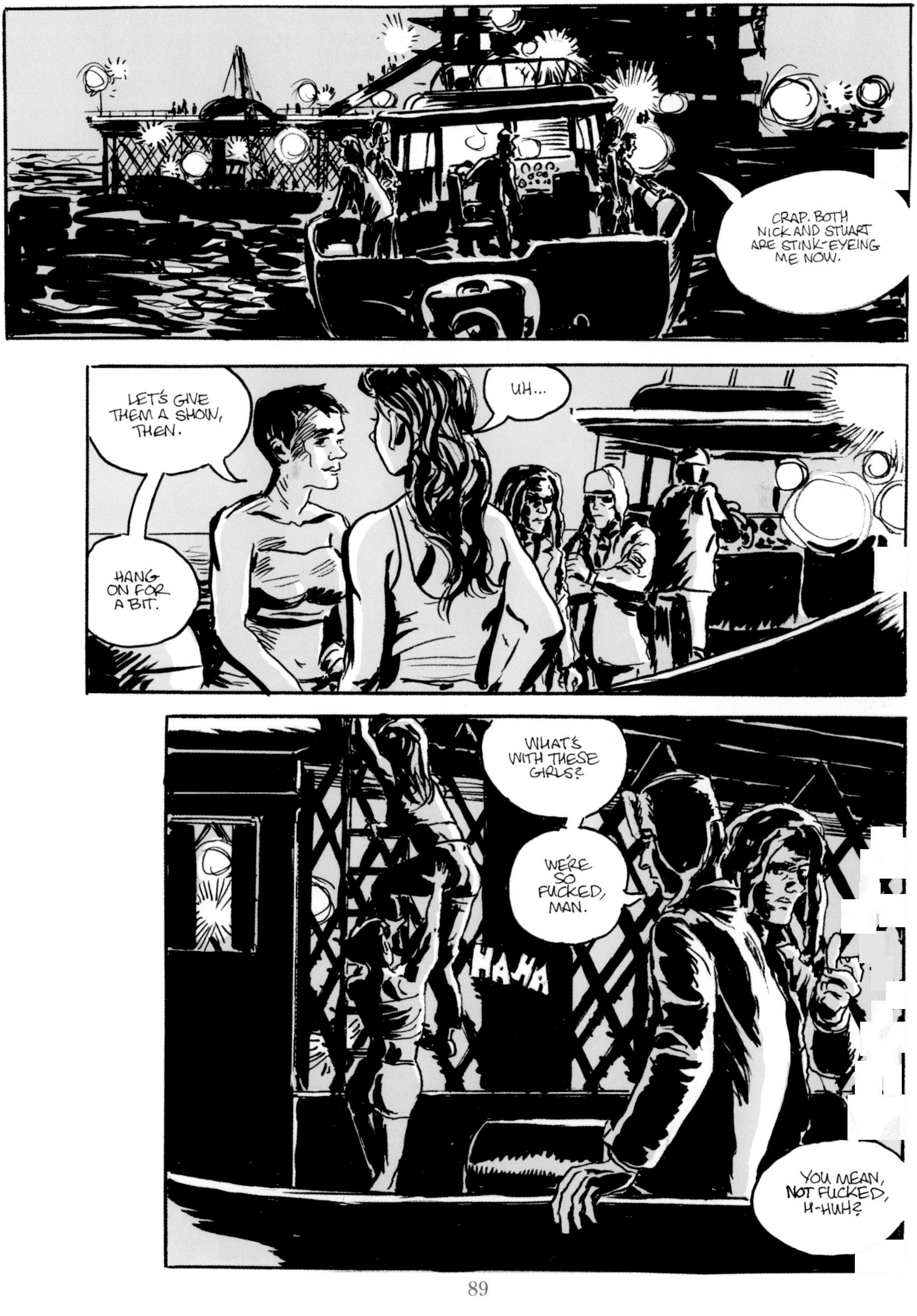
CRAP. BOTH NICK AND STUART ARE STINK-EYEING ME NOW.
LET'S GIVE THEM A SHOW, THEN.
UH...
HANG ON FOR A BIT.
WHAT'S WITH THESE GIRLS?
WE'RE SO FUCKED, MAN.
HAHA
YOU MEAN, NOT FUCKED, H-HUH?

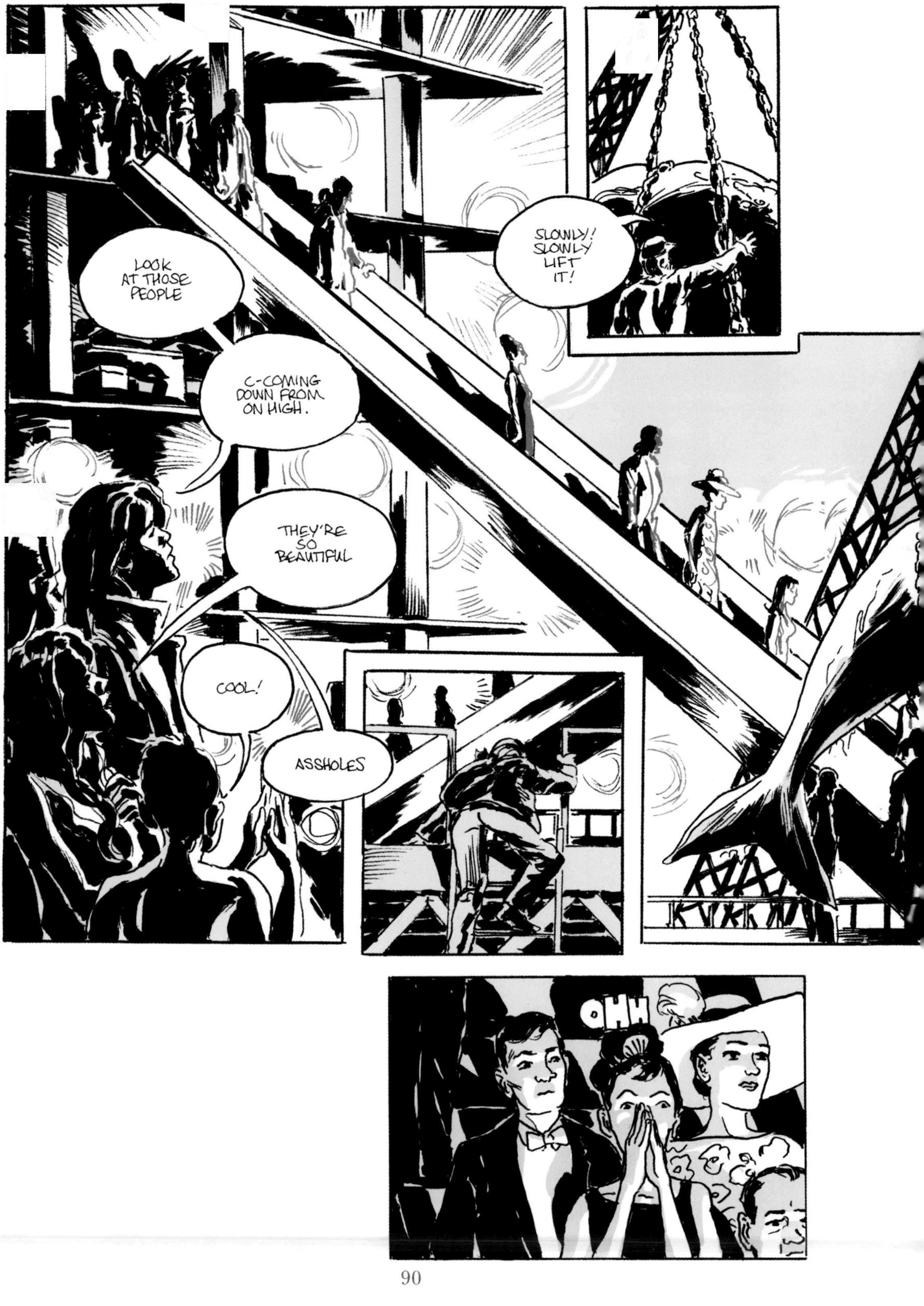
LOOK AT THOSE PEOPLE
C-COMING DOWN FROM ON HIGH.
THEY'RE SO BEAUTIFUL
COOL!
ASSHOLES
SLOWLY! SLOWLY LIFT IT!
OHH

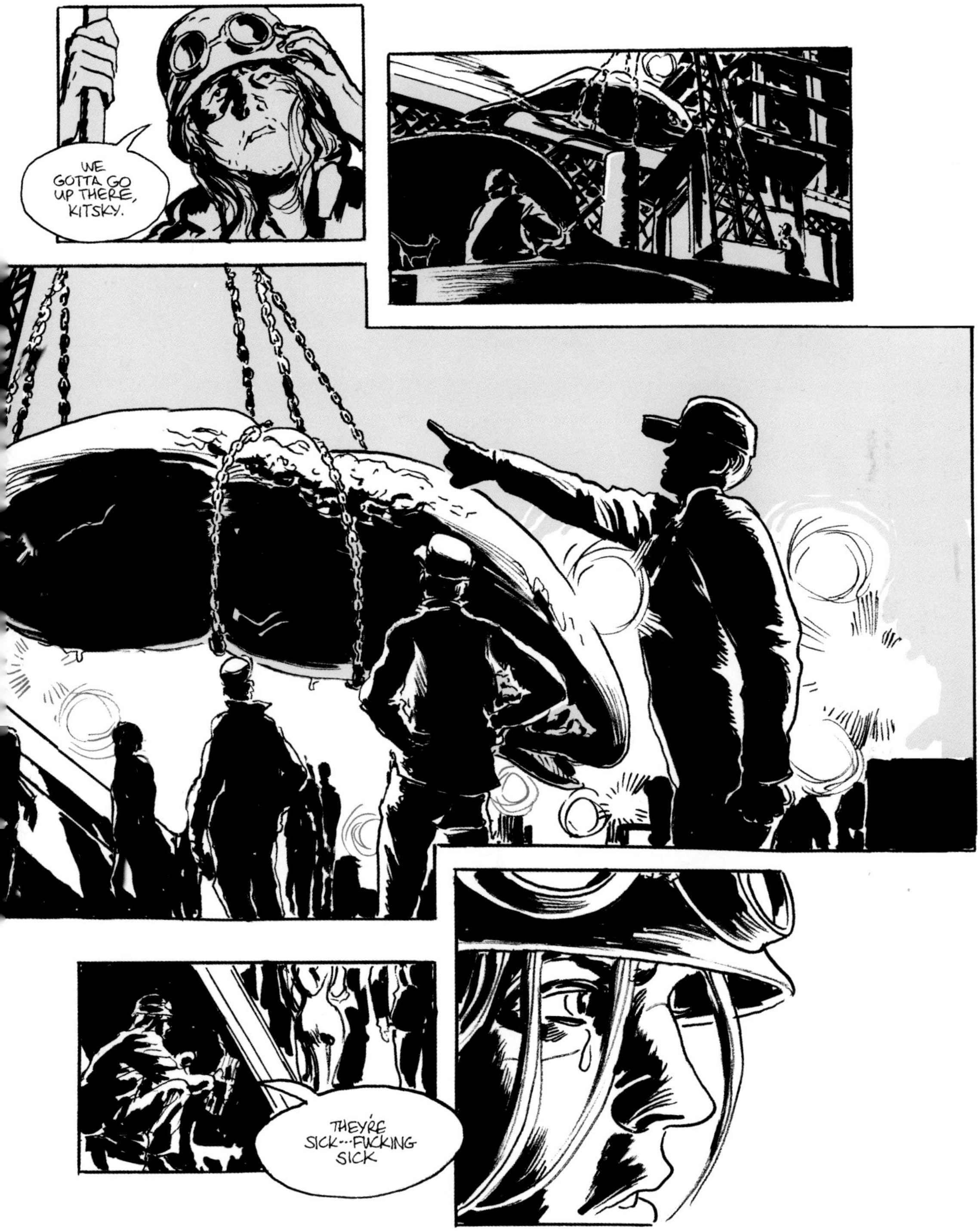
WE GOTTA GO UP THERE, KITSKY.
THEY'RE SICK···FUCKING SICK

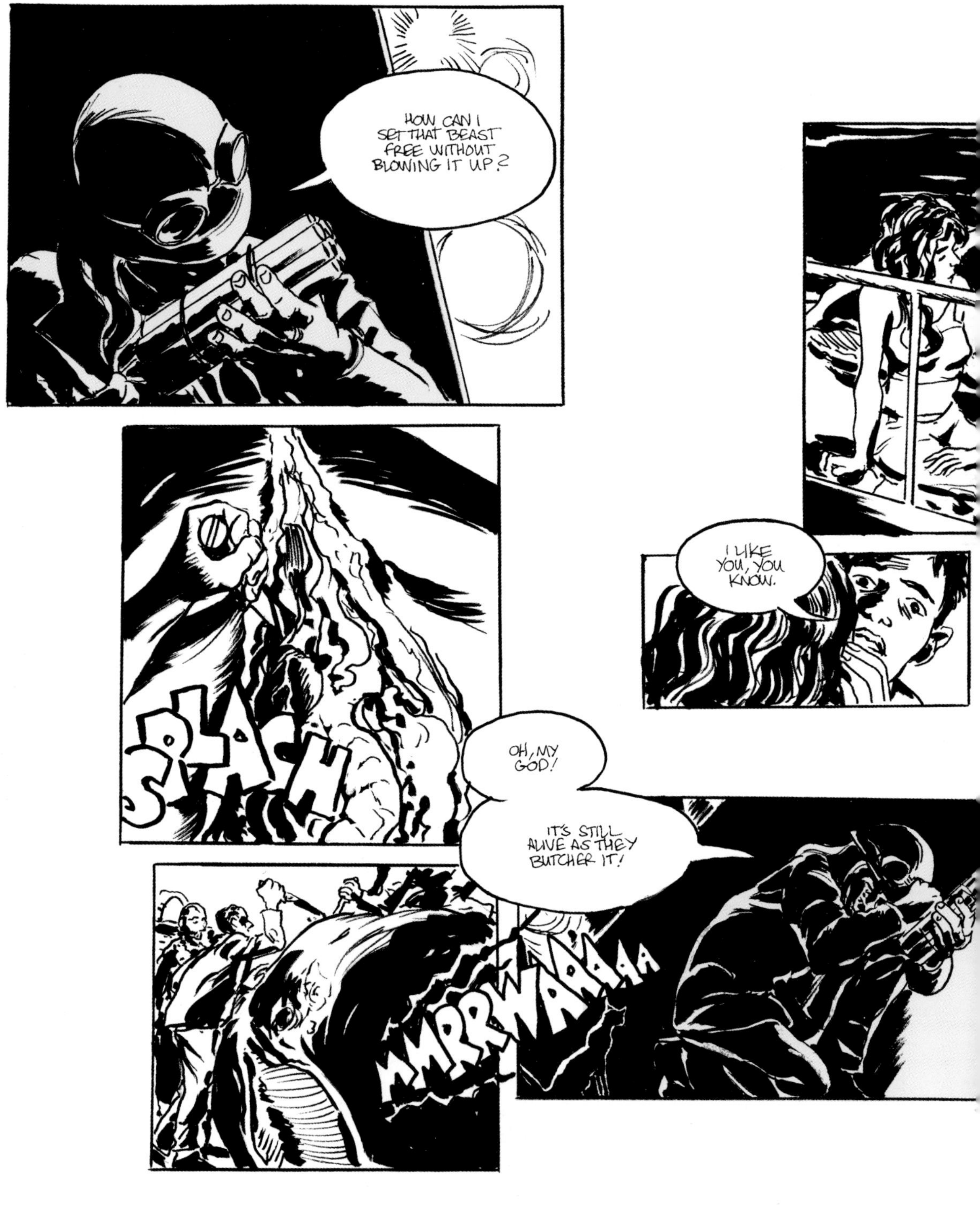
HOW CAN I SET THAT BEAST FREE WITHOUT BLOWING IT UP?
I LIKE YOU, YOU KNOW.
SPLASH
OH, MY GOD!
IT'S STILL ALIVE AS THEY BUTCHER IT!
MMRRWAAAAA

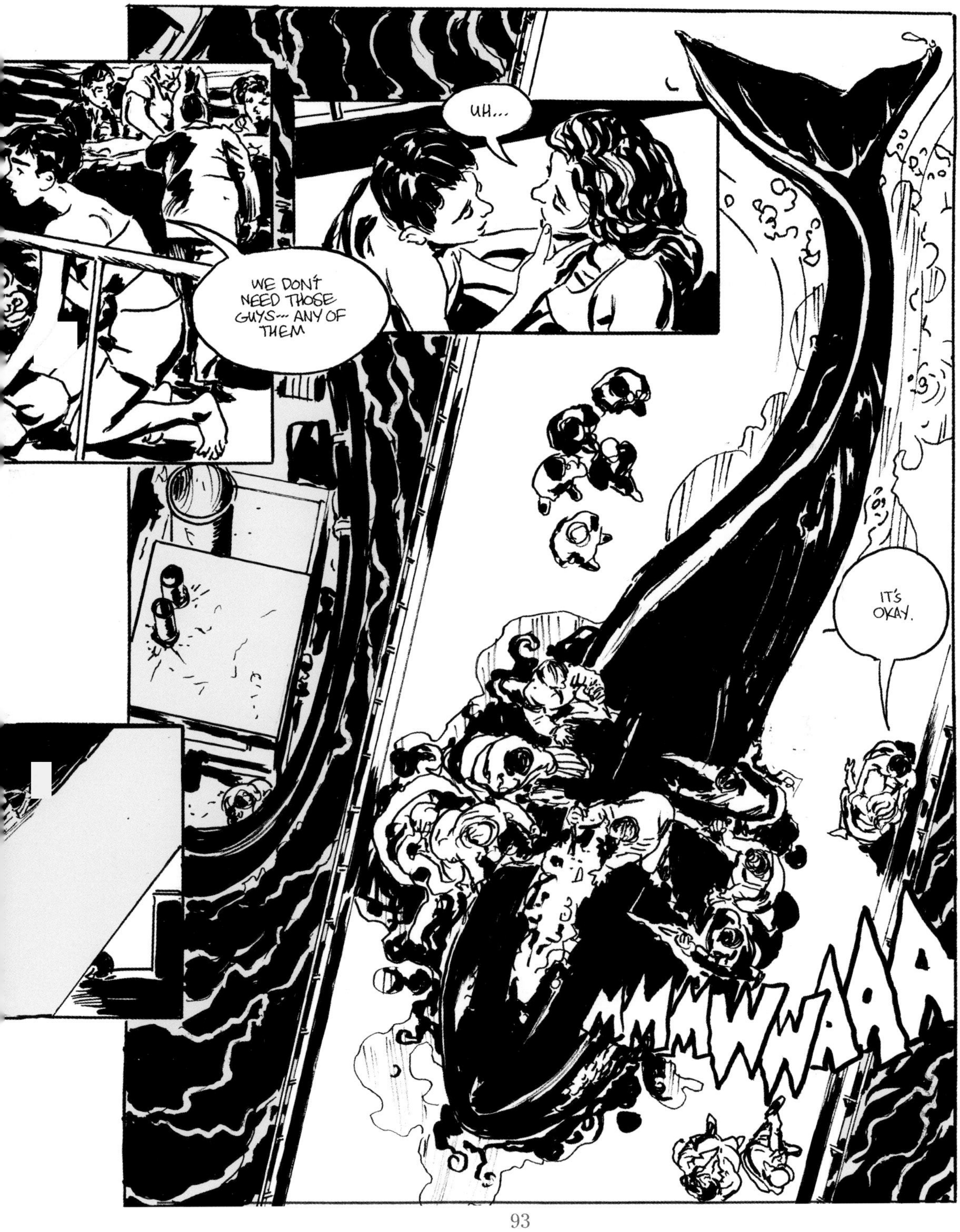
WE DON'T NEED THOSE GUYS--- ANY OF THEM
UH...
IT'S OKAY.

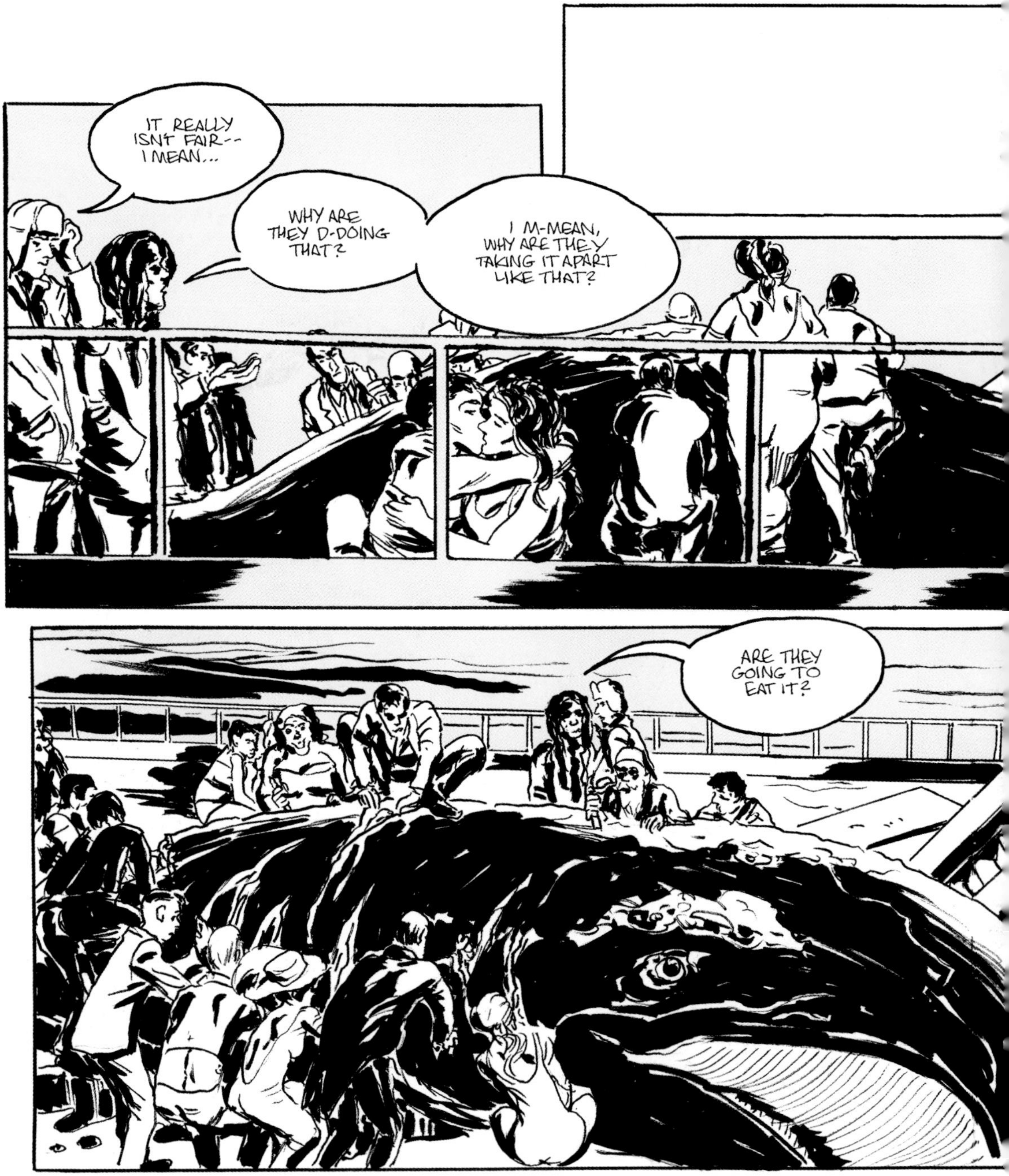
IT REALLY ISN'T FAIR-- I MEAN...
WHY ARE THEY D-DOING THAT?
I M-MEAN, WHY ARE THEY TAKING IT APART LIKE THAT?
ARE THEY GOING TO EAT IT?

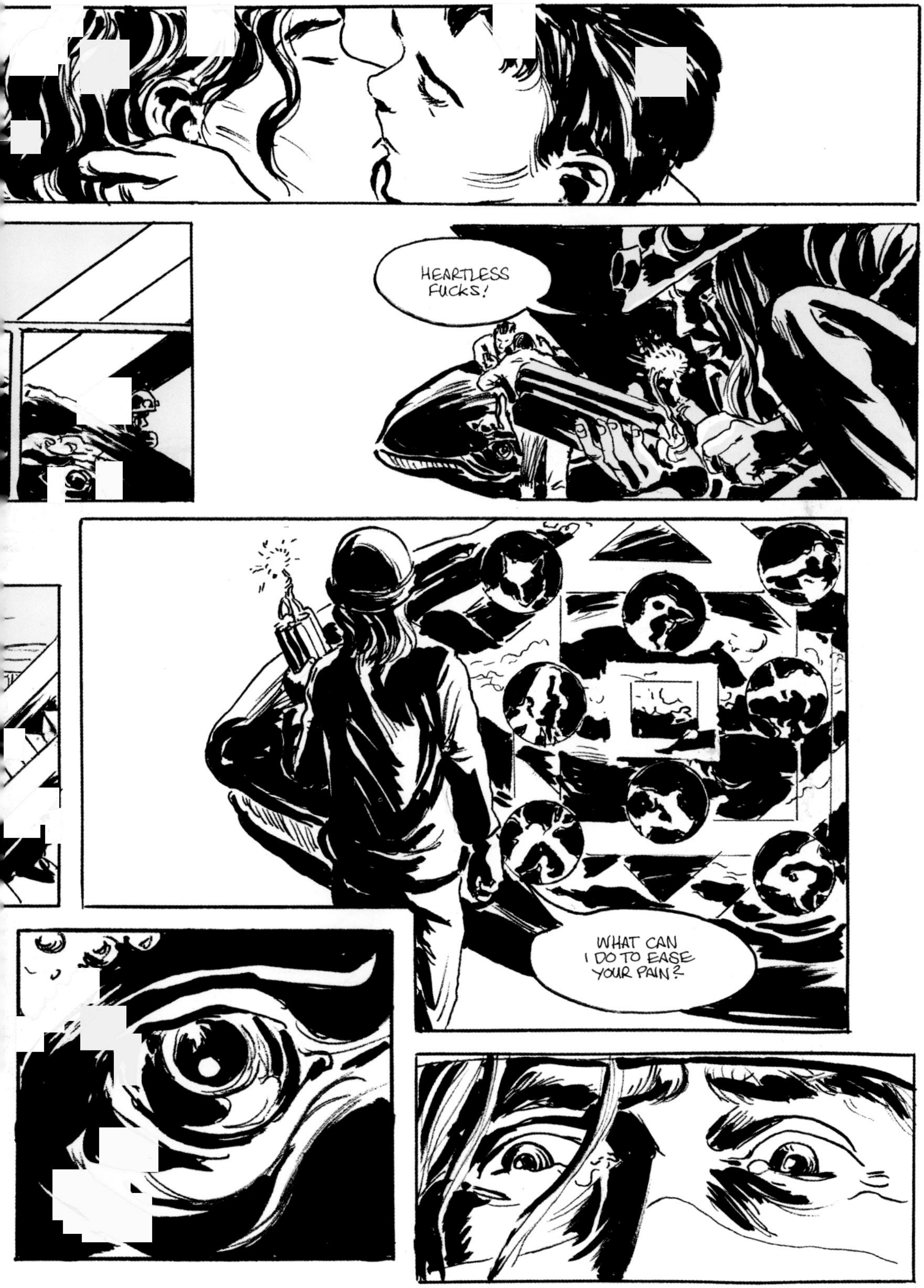
HEARTLESS FUCKS!
WHAT CAN I DO TO EASE YOUR PAIN?

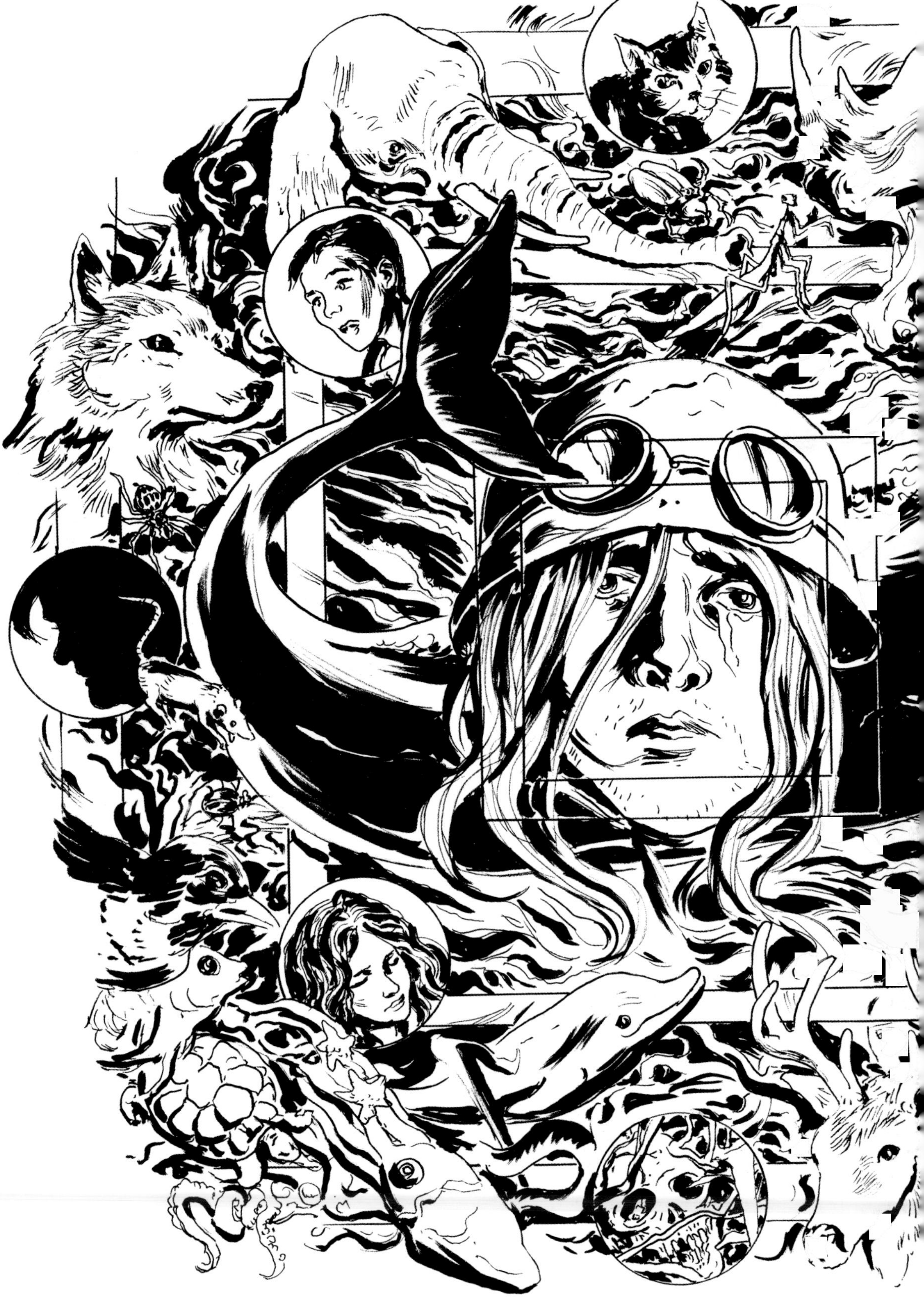

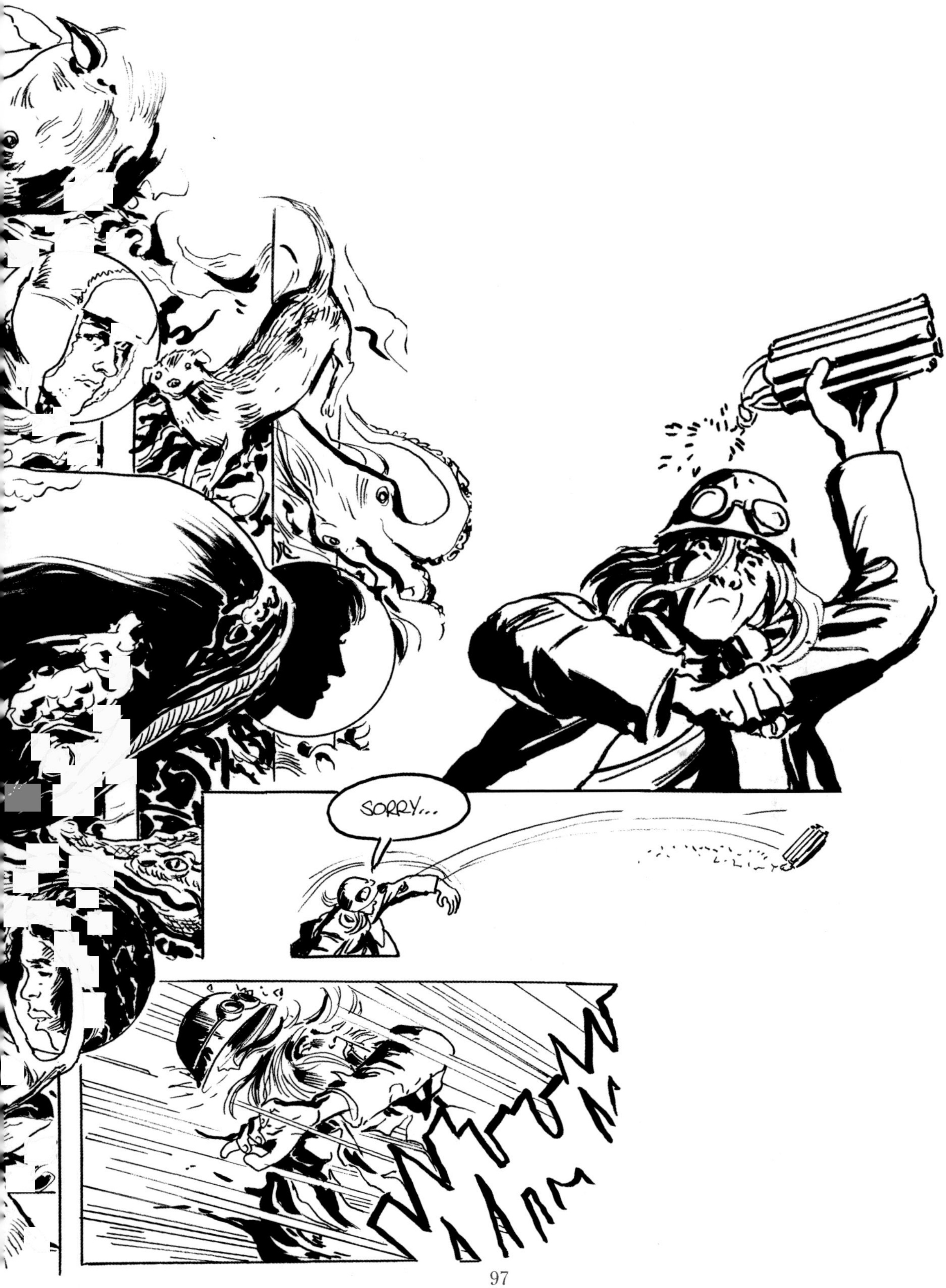
SORRY...

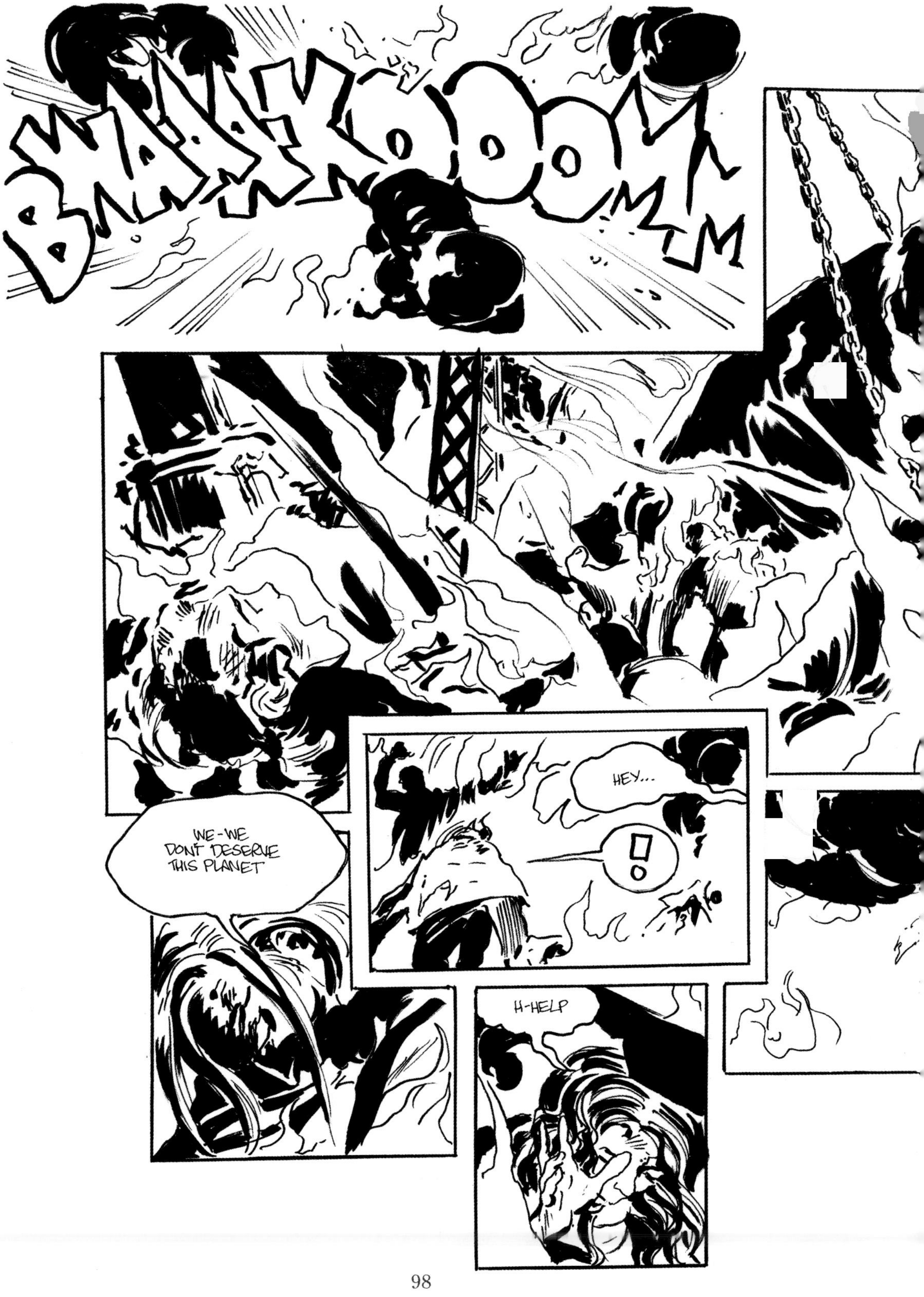
BWAKOOOOM
HEY...
!
WE-WE DON'T DESERVE THIS PLANET
H-HELP

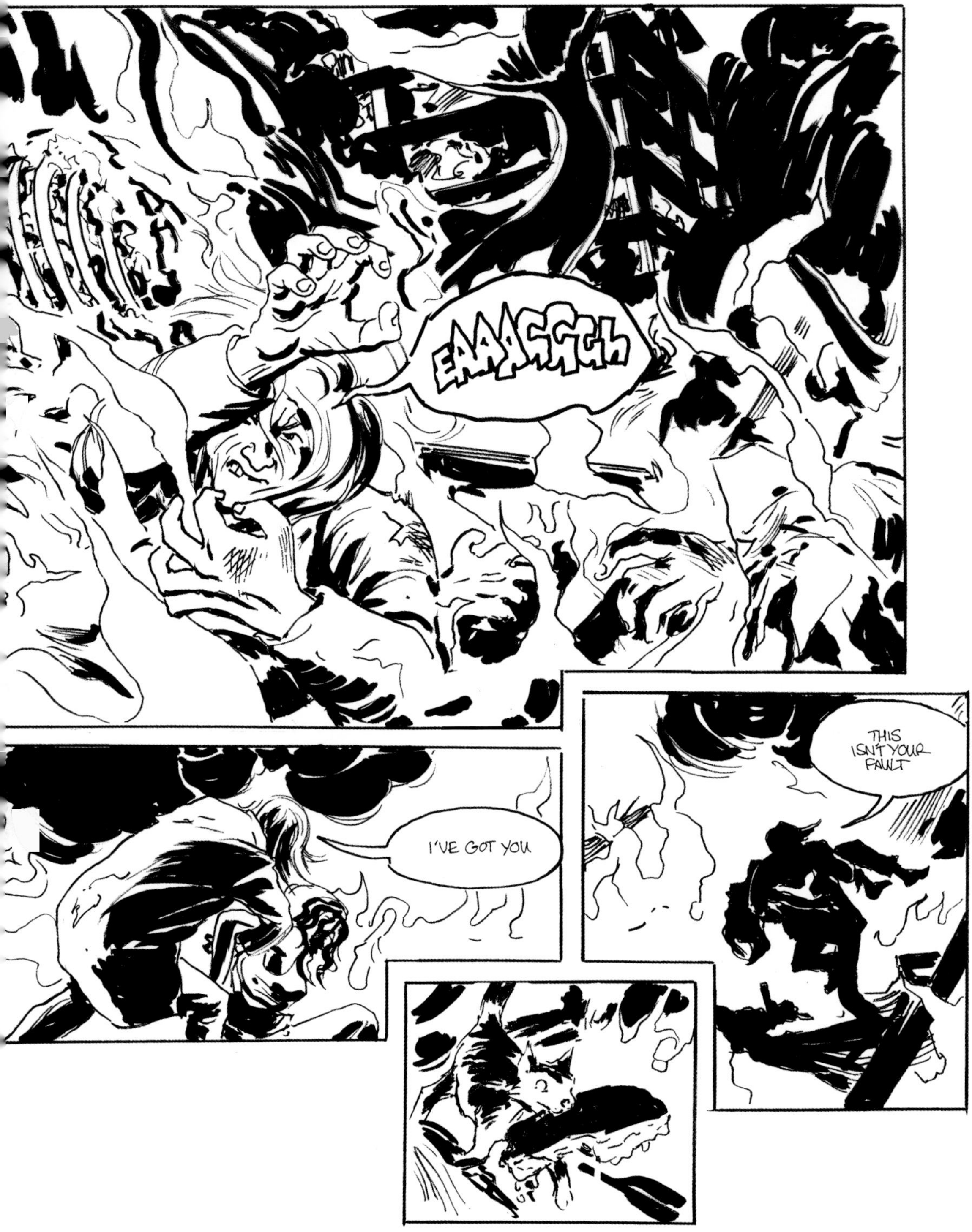
EAAAGGGH
I'VE GOT YOU
THIS ISN'T YOUR FAULT

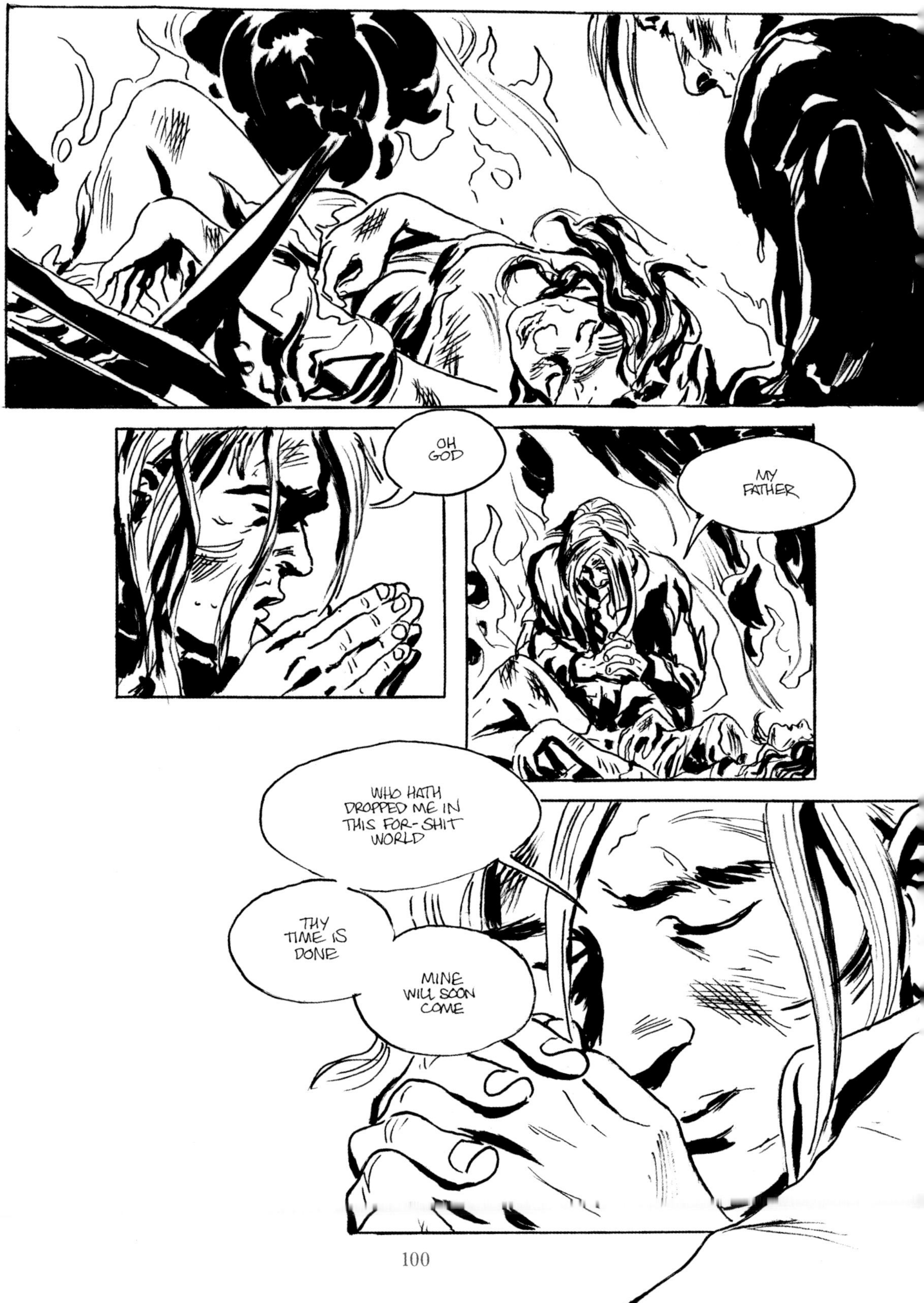
OH GOD
MY FATHER
WHO HATH DROPPED ME IN THIS FOR-SHIT WORLD
THY TIME IS DONE
MINE WILL SOON COME

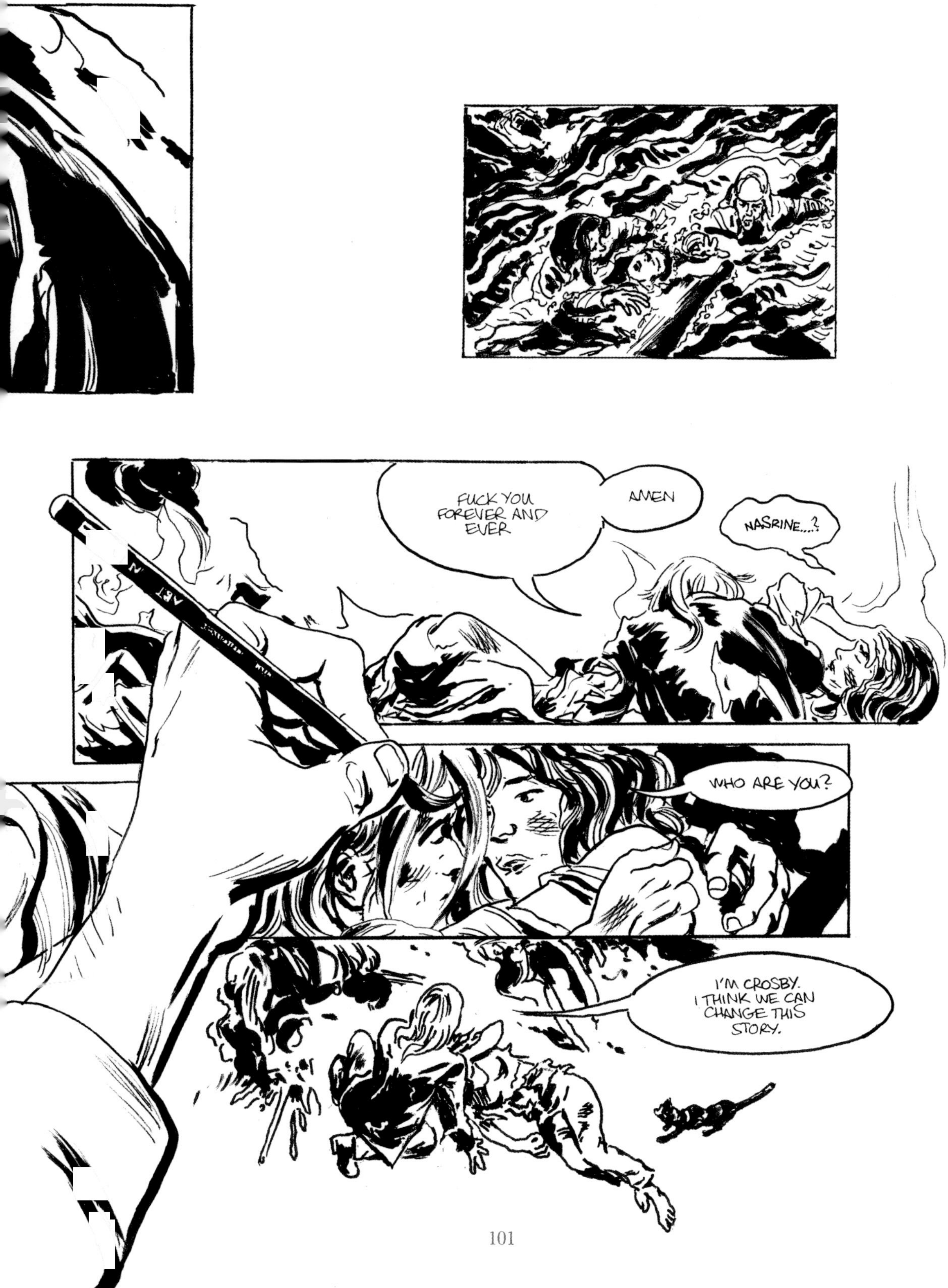
FUCK YOU FOREVER AND EVER
AMEN
NASRINE...?
WHO ARE YOU?
I'M CROSBY. I THINK WE CAN CHANGE THIS STORY.

POST YORK

IT FLOODED MY CITY, I DREAM ITS COMING TO GET ME
EACH WAVE CRASHES DOWN WHEN IT HITS ME,
BUT I'M NOT DREAMING, DON'T PINCH ME
HYDRANTS USED TO SPLASH THE CURB, NOW SKY SCRAPERS ARE HALF SUBMERGED
SOLID GROUND IS FAST A BLUR, I'M WALKING ON WATER, BUT THAT'S ABSURD
I NEVER THOUGHT IN A MILLION YEARS, I'D GET STUCK IN THESE BUILDINGS HERE
STREETS LOOKED LIKE THEY WERE FILLED WITH TEARS
BUT I'M STILL HERE FEELING WEIRD
WOULD YOU WATCH FROM ROOFTOPS, PEOPLE CARRIED FOR TWO BLOCKS
I SWEAR, I NEED A NEW DOCK AND A WATER PROOF WATCH
I FEEL NAKED AND ALONE, BUT I'LL MAKE IT ON MY OWN
WILL I SINK OR WILL I FLOAT, WHILE I THINK UP IN THIS BOAT
I GIVE IT MY HEART AND ALL MY SOUL, ALL I HAVE NOW IS THIS HOPE
THE WORLD IS JUST A BOTTLE OF WINE WITH NO CORK
MY BIG CITY OF DREAMS, POST YORK
I CAN'T SLEEP A PEEP, I FEEL SO DEAD
EVERY NIGHT THAT GOES BY, I WONDER WHEN IT WILL END
MY MOM USED TO SING A LULLABY TO ME IN BED
AND THERE'S NOT A DAY THAT GOES BY ITS NOT STUCK IN MY HEAD

ROW, ROW, ROW YOUR BOAT, GENTLY DOWN THE STREAM
MERRILY, MERRILY, MERRILY, MERRILY, LIFE IS BUT A DREAM

I'M JUST TRYIN TO KEEP DRY
I SET THE CITY ON FIRE

ALL THESE DAYS THAT I CAN'T GET BACK
AND THERE'S NO MAP AND I CAN'T KEEP TRACK
EVERY TALLY'S A DAY THAT I SCRATCH
LIVE WHAT I'M GIVEN NO WISHING IT BACK
THE LAST ONE TO LAUGH WITH A CASCADING GASP
I'M SCAVENGING SCRAPS TO ADD TO MY STASH
THE CITY COLLAPSED FROM A LIVID ATTACK
I ANCHOR MY PAST BUT THERE'S NOTHING ATTACHED
IT'S HARD BUT I STARTED A SPARK WITH A MATCH
KEROSENE ROPE AND I HOPE IT'LL CATCH
SO MAD I HANDLE MY PADDLE LIKE RAP
IF IT WASN'T FLOODED WITH NOTHING BUT CRAP
I'M COUNTING EACH LAP WHILE I'M SWIMMING WITH RATS
SURVIVING ALIVE IS MY VISION TO HAVE
I CAST THE LAST STONE ALONE IN A GLASS
SO I'M BOATING IT HOME TO KITSKI THE CAT
I'M MAKING A SPLASH

I'M JUST TRYIN TO KEEP DRY
I SET THE CITY ON FIRE

I WROTE THIS BY CANDLELIGHT AS I DREAMT
AS WHALES WEPT THROUGH THESE QUIET NIGHTS AS I SLEPT
I WAKE UP AND GET DRESSED, DRYING CLOTHES 'CAUSE THEY'RE WET
HELMET, GOGGLES A CHECK, WATER EVERYWHERE THAT I STEP
FASTEN STRAPS TO MY CHEST BEFORE I ROW IN MY VEST
'CAUSE IF I DROWN THEN I DROWN, AT LEAST I'LL FLOAT IN MY DEATH
IF GOD FORGOT US ALL, I WON'T FEEL ALONE WITH REGRETS
BUT I STILL PRAY EVERYDAY I'M NOT THE LAST SOUL TO FORGET
IF I'M ALL THAT IS LEFT, THEN I WON'T HOLD MY BREATH
I COULDN'T TELL YOU HOW MANY DAYS IN THIS BOAT THAT I'VE SPENT
THE COAST IS A MESS AND EVERYONE I'VE EVER KNOWN OF IS DEAD
AND I BET THESE TALL BUILDINGS HERE WERE OUR ONLY DEFENSE
THEY SAID THE SUN BROKE THE OZONE AT ITS BEST
BUT I WISH I COULD SEE IT LIKE A HOLE IN THE FENCE
JUST WHEN I THOUGHT THE WATER LEVEL COULDN'T GET HIGHER
I'M JUST TRYIN TO KEEP DRY, I SET THE CITY ON FIRE

I'M JUST TRYIN TO KEEP DRY
I SET THE CITY ON FIRE

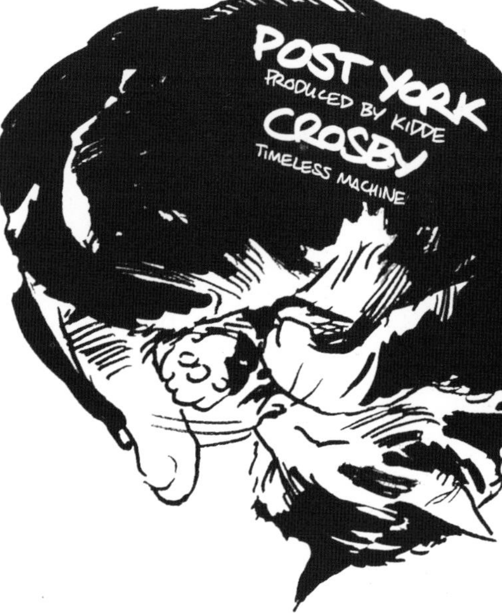
POST YORK
PRODUCED BY KIDDE
CROSBY
TIMELESS MACHINE

Mixed/mastered by Matthias Graf and Rastyle.
Additional vocals by Jordan Lane.
All lyrics written by Crosby.
Recorded at Alkaline Studios.

postyork.com

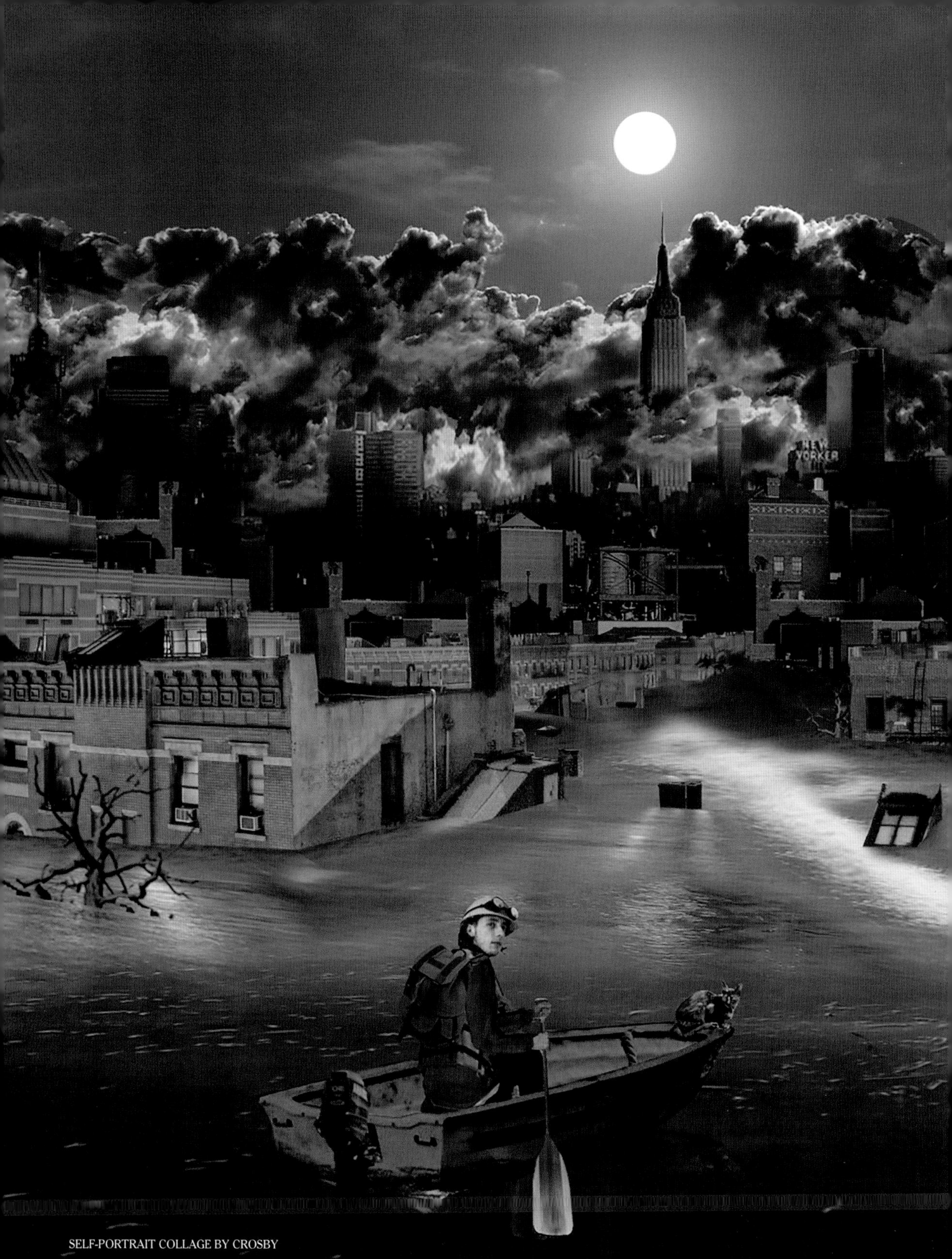
NEW
YORKER

SELF-PORTRAIT COLLAGE BY CROSBY

HIGHER GROUND

Post York **first began in 2009**

as an arty conceptual piece: a printed pamphlet and a performance at a poetry slam club about a group of nearly-insane artists living on a yacht anchored above what was once Harlem.

Over the next few years, I created other, grittier images and story vignettes about a lonely survivor based on my son Crosby, floating through Manhattan's submerged streets after the ice caps have melted.

I'd watched Crosby and his friends growing up in NYC Hip Hop culture pride themselves on freestyling, spitting impromptu lines to destroy their rap battle rivals. I borrowed that energy to freestyle the comics version of *Post York* in the act of drawing, without a script. For me, this approach to narrative is in sync with our visually-driven medium, as the improvisational "camera that writes" was for the cinematic French New Wave of the 1960s.

Post York reflects my fears about what Crosby and his contemporaries will face in the New York City that is coming. It is my apology to him for my own complicity in the current state of the world. Crosby is the star of this comic, and my wingman on the project; he is the only person I showed the pages to and asked for opinions. He made the self-portrait collage on the left, and he recorded a rap track, which was included as a flexi-disc in the 40-page *Post York* comic book that was published in 2012 by cartoonist Tom Kaczynski's Uncivilized Books–just a few days before Hurricane Sandy blasted the East Coast. The morning after the storm, Crosby stepped out of his tenement on Avenue C to see a police cruiser float by his stoop.

Nearly a decade after the one-shot comic, ex-Vertigo nexus Karen Berger enabled me to expand this ever-evolving concept into a full-length graphic novel at her Dark Horse imprint, with Crosby's lyrics inspiring a climactic fictional conflagration. But will anyone survive the very real looming disaster that we are allowing to happen?

As opposed to this fractured drama and romance, it is important to know how NYC could actually fare as global warming progresses. I approached the New York based sustainability think tank Unbuilt Labs with some questions about what the world's greatest city could look like in the near future. Their answers are terrifying. I condensed and paraphrased the large volume of raw data they sent me into a Q&A format and did some additional digging of my own.

1. How much will the oceans rise in the coming decades?

Our means of estimating the accelerating changes that global warming will effect are uncertain and variable. What we do know is that turgid waters will rise and fall at unpredictable intervals, depending on the weather. Unbuilt Labs researcher Lowell Clare remarked dryly about the *Post York* drawings, "looking down through clear water might be unlikely, as are consistent water levels at the heights portrayed for the next century at least." New York City is already experiencing a rapid acceleration of ocean rise, but the highest water levels are seen in storm surges. In the past 50 years, the sea level rose 6 inches in lower Manhattan, but scientists forecast that the ocean will rise that much in just the next 14 years; even this increase will greatly multiply catastrophic storm surges *(1a)*. Hurricane Sandy's storm surge was 9 feet. The world's glaciers are projected to melt entirely by the year 2100; the resulting worldwide sea rise will be 5 feet *(1b)*. Ocean currents will be drastically altered as the waters simultaneously have increasing acidity and lowered oxygen, suffused with highly toxic "harmful algal blooms" (HAB) *(1c)*.

These fearsome eventualities might be mitigated by sensible efforts to decrease destructive greenhouse gas emissions *(1d)*. But those actions must be actually taken, instead of being deliberately stopped by climate change deniers *(1e)*. At any rate, even if the emissions that cause global warming were ended today, by 2050 there will be yearly extreme and deadly coastal weather events that had previously only ever occurred once in a century *(1f)*.

2. Would the proposed but recently abandoned NYC seawall have been feasible?

After Hurricane Sandy, it became clear that New York City's positioning as a key port is no longer an advantage, but a liability. It inundated the subway system and every Manhattan road tunnel but the Holland. A recent study says by 2050, the tides will flood coastal parts of NYC twice daily and flood other low-lying areas permanently *(2a)*. In 2019, the Army Corps of Engineers determined that massive 6-mile-long sea barriers are needed to protect the Hudson River and New York Harbor from storm surges, but some consider their plan harmful to the local ecosystems and ineffectual against the enormity of nature's fury *(2b)*. At any rate, studies informing this effort were defunded by the Trump administration in February 2020.

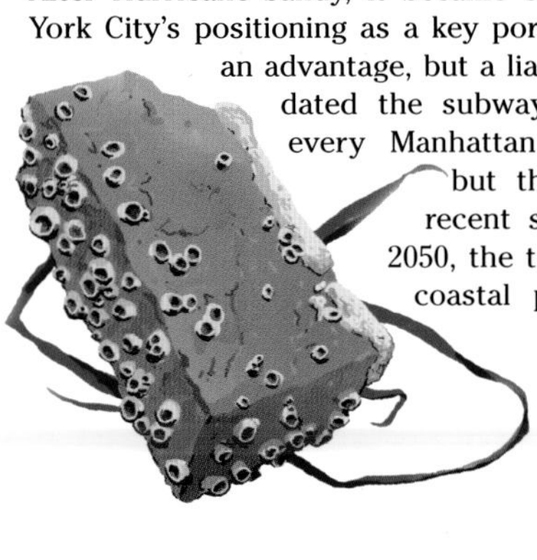

3. Would survivors even have fragments of buildings to cling to? Could the architecture of NYC withstand the pressures of massive flooding, ongoing storms or seismic events?

The rows of unreinforced brick buildings that make up 80% of NYC housing are terribly vulnerable to flooding and quakes; they rely on each other for stability and would collapse outwardly, starting at the corners of blocks *(3a)*. Chinatown and the Upper East Side are built on soft ground which might liquify. The East Village is built on a swamp and under duress its shoddy tenements would easily pancake down. New buildings are constructed to relatively high standards, but seismic activity was not accounted for in the New York City building code until 1995. NYC's worst earthquakes in 1737 and 1884 both measured 5 on the Richter scale. And there are numerous faults scattered near, or in, the city. One is the Ramapo Fault, a line quavering through New York, New Jersey, Pennsylvania, and possibly Connecticut that might generate a quake of a magnitude of 6 or 7, which would more than devastate NYC and perhaps destabilize the nearby Indian Point nuclear reactors *(3b)*.

4. If there were standing buildings, would they be festering with mold, as was the case in New Orleans after Katrina?

Yes. It's not for nothing that finding mold can cause a house to be condemned. It thrives in moisture and spreads on sheetrock, wood, and other organic surfaces. It attacks the immune system, inflames allergies, and causes asthma and other respiratory problems *(4a)*. Standing water also breeds mold–and mosquitos, a carrier of malaria and dengue fever. Warming waters also invite various types of the marine bacteria Vibrio, which can be ingested through contaminated shellfish or seep through open wounds underwater, and cause diseases like cholera and septicemia *(4b)*.

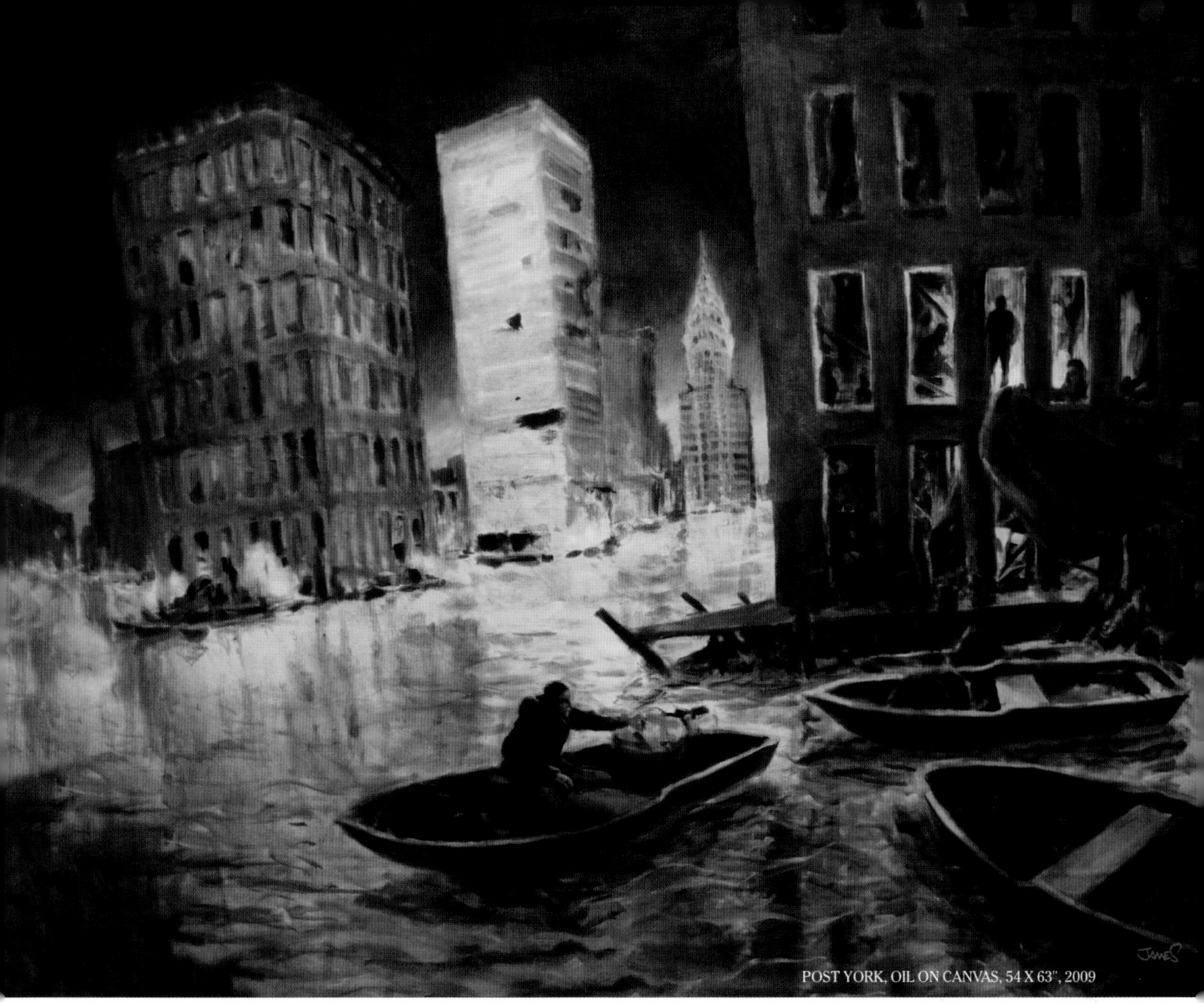

POST YORK, OIL ON CANVAS, 54 X 63", 2009

***5.** Despite what I drew of Ivy's theater, wouldn't there be extremely limited access to power sources? What about gas and solar generators?*

NYC only requires emergency backup power systems for high-volume buildings like malls, prisons, places of assembly and high-rises with elevators. The rest of us depend on the sense of our landlords. Generators are not cheap, so there are likely fewer in poor neighborhoods. Portable standby gasoline and diesel generators are built for emergency short-term use and only run for 1,000 to 2,000 hours in their lifetime *(5a)*. Solar generators are designed to power smaller household devices, and some stronger units can handle refrigerators and heaters. But solar batteries must be recharged between uses so several units to alternate are needed. Repair parts for anything will be hard to find. And at the best of times, the sun is an inconsistent recharger *(5b)*.

***6.** Would diseases like COVID-19 or worse be more prevalent, both from man-made biological agents set loose on the population by coastal disasters or ancient microbes released by the melting icecaps?*

As of 2020, there are 9 biosafety level 4 labs in the US; and 200 BSL-3s. Because of Federal regulatory restraints, we aren't told how many of those operate in NYC. However, we know that the BSL-3 laboratory on the Upper East Side at the Rockefeller University campus that is now studying tuberculosis is one of several labs in the city that specialize in researching inhalable, often lethal microbes. But even with high safety standards, containment can be compromised after a power loss from even one major hurricane or earthquake *(6a)*. As the ice caps melt, entrepreneurs might seek to appropriate the Northwest Passage and other fabled shipping routes. But global warming can also release bacteria and previously eradicated viruses from their project sites; the likes of Spanish flu and bubonic plague might infect their workers, who then share with their survivor circles *(6b)*. An anthrax-infected reindeer that was frozen in permafrost in Siberia for 75 years thawed in 2016 and newly infected 2,000 of its own species nearby, then some 73 humans *(6c)*.

7. *Would local sea life be a food source, or would it be degraded because of pollution and/or the widely circulating radioactivity from events like the Fukushima meltdown in 2011—or wiped out entirely? How many nuclear power plants are in coastal areas?*

If flooding occurs as deep as shown in *Post York*, you'd be risking your life to eat any sea species in the area. Fish and shellfish infected by toxic algae growth can cause illness, paralysis, and even death if ingested. Nuclear plants are built beside water sources for cooling purposes; there are 34 nuclear plants lying downstream from dams, all across America. NYC is in closest proximity to the Indian Point nuclear power plant, just 36 miles away. It is vulnerable to storms and perhaps also to a quake arising from the Ramapo fault, but it is being shut down in 2021. However, demolition won't be complete until 2033 and the radioactive materials will remain there until a viable disposal plan is conceived *(7)*.

8. *Survivors living on canned and bottled food is an enduring trope of dystopian fiction. In reality, would there be any food, canned, bottled, or otherwise for survivors to eat? Wouldn't most supermarkets and warehouses where preserved supplies like canned goods are stored be underwater?*

13,000 trucks a day bring more than half of NYC's food to the world's biggest food market, the Hunt's Point hub in the Bronx; it is hugely vulnerable to flooding because it lies low at a peninsula on the Bronx and East Rivers. If it ever shuts down, 22 million people will run out of food in 3 days *(8a)*. In our research, we have found no significant plans in NYC ordinances to address this potential calamity.

If massive flooding occurs, caution is called for. Water and other fluids in non-waterproof containers (i.e. anything with screw caps, snap lids, pull tops, and crimped caps) that have been in contact with flood waters are contaminated, as are rusty, swollen, or frozen cans. Most cans are stamped with their sell-by date and not safe to eat for long beyond that. Low-acid canned goods (like Spam, soups, vegetables, and spaghetti) are good for years longer than high-acid ones (such as citrus and other fruit juices, and foods treated with vinegar).

But regardless, cans are only viable for a few days after opening, even if refrigerated; the same goes for any of the options. Sealed "retort pouches" of processed meat, poultry, or fish store for a year and a half. Dry rice and cured meats like salami, jerky, and dry sausages are good for several years longer. A canned ham might be good for 5 years. If you are lucky enough to find military MREs (Meals Ready to Eat), they are edible for 7 years, and dried egg whites can be stored indefinitely, both as long as they are kept cool and dry *(8b)*. However, these options will definitely be in extremely short supply—which could make the hunt for them as dangerous as it is for Crosby. It would be advisable to vacate the area.

Based on research by Lowell Clare, Gauri Bahuguna, and Madeleine Tervet, overseen by Marvin Cheung and Marguerite Van Cook for UnbuiltLabs.com.

• Storyboard for proposed video for Crosby's *Post York* track •

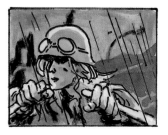

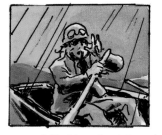

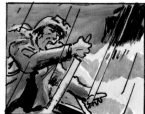

CU on Crosby rowing — Pull back to medium shot — rain, ocean roiling

I anchor my past but there's nothing attached — It's hard but I started a spark with a match

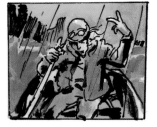

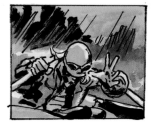

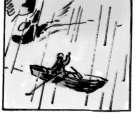

BG buildings slide L to R — Boat swivels, bobs in ocean

Kerosene rope and I hope it'll catch — I'm counting each lap while I'm swimming with rats — Surving alive is my vision to have

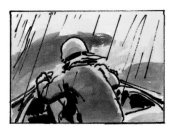

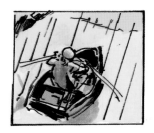

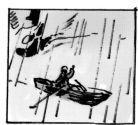

Around to rear view — and pull up to downshot

I cast the last stone alone in a glass — So I'm boating it home to Kitski the cat — I'm making a splash

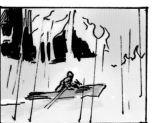

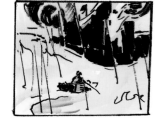

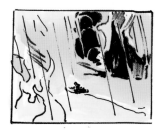

Flames slide L to R rain changes direction as boat swivels counterclockwise

I'm just tryin to keep dry — Set the city on fire

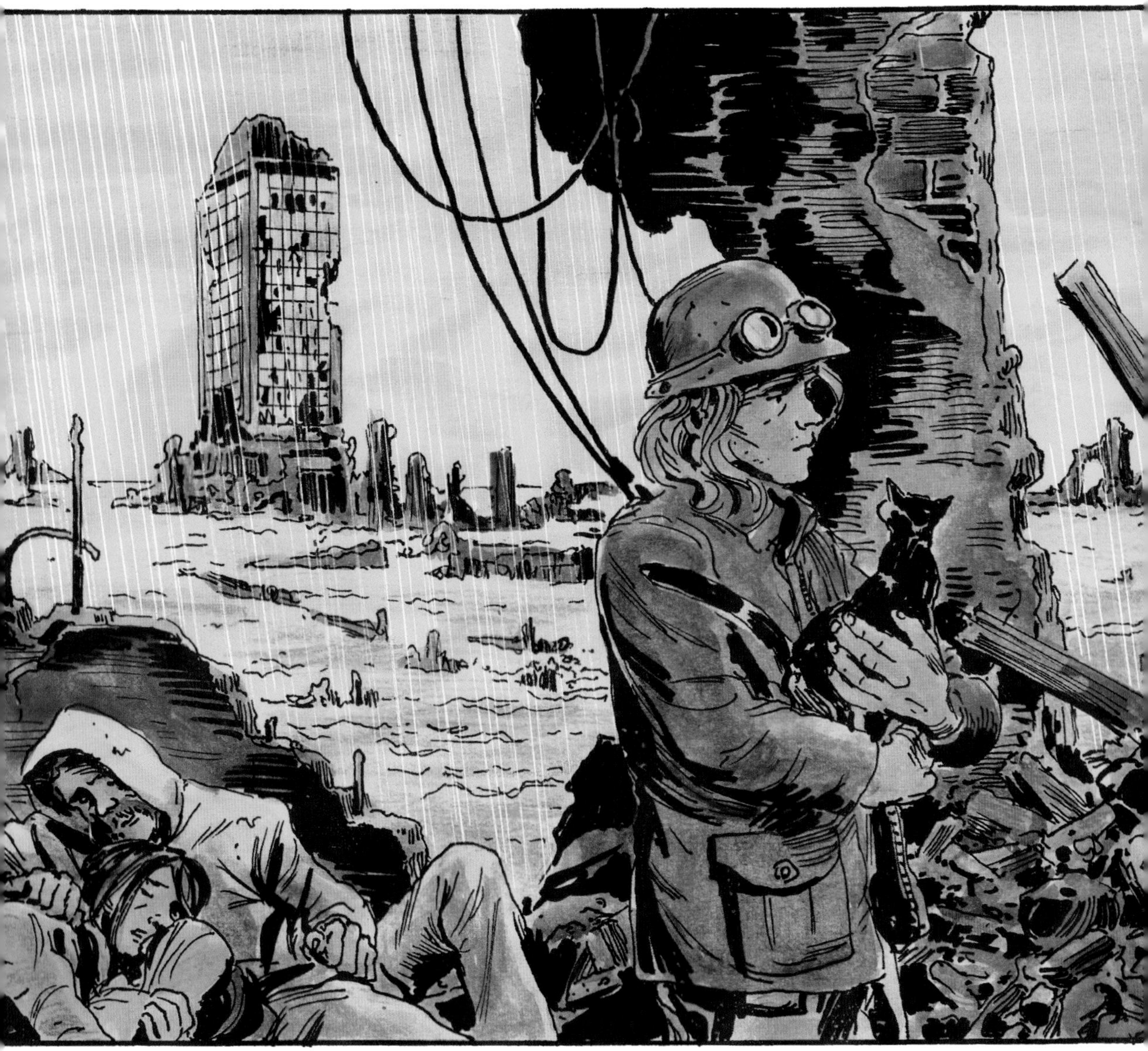

Selected sources:

1a. Sea Level Rise, 2016: https://sealevelrise.org/

1b. Yale University, 2019: https://e360.yale.edu/features/could-massive-storm-surge-barriers-end-the-hudson-rivers-revival/

1c. Center for NYC Neighborhoods, 2020: https://www.floodhelpny.org/

1d. NY Governor Cuomo's 2019 Climate Leadership and Community Protection Act: https://climate.ny.gov/

1e. Nature, 2020: https://www.nature.com/articles/d41586-020-02800-9

1f. International Panel on Climate Change, 2019: https://www.ipcc.ch/srocc/chapter/summary-for-policymakers/

2a. NYC's Mayor de Blasio's 2019 plan: https://www1.nyc.gov/office-of-the-mayor/news/140-19/mayor-de-blasio-resiliency-plan-protect-lower-manhattan-climate-change#/0

2b. New York Times, 2020: https://www.nytimes.com/2020/01/17/nyregion/sea-wall-nyc.html

3a. Verisk, 2020: https://www.verisk.com/insurance/covid-19/iso-insights/actually-it-can-happen-to-us-the-big-one-hits-new-york/

3b. Columbia University's Earth Institute, 2008: https://www.earth.columbia.edu/articles/view/2235/

4a. Habitat Magazine, 2004: https://randpc.com/ask/exterior-repair-and-maintenance/preventing-mold

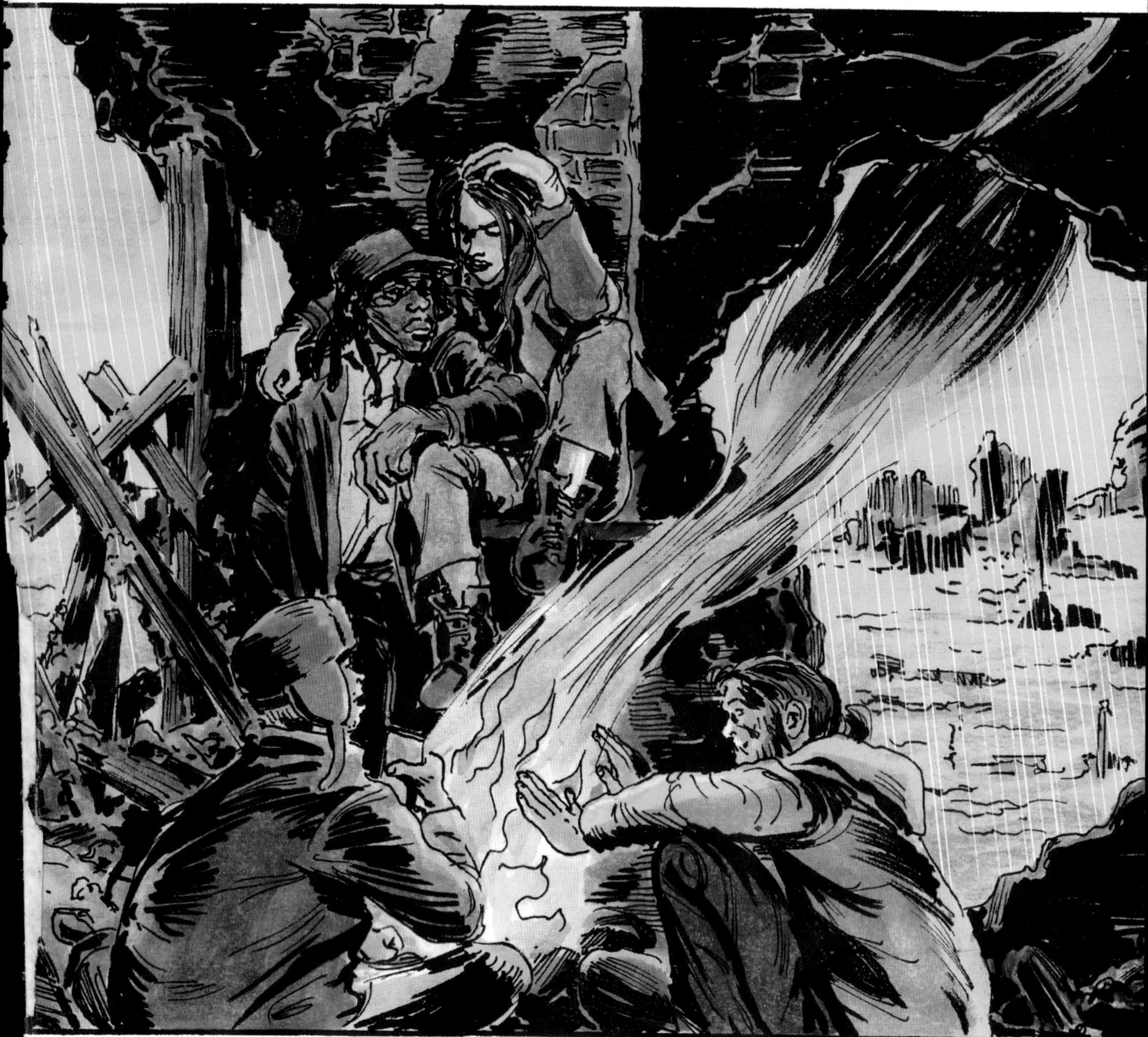

4b. Trends in Microbiology, 2017: https://doi.org/10.1016/j.tim.2016.09.008/

5a. All Time Power, 2020: https://www.alltimepower.com/learn-more/how-long-do-generators-last/

5b. Solar Reviews, 2020: https://www.solarreviews.com/blog/what-are-the-pros-and-cons-of-a-solar-generator

6a. New Yorker, 2020: https://www.newyorker.com/science/elements/the-risks-of-building-too-many-bio-labs

6b. World Health Organization, 2003: https://www.who.int/globalchange/publications/climchange.pdf

6c. National Public Radio, 2016: https://www.npr.org/sections/goatsandsoda/2016/08/03/488400947/anthrax-outbreak-in-russia-thought-to-be-result-of-thawing-permafrost

7. Reuters, 2011: https://www.reuters.com/article/idUS381697982020110502

8a. Hunter College NYC Food Policy Center, 2018: https://www.nycfoodpolicy.org/hunts-point-distribution-center-brief-overview-spotlight-produce-market/

8b. U.S. Food and Drug Administration, 2020: www.fda.gov/food/buy-store-serve-safe-food/food-and-water-safety-during-power-outages-and-floods/

JAMES ROMBERGER
is the artist of the graphic novels *7 Miles a Second*, *2020 Visions*, *Bronx Kill,* and *Aaron and Ahmed* for Vertigo/DC, and *The Late Child and Other Animals* for Fantagraphics. His most recent works are *For Real* for Uncivilized Books and his critical study *Steranko: The Self-Created Man* for Ground Zero Books. His pastel drawings are in many public collections including the Metropolitan Museum. He has taught at Parsons, Hunter College, and Marywood University.

jamesromberger.com

Photo by Marguerite Van Cook.

Crosby performing Post York *at Union Pool in Brooklyn, 2012*
Photo by Marguerite Van Cook.

CROSBY "ClockWork Cros"
is a designer, musician and conceptual artist based in New York City. His clocks and installations challenge ideas about time, celebrity, and aesthetics. He exhibits worldwide and in art fairs such as Art Basel Miami Beach and Armory Arts Week and Frieze in New York. He has managed marketing campaigns for Zac Posen, Swizz Beatz, and Alicia Keys.

clockworkcros.com

Karen Berger Editor
Rachel Boyadjis Assistant Editor
Richard Bruning Book Design
Adam Pruett Digital Art Technician
Mike Richardson President & Publisher

Cover Logo designed by James Romberger & Tom Kaczynski
Page 102-103 lyrics & page 104 collage ©2012 Crosby Romberger

First Edition: February 2021
eBook ISBN 978-50671-936-8
ISBN 978-1-50671-935-1
1 3 5 7 9 10 8 6 4 2
Printed in China
Library of Congress Control Number: 2020946878
DarkHorse.com ComicShopLocator.com

Published by Dark Horse Books,
a division of Dark Horse Comics LLC.
10956 SE Main Street, Milwaukie, Oregon 97222.